ROOSEVELT

THROUGH FOREIGN EYES

NICHOLAS HALASZ

ROOSEVELT

THROUGH FOREIGN EYES

D. VAN NOSTRAND COMPANY, INC.
PRINCETON, NEW JERSEY
TORONTO LONDON
NEW YORK

D. VAN NOSTRAND COMPANY, INC.
120 Alexander St., Princeton, New Jersey (*Principal office*)
24 West 40 Street, New York 18, New York

D. VAN NOSTRAND COMPANY, LTD.
358, Kensington High Street, London, W. 14, England

D. VAN NOSTRAND COMPANY (Canada), LTD.
25 Hollinger Road, Toronto 16, Canada

Published simultaneously in Canada by
D. VAN NOSTRAND COMPANY (Canada), LTD.

PRINTED IN THE UNITED STATES OF AMERICA

PREFACE

In the years between 1932 and 1936 a powerful argument for dictatorships asserted that democracy was incapable of coping with the economic crisis. When Franklin D. Roosevelt assumed the office of the Presidency, the choice for mankind seemed to be reduced to that between fascism and communism. From 1937 to 1941 the totalitarian propagandists propounded an even more powerful argument—that democracy, being in a state of decadence, was unwilling or unable to defend itself.

President Roosevelt made his reforms effective without impairing the democratic institutions, thus re-establishing democracy as an alternative to totalitarianism. The way the American war effort unfolded under Roosevelt's leadership demolished the argument that a democracy could not defend itself.

Roosevelt's personality, his long tenure in office, the many innovations of world significance presented in his name, and his leadership in the global war all contributed to a public identification of the United States with Roosevelt. His totalitarian opponents contributed to this image by their fondness for personalizing power even though they looked on his as evil. The life of no other American president can be so well reconstructed from the imprint he has left on world opinion. Working with my son Robert Halasz, I have attempted to tell the story of Franklin Roosevelt and his Presidency in the light of representative foreign reactions to him and his programs.

I am most grateful to Mrs. Eleanor Roosevelt for her gracious interest in this project and am in debt to all those I have quoted.

Also I wish to thank Mr. Herman Kahn, Director of the Franklin D. Roosevelt Library, Hyde Park, N.Y., for his reading the manuscript and his valuable suggestions. The staff of the library was very helpful in the completion of the book.

NICHOLAS HALASZ

New York, N.Y.
March, 1961

CONTENTS

1

THE AMERICAN DEPRESSION

The nineteenth century ended in America on that black Thursday, October 24, 1929, when the mirage of everlasting prosperity was swept away by a few hours trading in which time thirteen million shares were thrown for sale and could find buyers only "after wide vertical declines." A world which had ended for Europe in 1914 met its end on that day and during its aftermath. "Brokers wept and tore off their collars trying to keep abreast in selling orders . . . At the month's close fifteen billion dollars in market value had been obliterated, and before the end of the year losses reached an estimated forty billion." [1]

Strangers who had seen the Americans in high spirits before the crash, sharing a boisterous optimism, were baffled by the sight of the tired, humiliated, desperate crowds they met a year later. In the tough winter of 1930, long lines of unemployed waited at the doorways of the factories, some bundling their feet in rags to keep them from freezing. Harried masses thronged in front of the Salvation Army and other charitable institutions to get some food, aid, shelter. The philanthropic committees were overwhelmed; medicine for the sick ran out; the hospitals were bursting at the seams. In Chicago and Detroit the homeless were admitted to the prisons to stay overnight. The employment bureaus were besieged. For 100 positions, 299 candidates applied in 1929; by the winter of 1930, 2,861 applicants were available for every one hundred openings. People of wealth lacked ready cash to buy food. There was no way to sell for cash. The farmers, like the workers, had mortgaged their future income by buying on installment plans. It was the more difficult to get credit because over a thousand banks had shut their windows since the crash. In a year the consumption of electricity dropped twenty-five per cent; transportation on rail, nineteen per cent; production of steel, forty per cent; car production, sixty per cent. American industry as a whole was operating at less than half its maximum 1929 volume.[2] And the trend kept spiralling downwards.

There were no "cushions" to break the initial shock of the fall, let alone to bolster up a rudimentary sense of economic and social security among those who were already without a job or means. Family obligations and generosity from the neighbor were for many the only source of relief from destitution. The American people found themselves, after their heyday of prosperity, in much the same position as a visitor to a skyscraper in New York who had been induced by an apparently trustworthy elevator boy to ascend almost to the top floor only to have the whole building collapse beneath him.[3]

A year after delivery the President's proud words struck a sardonic echo:

"We in America today are nearer to the financial triumph over poverty than ever before in the history of our land. The poor man is vanishing from among us. Under these impulses, and the Republican protective system, our industrial output has increased as never before, and our wages have grown steadily in buying power. Our workers with their average weekly wages, can today buy two or even three times more bread and butter than any wage earner in Europe. At one time we demanded for our workers a full dinner pail. We have now gone far beyond that conception. Today we demand a larger comfort and greater participation in life and leisure."

These words of Herbert Hoover, Republican candidate for the Presidency, served to strengthen the general optimism. As he rode from the Capitol to the White House after his inauguration on March 4, 1929, the sun of prosperity was shining across the forty-eight States, and the nation exuded well-being and self-confidence. Calvin Coolidge had done such an outstanding job that the people did not want to let him go. But this small gentleman from Massachusetts had not really been the right man for strong, successful America. She needed at her head a representative who reflected her strength, a big man transpiring from all pores American self-confidence. The booming Coolidge era would be but a prelude. The nation was to accelerate now with a real leader in the driver's seat. No better leader could be found than Hoover, who had become rich from technical achievements, as had his country. He was known the world over as a great organizer, spreading America's faith in her prosperity with conviction. Hoover was the guarantee of billions of profit, the personified welfare-for-all, a warranty that no setbacks or crises would ever happen.[4] People cherished the gilt coins distributed during the election campaign of 1928, stamped on one face with the words "Hoover Lucky Piece," and "Good for four more years of prosperity" on the other. The nation acclaimed him precisely because he was to consolidate prosperity. The "promoters" stated that the prosperity of the Coolidge years had not been sufficiently exploited! They and the mass of Americans believed that it was possible to gamble on an infinite margin of progress boldly and abundantly. Was not the country on the road toward a period of opulence? The banks lent money without much difficulty. Those who had savings invested them readily, doubling and trebling their capital, since everything was on the rise.[5]

Optimism became a religion, the high priest being the multi-millionaire. He appeared to be not only omnipotent, but omniscient, wise, charitable, King Solomon himself. His opinion was requested not only in matters financial, but also in politics, art, literature, ethics, and philosophy. The opinions of these men on child education, the social role of painting, on the ways of writing a successful book, of behaving toward one's wife, filled volumes. Goethe's conversations with Eckermann had far fewer readers than the talks of a certain number of millionaires with a journalist named Barron, who published them in two volumes entitled "THEY told Barron." [6]

The men of finance appeared to deserve well their soaring prestige. They encouraged the boom by making possible selling on the installment plan. With this innovation the golden era seemed really to be unfolding.

A French author famous for his felicitous axioms found one for the dazzling perspective that expansion of the market by sales on the installment plan had opened. He observed that the age of exploration when the pioneers had moved West in a search for free soil, virgin forests, and untapped natural wealth was gone. Those settlers he called pioneers in space. The same pioneering now penetrated time through the system of sales against future payments, extending the market onto the future. The new pioneer in time was as optimistic, individualistic, chivalrous, childlike, and generous as his namesake in space had once been.[7]

As a general policy, selling on credit allowed the domestic market to keep pace with ever-increasing production, a steadily growing population, rising salaries and income, as well as with the supposedly unlimited desire of men for more and more comfort and wealth. The American people had come to believe that they had found the secret of perpetual prosperity. They were proud of the discovery and said so loudly.[8] They insisted that for the first time in history the masses were to enjoy abundance and luxury. The secret of this golden era lay in the steadily rising wage level which enabled the domestic market to consume the increasing production.[9] A foreign economist held everlasting prosperity to be within the realm of possibility. He wrote that before the war the natural wealth of the United States had not been sufficiently exploited because of the comparative lack of financial resources. Now, however, that they possessed a huge gold reserve and an improved credit system, all these resources could be turned to the benefit of the nation in the course of the next decade or two.[10]

This prosperity was believed to issue from and feed exclusively on the American domestic market. While misery and political subversion beset the world at large, America had isolated herself by shutting out immigrants, refusing to cooperate in organizing the postwar world, by high customs tariffs, by banning alien ideas, and by her very wealth. It was as if a new paradise had burgeoned on earth for the exclusive benefit of the Americans and that God had blessed them with the perpetual improvement of this providential condition.[11] They began to believe that in this matter of prosperity they were not as other men are, but instead somehow destined by miracle to go on from strength to strength while the rest of the world went under the harrow.[12]

In calm self-confidence and haughty optimism the Yankee businessmen walked among other peoples like demigods, preaching the American gospel on how to get rich.[13] They compared themselves to the ancient Roman conquerors who had visited Greece, surveying who and what was worth saving from a sinking civilization.

"It is perhaps human nature for us to gloat a little over America's present troubles—we have had so many of our own," an English magazine admitted.[14] The unmistakable malice in foreign comments on the American scene after the crash was the result of this arrogance.

Until 1927, the critical date, optimism was justified. From 1914, the beginning of World War I, until that date, the United States fed the whole world. The war gravely curtailed production in the belligerent countries and compelled them to buy in America what they could not manufacture. In the rest of the world, America met no European competition. Formerly Europe's food supplier, the war transformed America into the world's main source of both agricultural and industrial wares. In the face of this almost unlimitable market, America developed her productive capacities beyond measure.[15]

"The vast prairie that had been used for cattle raising before the war was turned into grain production. The combination of new methods of agriculture with new hybrid wheat and new machines enabled the United States in the years of 1925-1929 to extend by 3.6 million hectares. But in those same years, European agriculture again reached its pre-war level and even surpassed it. By 1926, it was able to resume exporting foodstuff and thus to compete with America on the world market." [16]

A recession was due to come in the year 1927.

In the same year, England began to feel the strain of returning to the gold standard. This act was the result of Europe's effort to restore international trade and economic affairs in general to the position it had had before the war. Stabilization of the various currencies was considered the basic condition for a return to old ways, since it guaranteed the foreign investor's interest and the foreign manufacturer's price.

The League of Nations was instrumental in pressing for stabilization of the currencies, believing it to be the all-important step toward the restoration of the world economy and a second line of defense for peace. The small and weak countries on the Continent literally starved themselves to reach the golden shores. For over a decade the restoration of the gold standard became a symbol of world solidarity. Currency was at the heart of the campaigns launched by Wall Street to overcome exchange problems and first to commercialize, then to mobilize, German reparations. But when Great Britain reverted to gold it became difficult for her to continue to lend to and help maintain the economies of the defeated nations in Europe as she had done before. It became apparent that the gold standard was forging a link between the small and poor East European countries, Germany, and the West. Eventually, the United States, the leading gold country, became silently concerned for the safety of the pound sterling. American support of the pound sterling in 1927 depended on a low rate of interest in New York in order to avert big movements of capital from London to New York. The Federal Reserve Board accordingly promised the Bank of England to keep its rate low; but presently America herself was in need of high rates as her own price system began to become perilously inflated. Thus, the preoccupation with the maintenance of the gold standard abroad brought America unexpectedly into the danger zone.[17]

The new, cheap money did not go into industry since American manufacturing just then was cutting back production in the face of the reappearance of European competition. Instead, the funds went into the Stock Exchange, where fast and high profits were expected. The speculators trusted in perpetual prosperity; [18] the speculative boom in Wall Street began.

Since the stock buyer needed only a marginal payment, small people were attracted to the market. This appeared to justify the general belief that the bull market would last. The boom was, to all appearances, self-sustaining. The man who sold made a profit since he had bought the stocks much cheaper; he who bought knew that he would sell at a profit a few weeks later; the broker made money on his commissions; the banker on the loans to the buyer and to the broker. Soon the reserves of industry also went into loans for stock market operations instead of production.

If any doubt persisted that the boom would never end, such authorities as E.H.H. Simmons, President of the New York Stock Exchange, were quick to berate the skeptic. Said he in September, 1929:

"Many people do not understand at all the facts that result in a surplus of capital in the country. They see inflation when what they observed was the continuous growth of financial transactions. They fail to understand that this is probably the end of the economic cycles as we have known them."[19]

As late as October 25, 1929, Charles M. Schwab, Chairman of the Board of Bethlehem Steel Corporation, said in an address before the American Iron and Steel Institute: "In my long association with the steel industry I have never known it to enjoy a greater stability or more promising outlook than it does today."

Millionaires like John J. Raskob wanted people to believe that the stock market could solve basic social problems. He called upon people of low income to follow the road to wealth:

"If a man saves $15 a week, and invests in good common stocks, and allows the dividends and rights to accumulate, at the end of twenty years he will have at least $80,000 and an income from investments of around $400 a month. He will be rich. And because income can do that, I am firm in my belief that anyone not only can be rich, but ought to be rich."

When the stock market crashed, the real values, the plants, the houses, the roads, were not wiped out; only the inflated figures attached to them. The prices of stocks had been driven to a height at which even the best stocks yielded disproportionately small dividends. The prices were not related to actual profits but to future profits which were supposed to become ever higher; in other words, to fantasy. It was this wealth of fantasy that collapsed in 1929.[20]

When the gold dust of illusion had been stripped away, a sober look at America's foundations revealed their moldy state.

America had ceased to be the country of unlimited opportunity as soon as the frontier had closed.

The high standard of living was a legend as far as it concerned the working population. In the years from 1919 to 1927, production per capita rose in the average three and a half per cent, but wages rose in the same period only two and four tenths per cent.[21]

The farmers were in chronic distress. Fifty thousand farmers went bankrupt between 1921 and 1929. Agricultural production in that period rose twenty-two per cent, but the value of farm commodities dropped twenty per cent.

The boom had not been justified by industry either. In the six years preceding the crash the yearly industrial output was estimated as amounting to seventy billion dollars. But huge quantities of goods could not be sold. At the end of each year, goods worth about twelve and a half billion remained in the factories and plants; five and a half billion more worth of goods stayed with the merchants.

Only in the highest brackets did incomes increase spectacularly. Revenue from the $10,000 to $150,000 a year bracket increased by thirteen per cent; taxes from those making above $150,000 doubled.[22]

The boom hid a grave maldistribution of wealth which made the rich richer and the poor poorer.

Until the economic depression began to show itself, still mildly in 1927 and then explosively in 1929, the American nation grew and developed its tremendous wealth. But in the past decades wealth had not been distributing itself lavishly among all the people; all the surplus wealth, all the savings had been amassed almost wholly by the very rich and the middle class, people who represented about one-fourth of the population.[23]

Before the crash, seven million families did not own a car; about twenty million had no radio. In the cities, more than four million families had no bathrooms; more than three million no running water in the kitchen. Thirteen million urban families had no telephone; four million no electricity in the years of prosperity.

The income of the corporations grew from 66 billion to 400 billion dollars net, the dividends from 38 to 375 billion dollars. But thirty per cent of the dividends was paid to other corporations as stockholders.[24]

It might have been the task of the government to reverse the trend of maldistribution of the national income through taxation and other appropriate means. But the idea was firmly ingrained in the public that the state was a parasite and that the best government was that which governed least. The dogma of American individualism refused to recognize the importance of the government. Civil service as a career was looked down upon by a public which considered getting rich as the highest aim of the individual. This principle generated a contemptuous indifference to politics as a profession of low calibre left to such people as incapable of making money in a more honorable way. While the masses neglected politics and had scant respect for the government, an oligarchy of big capitalists brought their influence to bear on it, often through the complicity of local politicians. They succeeded in acquiring titles for scandalous exploitation of public property and established business policies which reserved the bulk of the national income for a fraction of the citizenry.

They could not have done this, however, if the public at large had not approved of the preponderant influence of big business on politics. The public considered success as proof of the noblest qualities in man, and success in the financial field a top accomplishment of intelligence, foresight, and judgment. It was thus natural that these men should be called to lead America toward ever-increasing prosperity.[25]

This leadership failed the American people totally when the depression came.

Some economists insisted that a periodic, cyclical recession would sweep away unhealthy excesses, leaving business in better shape than before. Others believed that confidence in a fresh upturn would by itself start prosperity. They advised simple exorcising methods such as not recognizing the fact by substituting a smooth name for an ugly one. The word "crisis" was banned and "depression" used instead. This had also the advantage of evoking the image of a natural law. Therefore the depression made no headlines, being relegated to the back pages where it was counterbalanced by the statements of great men to the effect that the depression had reached bottom.[26] Throughout the first quarter of 1930, one side of Times Square in New York City carried an immense billboard bearing the legend, amusingly ingenious to the eyes of the foreigner unversed in American methods of handling the crisis: "Forward America! They can't beat US! Business is GOOD!" Smaller copies of this poster were to be found on other billboards and in the daily press.[27]

This faith in a depressionless economy had had a great share in the government's failure to devise protective measures during better times, while the constant optimism of experts convinced the public that the cycle was about to turn for the better again, and was responsible for the passivity of all concerned. The government's inaction stemmed from President Herbert Hoover's own convictions. He sincerely believed that government interference during the depression would do more harm than benefit, prolonging it by slowing down the inevitable process which eliminated the weak and unwholesome. He stood firm for laissez-faire. Even when the depth of the crisis revealed itself to be frightening and public pressure compelled him to take some steps, he acted reluctantly, he did too little too late. With regard to relief, Hoover "believed that the obligation for relief and reemployment began with the individual. Failing there, he might then call upon private organizations like the Red Cross, thence turn to municipal and state governments and, finally, as a last resort to the federal government—whose succor, in this ultimate extremity, should take the form of loans rather than gifts. Slowly and reluctantly Hoover was driven back trench by trench from what he conceived to be his defense of the public treasury." [28]

When a man asked him how a country could produce so much food that people starved, and so many manufactured goods that people had to do without them, Hoover branded it the dialectical invention of a cynic and warned: "There must be no place for cynicism in the creed of America."

But time passed and there was no improvement. The public recalled the optimistic statements of the President, the business leaders, and the predictions of the great economists "based on science." The first time the prophets of Wall Street declared that the depression was over, one was tempted to believe them, and when the first forecasts failed the American public was astonished. But as the breadlines grew longer, people shrugged their shoulders contemptuously at such predictions. Will Rogers, the humorist, implored the great economists to stop predicting the return of good times because, he said, it portends disaster.

Europeans were surprised by the total bankruptcy of the men of prestige and power in America in coping with the grave crisis. Europe had not believed that America had discovered the crisis-free economy. But they had expected that the Americans would know how to defend themselves against a setback with the utmost energy.[29] But the truth was that even the sales mechanism had failed in the predicament. The vast net of installment sales was showing astounding resistance to the depression; losses in the installment business were slight. The customers, the clerks, workers who had bought their phonograph, radio, furniture, and car on installment, were paying on time even if compelled to use up their last savings. But the salesmen lost their courage to take new orders.[30] They, like their bosses, were losing their heads. During the preceding years they had convinced themselves that the stupendous boom was the result of their own creative genius. Now they were forced to recognize that they had not been the deity controlling the winds, but rather the cork borne along helplessly on the crest of the wave.[31]

The crash of 1929 did not fail to affect adversely the rest of the world. Agriculture was in a world-wide depression, industrial raw materials slumping, industrial prices falling, stock exchange prices everywhere in a downward trend, and the banks were under the strain of heavy losses. Europe was going through a slowly grinding depression, less violent than its American counterpart only because the prosperity which had preceded it had not climbed to the dizzy American heights. The American depression made British financial problems easier by largely removing the danger of early reversion to dear money.[32]

In fact, the boom in the American stock market became one of the causes of the European slump. The huge profits made on loans to stock brokers had attracted American capital invested in Europe back to America. European capital also began to follow the way toward maximum profit and this movement started to drain the European money market.

Western Europe, particularly Britain, lent considerable amounts to the poor East European states to keep their currencies stable and so help sustain international trade. In 1931, the greatest bank of the former Hapsburg Empire, the Viennese Creditanstalt, which had important interests in the industries of the realm, was caught in difficulties. The British were ready to intervene in order to prevent the disastrous consequences of its inevitable collapse from spreading through Central Europe. France, however, opposed increased British influence in Eastern Central Europe. In September, the Creditanstalt defaulted.

English and especially American creditors became concerned for their capital in Central Europe. Above all, in Germany they hastened to withdraw their money. The inevitable consequence was that Germany and other countries stopped the transfer of moneys, introduced currency restrictions, and raised trade barriers. International creditors panicked eveywhere. Britain was so deeply involved by way of her credits in Central Europe that it was feared her own monetary position might be shaken by the crash. The Bank of England was obliged to go off the gold standard.

The blow to international trade caused a new wave of depression to flood America. Prices, production, and employment spiralled downward.

By the close of 1932, a great section of agriculture was already ruined; industrial prices had collapsed, the fall amounting to seventy to eighty per cent. In the capital goods industries, iron and steel plants worked at one-fifth of their productive capacity. Total payrolls had been reduced approximately sixty per cent.

One of every three persons still gainfully employed in 1931 was out of work by May, 1933; their number rose to fifteen million. Complacency gave way to bewilderment. The superstructure of prosperity crumbled with the foundations.[33] Many asked themselves whether the sick economy had not affected the very sources of life.[34] For the first time since the Pilgrims had landed on Plymouth Rock, Americans asked themselves in astonishment whether leisure might not become a duty. The "pioneer in time," like the "pioneer in space," appeared to be a species condemned by his own success.[35]

The pioneer and frontier mentality may have vanished in the period following the war, killed by death and the high standard of living.[36]

Many wondered about the future in the way a Mexican writer did, arguing that the United States, as well as other nations of the world, was facing a new situation in which human labor was no longer an essential factor. Since technical progress was of a permanent character and since nobody thought seriously of destroying the machines and of curbing scientific investigation, the problem of unemployment would also be permanent, unless new fields for expansion could be found or reforms in industrial methods were adopted to increase the demand for labor.[37]

Marxists, both socialist and communist, believed that this was the crisis of capitalism itself, perhaps its final crisis. From the opposite vantage point, but with the same tendency to overestimate its role in the development of human society, the organs of industrial capitalism in the European continent shared their apocalyptic views.

However, the Soviet Union did not encourage communists abroad. She was too absorbed in her first Five Year Plan. Any upheaval abroad might have necessitated intervention or increased armament and this would have delayed the accomplishment of the Plan. The Kremlin believed that the success of communist planning in Russia at the time when capitalist production was going bankrupt would spread communism all over the world.

Europe, however, was disillusioned with both America and

Russia. "When the earthquake of the world depression shook the economy of America as well as the Five Year Plan of Russia it made Europe sceptical about trusting either of these two prophets. Many who had turned toward Moscow and New York as the Meccas of new faiths overlooked the more intelligent middle of the road." [38]

"The depression revealed the truth of that early conclusion of Henry Adams that America had outlived her institutions, both economic and political," stated an English visitor.[39] The truth of the matter was that in the bountiful prosperity of her expanding market, which issued naturally from America's exploitation of the vast expanses of her continent from ocean to ocean, she had ignored the waste of her corrupt cities, her unstable banks, and her unsolved problems of democratic government in state and national regions alike. Now the public mind had at last realized that the optimism of nineteenth century expansion must give way to a reasoned examination of the ills of the body politic and economic—and that in the sphere of government, no less than in banking and manufacture, a new and more stable plan must be devised.

Arnold Toynbee had a much graver view of the crisis, believing it to be the moral crisis of modern civilization. Beyond American constitutional and business shortcomings, beyond the disharmony of technology and society, the historian saw the failure of Western man. "In A.D. 1932," he wrote, "it was patent that the potential gift of an undreamed wealth and leisure could only be grasped by Man at the price of an undreamed of fraternity and solidarity between every man and all his fellow human beings and this was a price which the living generation of Mankind seemed morally incompetent to pay." [40]

To understand the liberating effect of the Roosevelt era, a look backwards on the two years that preceded it, through the eyes of an English visitor, would be instructive:

"I landed in New York on December 24th, 1931.

"It was the difference from what I had met before that struck me most forcibly. Not only the difference from the glowing mood of everlasting prosperity of 1927 and 1928; but the difference, as marked, though of its own kind, from 1930.

"In 1930, people were, of course, dazed and reeling under the shock of the Wall Street and stock market collapse. . . . No one had expected it; few could, really, believe in it; nearly everybody then said that it was temporary. . . . Prosperity, in fact, as a line in a witty 1931 Broadway comedy put it with angry irony, was Hoovering round the corner. . . .

But in 1932, the author saw the same places disfigured by despair.

". . . In New York, one has only to pass outside the central island bounded by Lexington and Sixth Avenues to see hardship, misery, and degradation. . . . Times Square, at any hour of the day and late into the evening, offers an exhibit for the edification of the theatre-goer, for it is packed with shabby, utterly dumb, and apathetic-looking men. Nowhere, in New York or any other city, can one escape from the visible presence of those who with perhaps unconscious cruelty are called 'the idle.'

Was it America's happier past that made her despair in the face of disaster, while the long history of catastrophe behind the European nations hardened them toward misfortune?

"The American people are outraged and baffled by misfortune. . . . Misled in the onset by leaders . . . that American institutions were immune to the ills that had laid the countries of the rest of the world upon their backs; that prosperity was native to the soil of the Union . . . the nation now suffers from a despair of any and every kind of leadership. Every institution is assailed; even the sacred foundations of democracy are being undermined."[41]

Had the depression changed American thinking on economic issues?

An Englishman who had visited America yearly since 1928 answered the question in the negative in the fall of 1932. On his previous visits he had been impressed by the willingness of American businessmen to discuss the idea of planned economy, by the almost universal interest in Russia, and by the beginning of a sympathetic interest in unemployment insurance. A short upturn in early 1932 was enough for them, however, to think only of a rising stock market in which to recover some of the losses of the crash. The Americans as a whole had learned nothing from the depression, he concluded.[42]

Others sized up the reaction of the plain people to the demoralizing effects of the prolonged depression. They were impressed by the extent they had been able to adjust to their change in status. They found the secret hidden in certain features of the American scene not obvious to those who know only the sidewalks of New York. There was a great deal of neighborly feeling in small towns, and the small town was more typical of the United States than the few great cities which Europeans know mainly. There was not the same loss of caste, because no one believed that the reversal of fortune was anything but temporary. "Here is something which, speaking for myself, I find wholly admirable in the American," the visitor commented. "And this pioneering spirit, which refuses to believe that one can be finally down and out, is one of the main reasons for my belief that American recovery, once the corner has been definitely turned, will be very rapid." [43]

Neighborliness and mutual aid were not confined to the small towns. Paul Claudel, the great French poet and Ambassador to Washington, discovered that the Americans, feeling they were all in the same boat, had developed a true fraternity among themselves. "There is no other country," he said, "where the people are so much affected by the financial crisis, and nowhere have I seen so many examples of solidarity and kindness as I saw in America." [44]

Americans tried to weave a pattern of decent living on a much more primitive level than they had lived before the crash. That time now appeared ages away. The mighty and the successful of 1929 walked about "like emigrant grand dukes, only less romantic, their era about as real as the empire of the Romanoffs." [45] But the world economy might eventually be stabilized even on such a poor level, a Swiss delegate to an international conference in 1932 predicted, and no one protested. "Those who possess gold," he said, "will refuse to part with it. State debts will not be paid. Some kind of currency will be established within each State, and any kind will do the job if the money is not allowed to circulate outside the frontiers. Nations will import the exact value of their exports like the savages who exchange fur and ivory for some manufactured good. People will no more travel, and the West soon will be back where she started out centuries ago." [46]

Indeed, many households in America already were making soap, drying fruit, pickling, preserving, baking bread, brewing medicine from herbs, cleaning, dyeing, and cloth-making.[47] In Central Europe, horsedrawn omnibuses were remodeled to replace autobuses, since gasoline had to be paid for with scarce foreign currency. Agricultural machinery was also put out of use in order to let the unemployed earn some money. Human labor became the cheapest commodity everywhere. In this way did a civilization appear to be disintegrating; its triumph, the machines, stood unwanted, the industrial products they poured forth unsold, food rotted while people survived on a half-starvation level. This seemed to be the end of a civilization that had produced for profit, satisfying needs as a by-product, and calling this progress.

Europeans were startled at the total absence of riots or violent demonstrations of dissatisfaction by the American farmers and the unemployed.[48] "Disorientation did not drive the Americans to despair, or as the Germans, to metaphysical or even apocalyptic ideas. They remained basically optimistic and liked to hear whatever strengthened their optimism." [49] Yet some observers considered this stubborn optimism unhealthy and artificial. It meant that "the American public is collectively the victim of a Coué philosophy . . . which refuses to admit the existence of the unpleasant. The facts of our epoch must sooner or later correct this obstinate folly, which may be described as a faith in the future hardly less destructive of the national fibre than England's fatal reliance on the past." [50]

Another comment referred to John Dewey who wrote that "Christian Science rules American thought in business affairs; if we can be led to think that certain things do not exist, they perforce have not happened," but it also attributed the "conspiracy of opimism" to the press and the business associations, "Mr. Hoover himself contributing to the blinding of the American public." [51] Whatever its cause this disproved the forecast of Lord Macauley, the great liberal who was terrified by the prospect of democracy. He wrote to an American friend: "I seriously apprehend that you will in some . . . season of adversity . . . act like people who in a year of scarcity, devour all the seed corn, and thus make the next year not of scarcity, but of absolute famine. There will be, I fear, spoliation. The spoliation will increase the distress. The distress will produce fresh spoliation. . . . When society has entered on this downward progress, either civilization or liberty must perish. . . . There is nothing to stop you. Your Constitution is all sail and no anchor . . ." [52]

Yet it was the consciousness that the Constitution had given them the right and the opportunity to throw their government out of office and to sweep clean the Administration and Congress of those who had proved to be incompetent and impotent that kept Americans from revolting. The Constitution had given them the power to make a legal revolution. As long as this power remained intact, there was no urgent need to overthrow the government by force.

The Constitution invested the person of the President with a "blinding predominance." He had to pay for it in times of adversity, and Herbert Hoover was paying for it. "Adulated for a prosperity he had not made, he was condemned for an adversity he could not cure." [53] Was he unfit for the high office at times of crisis?

"As Secretary of Commerce for seven years, and the master of the new technique, Mr. Hoover gained a knowledge of American industry and trade greater than that of any cabinet member known to this generation. It was understood that he was particularly interested in the phenomenon of trade cycles, and the public could take for granted that, in the event of financial or commercial disaster, he would be prepared for immediate action." [54]

"Mr. Hoover . . . was the first President to be known as a

representative of modern business and of industrial organization. To the confusion of the politicians of the old order he was explained and acclaimed as the Great Engineer." [55] His qualifications appeared, however, insufficient for a leader of a nation in an emergency. Less than two years after his assuming the Presidency, "the rueful Republicans are reflecting, it would seem that this is exactly what the President is, a great engineer." [56]

Others were less severe toward Hoover. "Through colossal ill-luck," a German wrote of him, "Hoover has become the most unpopular man in America." [57] Two years after his inauguration he was subjected to disparaging criticism by the press, by all sections of business to an extent that no other President had experienced. Some had been hated by the industrialists, by the rich, or by the poor, in the North or in the South, but no one had ever aroused such a universal hostility as he. Not even his closest party friends dared plead for him lest they share his unpopularity.[58]

He did take effective measures against the depression, but only after long and futile battles and then with deep conviction that he was doing the wrong thing. In 1930 he accorded aid to the victims of drought and made money available for local public works. But he stubbornly refused government aid to the unemployed. Charity and local authorities caved in under their tremendous burden, but still Hoover feared to injure the moral integrity of the men who would accept aid. He was not callous to human misery, but remained true to the dogma of laissez-faire.

When it was unavoidable, Hoover granted credits to the farmers as an advance on their income from the next crop, and he allotted funds to the Red Cross for distribution. He was eventually compelled to establish the Reconstruction Finance Corporation for the purpose of lending federal money to the states so that they might distribute help among the needy. This expediency did not impair Hoover's disapproval of government intervention in the economy.

The governor of one state challenged Hoover to act in 1930. On the basis of a different philosophy of government, which clearly established the responsibility of the government for the welfare of its citizens, Franklin Delano Roosevelt reproached Hoover for his inactivity in the face of utter emergency. "Although the times called for quick and decisive action by the Federal government, nothing happened but words," he charged. "[Now] was the time, if ever, when government projects should have been accelerated. That was the time, if ever, when public works should have been pushed so as to provide employment. That was the time, if ever, that increasing appropriations for federal aid, roads, river and harbor improvements, veterans' hospitals, military constructions, and public buildings should have been speeded up." [59]

2

FORGOTTEN MAN'S MAN

On November 6, 1932, the people elected Franklin D. Roosevelt President.

By 11:30 P.M. the election was over. Roosevelt had carried forty-two states and 472 electoral votes. One had the feeling that a crisis of nerve was finally vanishing, a French journalist who spent the evening in New York reported. "People blow trumpets, strike the bells, stir the rattles, peddlers pop up on every corner, selling bizarre objects which all make noise, young people start singing and take to dancing as at a carnival. I don't buy whistles, but I also burst with gaiety. Not as if I am taking part; I'm not. But I attempt to understand the passions let loose about me; I understand them through sympathy. This is an explosion between two inhibitions: that of yesterday and that of tomorrow; this is the exuberance of the young soul of America that has nothing in common with the skeptical and blasé soul of Old Europe." [1]

"For the first time in half a generation the American people have elected a President who gives his fellow citizens the heartening picture of a joyous American, working with zest, talking copiously, and smiling as though he had no misgivings for the future of the United States," [2] an Englishman wrote.

"In personality and associations he makes a striking contrast to each one of his predecessors since Wilson. Warren Harding was a painfully limited politician, the frightened creature of an Ohio gang. Calvin Coolidge, a New England Republican of remarkable steadiness, was an example of that 'availability' which in easy times exemplifies the smooth running of a national political machine. Herbert Hoover, attaining the Presidency after a professional career in which the politics of democracy played no part at all, has afforded the American people their first experience of a specialist organizer as Chief Executive. Governor Roosevelt is as thoroughgoing a politician as either Harding or Coolidge, but he belongs to the class of gentlemen-politicians which in contemporary America is an exceedingly small class."

The writer summed up the public career of the President-elect.

"Elected to the State Senate while still in his twenties, he made an early reputation at Albany by leading an effective revolt against the Democratic party bosses. He was active in the Wilson presidential campaign, and was rewarded with the Under-Secretaryship of the Navy, a post for which, by a coincidence almost unheard of in modern Washington, he had been prepared by the extensive study of naval history. At the close of the second Wilson term no man in the Democratic party seemed more assured of advancement than this vigorous and expansive New Yorker, who had done his administrative job to admiration.

"But he was stricken down. In 1921, after swimming in the icy waters of the Bay of Fundy, he was attacked by poliomyelitis, the deadly scourge that most people know as infantile paralysis. It caused a complete crippling of the legs, and for any man of less courage and resilience it might well have meant the end of all active life.

"Mr. Roosevelt refused to be beaten. He started on a course of the most rigorous treatment, returned to his law practice, and by 1928, when virtually compelled by his political associates to become a candidate for the governorship of New York, he was far on the way to recovery. He walks now with the aid of two sticks, displaying in his large frame all the evidences of perfect health. . . ."[3]

One man who had visited the young Roosevelt in Washington during World War I, when the latter served under President Wilson as Assistant Secretary of the Navy, hastened to publish his recollection of that meeting:

"Secretary Roosevelt's parlor was decorated with models of vessels, ancient and modern. He cut a magnificent figure, talked with gusto, and disarmed rather than convinced the visitor as he presented his arguments with lively gestures and a contagious smile. His sheer appearance created immediate good feelings and ease; it suggested the presence of a man who enjoyed life, knew how to go about it and also how to extend his exuberance to other people." [4]

European democrats, who feared not only their own dour ideologists but also American moralists of the Wilsonian type, hailed the election of a man who reflected the self-confidence of a young and strong country. They liked his almost naïve common-sense attack on the ugly complex of the depression, his pragmatism in promising to find one method or another for the people "to get the things to satisfy their needs." In essence, he promised but one thing, that he would keep on trying. "He is sensible enough not to pose as a superman," a Frenchman wrote.[5]

Some foreign papers warned that it would be a mistake to attribute too much importance to the personality of the President-elect or too great a part in the victory to the victor himself. His election was a demonstration of anger and disillusionment.[6] "The army of ten million unemployed, the three million more men and women who may be out of jobs this winter, the hundreds of thousands who have seen their capital savings disappear into the thin air. From them came Roosevelt's huge majority. Their disillusionment, their despair accrued to him." [7]

"He was elected by 'the forgotten man,' to whom he had promised to lead the United States back onto the road of clear reason." [8]

The vote belied those who a year before had insisted that the American people would never elect a cripple to the Presidency. There was instinctual logic, however, in electing a man handicapped, who had given such a luminous example of triumph over disability, to the task of leading the stricken country back to health.[9] By electing him the American people took a long step toward psychological and moral health. In the time of the unlimited-success myth and prosperity craze, mishap and misfortune had been considered un-American and ruled out of place in public life, unmentionable in decent company. Roosevelt re-introduced misfortune, albeit a conquered one, into American life.[10] Roosevelt's paralysis had created a new trait in his own character which became essential in his personality: an understanding of humiliation in life. Before fate struck him down, Roosevelt had walked on the heights of this world. He could become a sponsor of the "forgotten man" only after fate had humiliated him and thrown him into the depths of misery.[11]

An Englishman, like so many who watched the President, was startled at his unconcern with the public display of his disability. "I watched with interest," the British M.P. wrote, "his approach to the platform. Very slowly, painfully slowly, he shuffled down an interminable gangway, leaning on the shoulder of his young son and on a stick, dragging one limb after another until he reached the inclined ramp which, for his benefit, had been substituted for the four steps that led to the platform. It ought to have been rather embarrassing, but I remember that I was unconscious of any feeling of embarrassment. There was something in the poise of the head on the broad shoulders which made one forget the nearly helpless limbs beneath. There was an expression on the face of relaxed good will, of unconcern, of utter unselfconsciousness, which made it impossible for the onlooker to be aware of a disability of which the victim himself was so supremely unaware." [12]

International opinion concurred in recognizing the significance of the 1932 election for the whole world. When a country of 120 million people, responsible for forty per cent of the world's production and associated with the most advanced capitalist economy, set about the task of forcing its way out of the economic morass, no part of the world could fail to be directly affected by the eventual outcome of the experiment.[13] Yet people wondered: Would things get better? Was the capitalistic world strong enough to rise again? Everybody was aware that these questions would be answered in the United States and nowhere else. America, the strongest representative of the system, was called upon to demonstrate its ability to recover and its capacity for self-help. From the success of the strong, the weaker ones would draw hope and strength.[14]

The new President assumed office on March 4, 1933. "Under a heavy sky, a powerful automobile drove through the principal avenue of Washington, preceded by a howling swarm of motorcyclists zooming in the direction of the Capitol. A massive row of people silently viewed the two figures in the car. On the right, a mask famous over the whole world in the last four years . . . pressed in vain his strong jaw; a deeply disappointed nation had no interest in his sagging face and nervously trembling lips. All eyes have turned upon his successor, Franklin D. Roosevelt." [15]

"Who is Franklin D. Roosevelt?" a Swiss paper asked. "Will he become the leader that the United States now more urgently needs than ever?" Reviewing his public career, the paper cited his assets: "Only 31 years old, the fiery Franklin sat in the Navy Department as Under-Secretary, where he is still remembered for turning the 'white elephant' Navy wharves into a working proposition. It is said also that his indefatigable activity was responsible for the fact that the Navy met the requirements of the World War. The Labor Board was his creation and he who examines the history of American labor unions will find much to Roosevelt's credit. Whether he will be able to fulfil his promises nobody can foretell. Time will work against him as it has worked against Hoover, but his advantage over Hoover is the refreshing optimism that animates him." [16]

Since his personality was to be of immense consequence, the foreign correspondents tried to penetrate it and to convey their analysis to the public back home. A French journalist wrote, ". . . Roosevelt is very different from the pictures with which the magazines are full, showing him as an average, decent American, off the assembly line, so to say. Actually there is something very peculiar and very original in his features . . . which are irradiated with a magnetism which captivates all who confront him. . . . The agility of his speech is remarkable. Memories and anecdotes come crowding into his mind. Of all American statesmen, he is undoubtedly the most familiar with matters European, a precious quality that will amply aid him during his Presidency. He speaks excellent French, as one who learned the language as a child, and he visibly enjoys talking it. I do not know any other American politician, although I know many, of whom I could say the same." [17] "He is of great charm but superficial rather than profound," another observer ventured.

The radio waves carried Roosevelt's inauguration speech to the four corners of the world. The German voters, on the eve of their own fateful election, probably drew from the speech of the new American president the conclusion that a new era was to begin across the Atlantic also.

". . . first of all, let me assert my firm belief that the only thing we have to fear is fear itself—nameless, unreasoning, unjustified terror which paralyzes needed efforts to convert retreat into advance . . . our distress comes from no failure of substance. We are stricken by no plague of locusts. . . . Plenty is at our doorsteps, but a generous use of it languishes in the very sight of the supply. Primarily this is because rulers of the exchange of mankind's goods have failed, through their own stubbornness and their own incompetence, have admitted their failure, and abdicated. Practices of the unscrupulous money changers stand indicted in the court of public opinion, rejected by the hearts and minds of men. . . . If I read the temper of our people correctly, we now realize as we have never realized before our interdependence on each other; that we cannot merely take but we must give as well; that if we are to go forward, we must move as a trained and loyal army willing to sacrifice for the good of a common discipline, because without such discipline no progress is made, no leadership becomes effective. . . . I am prepared under my constitutional duty to recommend the measures that a stricken nation in the midst of a stricken world may require. . . . But in the event that the Congress shall fail to take [action] . . . I shall not evade the clear course of duty that will then confront me. I shall ask the Congress . . . broad Executive power to wage a war against the emergency, as great as the power that would be given to me if we were in fact invaded by a foreign foe.

"For the trust reposed in me I will return the courage and the devotion that befit me. I can do no less.

". . . We do not distrust the future of essential democracy. The people of the United States have not failed. In their need they have registered a mandate that they want direct, vigorous action. They have asked for discipline and direction under leadership. They have made me the present instrument of their wishes. In the spirit of the gift I take it."

As the Governor, in a message to the Legislative Assembly of the State of New York, the President had much earlier spelled out his philosophy of government:

"In broad terms I assert that modern society, acting through its government, owes the definite obligation to prevent the starvation or the dire want of any of its fellow men and women who try to maintain themselves but cannot . . . the same responsibility of the State undoubtedly applies when widespread economic conditions render large numbers of men and women incapable of supporting either themselves or their families because of circumstances beyond their control which make it impossible for them to find remunerative labor. To these unfortunate citizens aid must be extended by the Government, not as a matter of charity, but as a matter of social duty."

In another speech, on July 2nd, 1932, Roosevelt had drawn a sharp line between himself and nineteenth century *laissez-faire*. He refused to accept economic laws as unchangeable when they caused men and women to starve amidst plenty. He challenged those laws: "We must lay hold of the fact that economic laws are not made by nature. They are made by human beings." The statement implied that what was made by men could also be altered by men, and if the current economic laws involved periodic panic and general misery, the laws had to be and could be changed.

On March 5, a day after Roosevelt's inauguration, the Nazis hailed the result of the German election. Yet the country failed to return Hitler's party by an absolute majority.

Hitler had been Chancellor since January 1933 when Marshal-President Hindenberg asked him to head a coalition government. Upon taking office, Hitler promptly dissolved the Reichstag and ordered new elections for the following March in the hope that his party would gain absolute power by a clear election majority. A violent campaign culminated in a huge Reichstag fire which Hitler denounced as part of a Communist plot. Goering and other party workers drove the peasantry and middle class into a frenzy of fear with their stories about other communist plots to poison all the food and burn the granaries all over the Reich.

Despite all of this the National Socialists received only forty-four per cent of the votes in the March 5th election.

Both Roosevelt's New Deal and Hitler's program attacked international banking's hold on their countries' budgetary policies. Roosevelt's campaign against Wall Street and Hitler's condemnation of "interest slavery" issued from the same necessity of freeing the government's hand in order to take measures against unemployment and economic crisis. In Germany, however, this policy was charged with emotional explosives. International banking had assumed control of the German budget to insure reparation payments accruing from World War I. In the final analysis, the inflation, the fall of the German rentier class, tight money and the resulting crippling unemployment, even the spread of foreign-owned department stores, issued from the same catastrophe—defeat in the war. At least, it was easy for the Nazi program, a remarkable concoction of the follies and phobias of the middle class, to impute all later misfortunes to the defeat. The Nazis promised to wipe out Marxism and capitalism as well, but in the hatred of the Jews the contradiction dissolved.

There was nothing sinister in the change that was discernible in Washington as Herbert Hoover's successor moved into the White House. "His presence wiped out with a single stroke the atmosphere of rigidity and solemn dullness that hung upon it under the preceding presidents. The warmhearted and lively temperament of the new landlord, his joy in life and cheerful humanity turned the august residence into the pulsing center of a reviving nation," said an observer.[18]

His was not to be a businessmen's government nor was it to be one directed against them. The new president gathered round himself a far more diversified group than had any other president before him. A group of businessmen had formed before the election to support him, partly from personal loyalty, for many old friends were among them, partly from opportunism. But some welcomed the change represented by Roosevelt's election either as long overdue or as a prevention of something worse. Along with the people the party machinery selected to get a share in the spoils, these businessmen represented the traditional element in a victorious party. A newspaper reproached Roosevelt for failing to free American political life from the old machine politicians, "who often do not excel either in moral or intellectual qualifications." But, the paper added: "America knows that a new day has dawned and that her most important heritage, freedom and respect for the individual, has a better support in the popular-liberal concept of Roosevelt than in the theoretical principles of the Republican protectors of freedom." [19]

Right behind the President's study a group of bright young men settled down and proceeded to inform the President as they had done when he was campaigning, discussing with him bills, new organizations, economic theories, and their applications. The group was called the "brain trust." The President wanted idealists and realists in his inner circle. The fact alone that Roosevelt was selecting academic men augured the dawn of a new order. By principle and necessity the Federal government had to take on new functions. Soon new agencies were organizing for what were believed to be unorthodox or temporary assignments. Professors and intellectuals headed for Washington.

From his first moment in the White House, Roosevelt "humanized . . . the economic and political life of the country so as to make it more tender, more hospitable to man." [20] Instead of theories, "a human factor guided his thinking even in economics, where it had been neglected for a long time." These were "the social values more noble than mere monetary profit" he had spoken of in his inaugural address.

Roosevelt kept in direct touch with the people by means of press conferences. They became the forum for a mutual exchange of ideas between the government and the public; a source of first hand information and a platform for releasing trial balloons. Roosevelt's fireside chats brought into all homes the confidence, humanity, and friendliness of the President. After listening to him talk, people knew that their case was in strong hands.

On Sunday, his first day in the White House, the President

ordered all banks in the country to remain closed till Thursday, when Congress was to meet and approve the measure.

Many banks had already been closed as a consequence of runs on them by their depositors or by state authorities attempting to prevent a run from materializing. Nevertheless, the presidential order made a mighty impression, perhaps because it came so promptly, or just because it was action. Roosevelt promised that the solvent banks would soon re-open. At the same time, he prohibited dealings in gold, including its export. There was a general feeling of relief in having a President determined to cope with the crisis.

Psychologically, the effect of the President's first acts had been masterfully, though perhaps not consciously, prepared. He had refused to share any responsibility with Hoover for emergency actions between the time of his election and his assumption of the Presidency. During the interim, the situation continued to deteriorate. The whole economy seemed to be sinking indefinitely and there was no one to hold back disaster. Roosevelt's order on his first day in the White House resolved an almost unbearable tension. During the following days, when the President's reassuring voice first spoke to the people from the fireside, and through the questions and answers of his first press conference, his serene confidence instilled new life in the native optimism of the American public. On Thursday, people ran to the banks—to redeposit their money.

During the famous Hundred Days after Roosevelt's inauguration, bills coping with the emergency rained on the Congress, which hastened to invest them with the power of law. Even these temporary measures reflected the President's great concern for the dignity of the people, for the morale and self-confidence of the youth, and for the conservation of natural resources. A banking law established control over the banks and instituted obligatory insurance of deposits. The Federal government instituted direct aid to the states and municipalities for distribution among the needy. Youths were recruited for the Civilian Conservation Corps, which was engaged in various public works projects. Other public works were financed as a means of providing money and work for the unemployed. Home loans were organized to save small property owners. The Agricultural Adjustment Act guaranteed a certain return for basic commodities and reimbursed the farmer for the loss resulting from his voluntary limitation of production.

Sensing the enthusiasm of the public as the prodding actions simultaneously galvanized every segment of the economy and population, the President and his advisers resolved to change their schedule, which had originally provided for immediate emergency measures, with a more complete reform program planned for later consideration.

These emergency measures already represented a radical break with American tradition. The federal government's aid to the unemployed, even though distributed through the states and the municipalities; its direct intervention in the field of agricultural production and prices; its crucial role in fixing prices and wages; and its support for collective bargaining marked the beginning of a new era. But this program also introduced a change in philosophy, in the American way of life. The New Deal legislation was inspired by the general, deep desire for security. From this desire stemmed the program of unemployment insurance, minimum wages, the prohibition of child labor, collective bargaining, social security, conservation programs, etc. Enthusiastic approval by the public suggested to the President that he might deviate from his timetable and introduce reform legislation planned for later as long as the public's enthusiasm could be sustained. He was aided by the general hostility felt toward the old industrial and financial system, the utter discredit of business leadership, "and a considerable degree of liberty of action facilitated by the extreme diversity of the remedies." And time was of the essence.

As the numerous bills of the Administration began to appear on the House and Senate floors, it was plain that it was the view of the President that his power to complete the task he had set for himself depended greatly upon a public opinion cowed into acquiescence by the continuance of the very depression he was trying to eliminate.[21] For, meanwhile, business continued to get worse, even though morale everywhere was so much better. "To the ardent reformers in his party quick action on all fronts was welcome. Here was a catalogue of ancient wrongs inflamed by the savage injustice of the Machine Age. Here were problems which wrung the heart and taxed the intellect; opportunities which quickened the imagination and fed ambition; noble visions of a new and splendid social order; and a vast discomfited people ripe for salvation if only it would come quickly." [22]

The great program was embodied in the National Recovery Administration. The idea originated with General Johnson, its first chairman, who had adapted Mussolini's corporation idea in which labor, management, and government had cooperated—at least on paper. Here was an ambitious project that would lay the foundation for a self-regulating economy. Each industry would establish its code, set prices, agree on wages and working hours. Labor, management, and representatives of the consumers would cooperate in establishing the codes, with government approval giving the power of law to them. The NRA gave a very small role to the government, but the President and his advisers wanted it that way. They feared being accused of launching a fascist state. But the NRA practically thrust aside the anti-trust laws and legally established collective bargaining for labor. The Public Works Administration received federal funds for large-scale public works. A simultaneous pick-up in all industries and resultant higher employment gave a powerful impulse to the entire economy. A huge army of unemployed was put to work, though at less than standard wages. Eventually they produced roads, hundreds of military airports, bridges and viaducts, over a hundred thousand schools, libraries, laboratories, hospitals, court houses, etc., and warships.[23]

Above all the public works, the creation of the Tennessee Valley Authority stood out. It was a multi-purpose regional cooperative development based on a great river. It was to become an instrument of flood control, navigation, irrigation, reforestation, soil conservation, and a generator of cheap electricity for the inhabitants of the region and for industries that would be attracted there. Its outstanding success has been an example of an American solution to the problem of combined private and community ownership and a beam of hope to underdeveloped peoples trying to rise from poverty.

"If America succeeds it will do the world a great deal of good; if she fails the whole world is bound to feel its repercussions," the *Bombay Chronicle* wrote on September 30, 1933. While the world weighed the chances of the American experiment, Sir Robert Horne, former Chancellor of the Exchequer, stated as early as November 3, 1933, that Roosevelt "succeeded in restoring confidence in the prospects of recovery and to the American citizen the belief in himself."

By the end of 1933, Roosevelt's popularity was still so overwhelming that a foreign observer heard no dissent. "His popularity has only one precedent in the history of the United States," the writer reported, "that of George Washington. It cannot be justified by the results obtained here and there, not even by the hopes. . . . The docility of the Congress is an index sufficiently convincing. Senators and Representatives obey the will of the people manifesting itself through their daily mail, in which the voters insist that they follow 'our President.' A humorist went so far as to pretend that if Mr. Roosevelt requested a law prescribing the sterilization of the members of Congress they would not dare oppose it. . . . Thus the man, and his policy in which a year before the highest hopes of salvation had been put, have not disappointed."[24]

"In America, not in form but in spirit, the same has come to pass as in ancient Rome when power was transferred to a dictator, but only for a limited period in order to save the Republic. The Romans renounced temporarily democratic rights in order to save Democracy itself. This is in contrast to Germany where the people have never made a similar political decision and where, therefore, the clamor for an authoritative *régime* surely signifies more than a temporary measure," a Swiss daily commented.[25]

Men as distant in character and action as Lloyd George and Paul Claudel praised the President, each in his own way. "The American government when faced with a panic did not stand with chattering teeth in the face of the emergency but dealt with it firmly and boldly," the British statesman said on May 16, 1933. "Roosevelt is a great man," the French poet-ambassador stated on May 4, 1933, "not only because he has a great mind but because he has a wonderful technique in handling men. He believes rightly that in time of depression anything is better than remaining in the same place, and that it is better to move in one direction than in several directions at the same time."

Few appreciated the full meaning of the President's resolution to quit the gold standard as much as a Frenchman who warned: "No matter how uncertain the future seems to be, one point has been established: The United States took the measure of directing the dollar. It is the government that has taken hold of the wheel of the monetary command. Elsewhere it is held by the Central Bank which is mostly the agent of the great financial powers. In America now the state is master of its money. A capital event, practically a revolution." [26]

But Roosevelt's decision augured ill for the World Economic Conference, set for London on June 12, 1933. The Europeans had hoped for a general agreement on the stabilization of the currencies. Roosevelt had given enough reason for European statesmen visiting Washington in the Spring to misunderstand him. Also, his appeal to the sovereigns of the world had made them believe that he was looking for an international solution of the monetary crisis. He had probably not made a final resolution when the Conference opened. The *Times* of London rightly complained that the President had not had enough time from March to June to "reach a solution of the complicated tangle," but the delegates assembled from all over the world. "The somber black in which they were universally garbed gave them the appearance of being in mourning for the world's financial condition. Pessimism [was] a strong undertone of the preliminary utterances. . . . There are said to be at least thirty million unemployed workers throughout the world whose hope for re-employment must rest largely upon what this conference of nations can agree upon." [27]

Even more disquieting was the obvious fact that the American delegation, headed by Cordell Hull, Secretary of State, was not interpreting the President's stand correctly, unless Roosevelt had undergone a change of heart while Hull was on his way to the conference. The President's message put an end to the uncertainty. He could not sacrifice his freedom of action to manipulate the price of the dollar in terms of gold, nor could he agree on a level of stabilization of currencies that favored vast imports from the European continent. His message dissipated unrealistic expectations as it read: "The sound economic system of a nation is a greater factor in its well being than the price of its currency in changing terms of the curriencies of other nations."

The new American President thus appeared to be no less isolationist than his two previous predecessors. A Frenchman had warned the public back home prior to the Conference. It might be illogical, surely regrettable, perhaps deplorable for her as well as for Europe, he wrote, but the truth was that the United States, since the end of World War I, had not wanted a European policy. Even if the President was inclined to cooperate with Europe, the Senate would resist such a policy. He compared the making of American foreign policy with Plato's famous myth of the human soul which he compared with a quadriga of black and white horses, the latter pulling it skywards, the former down toward realities.[28]

A German called "international illusionists" those who had expected the President to become a partner to an agreement on monetary stabilization as a first step toward economic collaboration.[29] Unorthodox experts fully approved of the temporary avoidance of international commitments. John Maynard Keynes saw in it a guarantee of freedom from international finance. "The policy of national self-sufficiency," he wrote, "although not an ideal in itself or in the long run, is needed for the immediate future to guarantee each country its freedom while attempting to find a new mode of political economy. . . . Ideas, knowledge, science, hospitality, travel—these are the things which should of their nature be international. . . . But let goods be homespun, whenever it is reasonably possible, and above all, let finance be primarily national." [30]

It is rare to find among the contemporary publications the perspicacity with which one of them caught the exact meaning of the President's stand with respect to an international monetary agreement. An article in an English magazine expounded on the significance of the change in Washington. The initiative, like the administraton, it asserted, had passed from the hands of the creditors to the hands of the debtors. This change of the guards was more obvious abroad than in the United States. On the Continent it was consistently developing into the *Diktat* of the debtors. Gone were the times when the governments sent warships to the defaulting debtor countries' main harbors, enforcing submission. Now Hitler's government began buying food and industrial raw materials from the hard hit Continental countries first on barter, then on credit, while the small creditor countries trembled that he might stop buying and upset the whole economy. Still, to follow a debtor's policy might have been understandable on the part of an internationally indebted country like Germany, but made little sense in the case of America, a par excellence creditor country. However, Roosevelt had switched to the debtor because, as Frances Perkins put it, though the minority often turns out to be right and Roosevelt knew that, he was always tempted to go along with the great majority.[31]

The President switched to the point of view of the debtor in the international field so he could choose his internal economic measures independent of the rules of international finance. The English magazine cautioned its readers against identifying the rule of finance with democracy, with laissez-faire, or even with capitalism. "We might do better to consider how far democracy has gone down on its own merits and how far it has succumbed because it could or would not give up serving as a mask for the type of unplanned, rapacious capitalism which is obsolete and dying." [32]

Yet this was exactly the mistake that the Western European governments and their supporters made in defending democracy from the propaganda onslaught of the dictators. When these latter conveniently called that kind of democracy decadent and obsolete, it rang true to many within the Western democracies.

When the danger of war became serious, people began to question whether they had anything to fight for. Roosevelt's break with international finance won general approval in Western Europe after it became clear that he had at the same time preserved intact the democratic institutions of the country. The dictators, however, were convinced that Roosevelt, to save his reform plans, would be compelled to shift to autocratic methods.

Roosevelt's message ended the Economic Conference. Autarchy became the economic self-defense of the continental countries. They manipulated currency, levied import restrictions, made barter agreements. For Italy and Germany, autarchy provided an immunity from international restrictions and facilitated their preparations for war.

The end of the Economic Conference led to the end of the Disarmament Conference.

The Survey of International Affairs of 1933 ascribed the "portentous failures" of the two conferences to Germany as well as to the United States. "Two countries were at crucial points in the world battlefield." The most prominent single cause of the breakdown of the Disarmament Conference was "Germany's self-centered determination to recover, at all costs, her lost equality with other Great Powers of the World, while the most prominent single cause of the breakdown of the Economic Conference was the similarly self-centered determination of the United States to restore, at all costs, her lost international economic equilibrium."

In the fall of 1933, Roosevelt lowered the gold value of the dollar in order to raise prices, especially those of agricultural products. The gold standard countries, headed by France, execrated and heaped abuse on America and Roosevelt. Roosevelt was accused of engaging the richest nation on earth "in a demoralizing wave of speculation and in encouraging the violation of contracts." [33]

This accusation was rather strange, coming from a country which had just defaulted paying her war debts to America. But the fact was that France had suffered great damage in lives and material in the war against Germany and she considered the loans to her as a contribution to the common cause by an America which had come to the battlefield on the eve of victory. She had been ready to transfer to America the reparations payments owed to France by Germany, but America had refused to tie one debt to the other. Nevertheless, when Germany stopped payment on reparations, American emissaries of Hoover's government had persuaded France, England and the lesser beneficiaries of reparations to accept a ninety per cent cut in reparations. It was understood but not spelled out that the Allied debts to America would be cut in the same proportion. This settlement had enabled American private creditors to receive their money from Germany. Hoover might have carried through the tacit understanding and reduced the war debts but for the fact that meanwhile the Democrats had won control of Congress and there was not the slightest inclination there to lighten war debts. The Western Europeans thus defaulted entirely or made only token payments. France refused, however, to consider herself as having defaulted or even as a debtor country.

When Roosevelt devalued the dollar to raise prices, French papers branded it as sheer demagogy. They doubted that economic recovery could come from currency operations. "If a heat wave falls upon the United States one cannot refresh the atmosphere," a French magazine mused, "by decreeing a modification of the thermometer. The heat does not obey the instruments of its measurements but it obeys the sun." [34] The argument was legitimate except for the fact that shortly before it had been the French who had insisted the Economic Conference agree on monetary stabilization prior to international trade agreements and price settlements.

The French went far back in history to remind America that she had once asked them for leniency when America had defaulted on her Revolutionary War debts. A writer quoted Thomas Jefferson berating the French: "The possibility that the buyer will be able to pay is one of the motives of the contract at the time of the buying. If the creditor destroys that possibility he cannot complain in good faith that the debtor was amiss with his payments, since the delay had been the effect of his own action." [35]

The devaluation of the dollar did raise prices, but unfortunately it also decreased the purchasing power of wages. By the end of 1933 the economic situation had improved or remained unhealthy, depending on what section of the population one studied.

Between the two goals of the New Deal, recovery and reform, political realities forced the Administration to give preference to recovery to avoid disaster. The situation of the farmers improved, industry and trade in consumption goods revived, while capital industry lagged. The number of unemployed decreased to one third of that in 1932. Banking was entirely restored to health. Judging by facts and figures, the crisis had not yet been solved but the solution was rapidly on the way.

As against this opinion of the partisans of the New Deal, its enemies summed up the situation differently. They thought the progress was undeniable but artificial. The improvement was attributable to the mechanism of inflation which was going to proceed at an accelerated pace until it got entirely out of control. Possibly, the recovery was due only to government action in many economic spheres. If such government intervention lasted a few months more it would lead to financial disaster, followed closely by economic disaster. However, if government intervention should cease total collapse would follow rapidly.[36]

3

THE FIRST NEW DEAL

Roosevelt's recovery measures, usually called the First New Deal, coped with the national emergency under the slogan of national unity. His inaugural speech indeed called upon the nation to close ranks "as a trained and loyal army" and declared war on the depression.

The National Industrial Recovery Administration was to provide a framework for increased production through national cooperation. The representatives of industry, labor, and consumers were empowered to regulate production, prices, wages, and working hours in the spirit of sacrificing special interest to the common good. Although their agreements attained the force of law by being approved by the government, the President wished the organization to retain the character of economic self-government and he brought no pressure to bear on the participants to balance their interests in the cooperative venture. Without the balancing action of the government, industry, as the most powerful group, gained predominance over labor, and both gained over the loose, almost nominal representation of the consumers. As a result, even the collective bargaining position of labor was put in jeopardy by the acceptance of company unions as representatives of workers. During the negotiating of prices and wages little regard was shown for the consumers. Although such measures as minimum wages and maximum working hours benefitted labor, industry made use of the suspension of the anti-trust laws to engage in price fixing and to make agreements to the detriment of small business and the consumers. The President did nothing to remedy the situation. In this recovery phase of the New Deal, there was nothing more imperative than wiping out unemployment. Big industry could do most in the way of resuming production while government public works projects were still in the planning stage. Favoring big industry, however, was the price for its cooperation, as the example of European fascist dictators clearly demonstrated.

Similarly, under the Agricultural Adjustment Act, the large and efficient farms, owned mostly by banks and insurance companies, benefitted most. Dissatisfation began to mount and spread. Demagogues appeared to harness the dissatisfaction into popular movements, giving political power to the discontented. In the South, Senator Huey Long promised a limitation of fortunes and a share the wealth plan; in the West, Dr. Francis Townsend mobilized people concerned with security in old age for a monthly two hundred dollar pension program; in Detroit, Father Coughlin exhorted millions of his nationwide broadcast audience against plutocracy and for nationalization of the country's wealth. Long and Coughlin had supported Roosevelt during the 1932 campaign, but they were becoming disillusioned with him. Huey Long alone possessed the attributes of a great demagogue who might mold all radicalism into a national movement.

Roosevelt tried to get along with these men, since he knew that they thrived on a genuine grass roots desire for security. But he was confident that his bills for unemployment insurance and social security, so long in drafting, would eventually take the wind from the sails of these agitators.

In 1934, however, hostilities broke out between the New Deal and the Right. The Liberty League, launched in August, demanded, in effect, the restoration of *laissez-faire* as the essence of constitutional government. Big industrialists, bankers, corporate lawyers found support even among Democrats and Roosevelt's old friends. The League was a powerful group but had no chance of getting mass support at that time. Many industrialists, who were still targets of popular hostility as the men responsible for the depression, refused to join. Their instinct was right, since the Liberty League's attack eventually gave rise to a new wave of support for the President. The off-year elections that took place in November, 1934, represented a victory for the Left.

This was the reverse of what informed public abroad had expected.

"One might describe the mood of agriculture as aggressive, of industry as defensive, and of Wall Street as defeatist," a great English magazine reported.[1] It warned that "a sweeping programme hastily adopted under pressure would inevitably encounter demands for revision as the immediate emergency had passed, and as soon as its implications began to be felt."

"For the first time since the Civil War, the Party in power suffered no losses in the interim elections but on the contrary was returned in larger majorities in both Houses," a Swiss newspaper [2] commented. This was, in the view of the paper, the more remarkable since Roosevelt's economic policy "has introduced a host of experiments that ran into deeprooted prejudices and often against important interests. It was to be expected that after the end of an era in which bold and not always successful measures had been applied dissatisfaction would raise its head at the first opportunity when people could express their opinions through the vote. Yet the result is that Roosevelt's star is again on the rise. His opponents have not been able to recover from the grave defeat of Hoover and have now suffered a new blow to their prestige. The prosperity that fascinated the Americans during the Coolidge era and that collapsed after Hoover's second year in the Presidency is obviously no more the aim of the American people.

"The way to reconstruction is not to go back on the road of the lost 'economic paradise' but a real 'new order' in which the outgrowth of powerful interests will no more be tolerated and the interests of the thus far 'forgotten man' will be protected. This is the road Roosevelt has taken and the accomplishments justify his pride in heading a government of great reforms."

But the big conservative Swiss paper felt the danger to Roosevelt's reconstruction program ". . . to be in his own party. Although no revolution threatens the United States the radicalism of a section of the Democratic Party may infect the reform program. Here is the chance for the Republican Party to bury the old order and help the unavoidable New Deal prevail over revolutionary tendencies."

The President had not believed that the election would return his party to Congress with majorities like those of 1932.[3] His doubts were only too well justified by the failure of his recovery measures to wipe out unemployment. The NRA's record was disappointing. By September, 1933, over six hundred "codes" were in operation, but production had declined while prices continued to rise. Later in the fall, employment also began to decline.[4] Moreover, agricultural prices started to fall, an event that put the whole recovery program in jeopardy, since the simultaneous rise of the prices of industrial goods undermined any improvement in the farmers' situation. The President had to resort to the forced devaluation of the dollar to make prices fall in terms of foreign currencies and to create a demand for American goods, at least abroad. Such a step was bound to be resented by other countries as openly defying international cooperation and, indeed, making it impossible. Since fascism and Nazism relied on economic nationalism, completely disregarding the interests of other countres, Roosevelt's monetary manipulations gave moral support to the enemies of democracy. It may have halted further deterioration of the domestic price and employment situation, but it led to a break with some very influential members of the President's party, among them Al Smith, Dean Acheson, and Bernard Baruch.

In 1934, however, the President gave unmistakable evidence that only the extreme emergency of the depression had detracted him from international economic cooperation. He hastened to stabilize the dollar and pushed through Congress the Reciprocity Trade Agreement Act, enabling him to enter international agreements.

Nineteen thirty-five was the year of the Second New Deal and its reforms that have permanently changed the life of the country. It was the year of the Social Security legislation, of Unemployment Insurance, of the Wagner Labor Relations Act. This was the year the Works Progress Administration received four billions for public projects under direct federal contracts and the year the Rural Electrification Administration extended power lines to farmers on cheap loans. The President indicated in his annual message that he would move as rapidly as possible to see the unemployed shifted from direct relief to publicly supported work and, from that, to restoration in private employment. Since huge public works required finished goods from heavy industry, from practically all industries, and a large array of industrial raw materials, the WPA and PWA raised purchasing power both directly and indirectly.

In the view of an Englishman, the President "saw the potential danger to the United States from the triangular battle for control between the three European systems: old-fashioned capitalism, represented by the Bank of England; new fashioned capitalism, espoused by the Fascists; and the communism in Russia." [5]

The democrats and liberals in Europe feared the success of the Soviet Five Year Plan and watched with increasing anxiety the new danger in the heart of Europe, Hitler's Nazism. Should the latter succeed in solving the economic crisis in Germany and should the most powerful democracy, the United States, also choose a system other than capitalism to master the depression, they thought it would herald the end of democracy everywhere.

Roosevelt's intentions remained a puzzle abroad. It was difficult to get a coherent picture of his personality and of his stand with respect to the formidable currents of ideologies that seemed to be geared for a final battle. True, his closest political folowers and collaborators also often wondered about the motives of such contradictory actions as his break with tradition in early 1933 and his conservatism in 1934. Once he characterized himself as a Christian and a democrat. One of his collaborators, highly competent to define the President's outlook on the world, Rexford G. Tugwell, called him a humanitarian and a conservative reformer of capitalism. "He spoke feelingly of the unfortunate," Tugwell wrote, "yet he understood and did not expect any rapid change in the existing class relationship. But he did mean to raise the minimum levels. He thought every child ought to have opportunity; he interpreted the profit system as fair pay for honest effort; he believed that minima ought to be established and protected, and he thought that the helpless members of the community—children, mothers, the aged, the crippled, and the unemployed—should be public charges. This noblesse was an integral part of his system of intentions. A large portion of his time and energy during the earlier years of his presidency was given to planning, intrigue, manoeuver, and bargaining in the interest of these ends."[6]

A French correspondent described him in much the same way. "Roosevelt is in the literal sense of the term an opportunist. He has no ideas, no system, or set program in matters financial and economic. He is not doctrinaire to any degree. When I had the privilege of being received by him, he gave me the impression of being an intelligent man, of good will, charming, fine, absorbed in his work, ready to move everything to pull his country out of the abyss into which the mistakes and follies of Wall Street had threatened to drag her."[7]

Roosevelt may not have had a set program, or even definite ideas on the means, but he well knew the essence of the problem his country faced. He described it in these words: "Where Jefferson had feared the encroachment of political power on the lives of individuals, Wilson knew that the new power was financial. He saw, in the highly centralized economic system, the despot of the twentieth century, on whom great masses of individuals relied for their safety and their livelihood, and whose irresponsibility and greed (if it were not controlled) would reduce them to starvation and penury."[8]

His admirers abroad would never admit that there was no consistently thought out theory behind the New Deal. An Argentine insisted: "I admire President Roosevelt more for what I see in him as a humanitarian thinker than for what circumstances have compelled him to say or do as a politician. He knows, I presume, that his country is not yet sufficiently indoctrinated with the theories implicit in the New Deal. The people have been led to accept whatever brings immediate relief, but not what implies a change in the economic or political pattern. . . . Whatever the political destiny of the New Deal may be, its fundamental idea will remain; it will be a conception of the new function of the State, at least in time of emergency. But I do not think that the extent of this experiment in national thinking will stop here. I believe the idea will gain ground that State intervention should not wait for an emergency to force private interests to yield to public interests in the economic field." [9]

Meanwhile, others tried to interpret his actions against the general situation or in terms of their knowledge of the American background.

A Mexican writer thought that America was on the crossroads after the 1934 elections. He wrote ". . . the dilemma before the American people now can be stated as follows: unorganized economy with the danger of continued depression and further political disturbances, as a natural result of public discontent, or organized economy with the danger of retarding recovery on account of new economic adjustments and the possibility of the state being a despotic factor in the conduct of business." [10]

A Frenchman wrote, "It is not an exaggeration to consider the present politics of the United States as much a capital event in the history of human institutions as Italian fascism or Russian bolshevism. Moreover, the American experiment interests us particularly because it was not performed through a coup d'etat, to the sound of fanfare and drums. . . . Nor is it tied to the destiny of one man, of an omnipotent dictator." [11]

In 1934, when it appeared that big industry was back in the driver's seat directing the NRA economic policies, a Far Eastern observer commented: "Mr. Roosevelt's mandate was to restore the old system to prosperity, not to change the social order. It was an impossible mandate, a contradiction in terms. He was commissioned to redeal the old marked deck at a table surrounded by the same innocents and the same sharks. Is it surprising that the aces have fallen right where they were before?" [12]

Another writer was not misled by the retreat of the President from more drastic reforms. "Can a wheel that has turned so far be forced back again in the old direction?" he asked. "Or may it be that what America has experienced since March, 1933 is only the introduction to a new economic era and thereby to a spiritual revolution? In all events, it is a huge economic experiment, comparable in violence and extent, though not in program, to the Russian experiment." [13]

The *London Times* related as a fact that Britain's own difficulties would be lightened or increased in proportion as Roosevelt succeeded or failed. "For the Empire as a whole, indeed, the great American departure in policy lights up opportunities which now lie before its constituent countries." [14] In the view of another English paper, the New Deal would have an even broader significance. If it succeeds "not in every particular, but as a whole—it will spread to every civilized country and there will in reality be a new earth. If it fails, then not only America but the world will have to begin all over again." [15]

For an Argentine, America offered a poor show. He [16] had respect for the President, stating that he "is the first United States President whose personality and acts have had that dramatic element which makes the Latins sit up and take notice." But otherwise he thought that America was about where Germany had been in 1931, facing a choice between chaos and dictatorship. In his opinion, the spirit of competition prevented the Americans from cooperating, but it was impossible "to live on a *sauve qui peut* basis forever." The Americans would either learn to cooperate or be forced to do so by a dictatorship of the Right or Left. The alternative was ruin, since the frontier was closed and competition had reached a ruinous stage.

Mussolini's attitude was sympathetic. The Duce told Anne O'Hare McCormick: "The whole world is in revolution. Events themselves are a tremendous force, pushing us on like some implacable will. Your new plan for coordination of industry follows precisely the lines of our cooperation. It is inevitable that the complex social and economic problems of today should force a new order—neither capital in control nor labor in control, but both in proper balance with the State as the program." [17]

On the other hand, Edouard Herriot, the French Liberal, resolutely denied any trend toward fascism in Roosevelt and the New Deal. After visiting the President, he said: "There is a whole world of difference between Roosevelt's conceptions and those of fascism. He has done and is doing nothing which infringes on political liberty. He is making no appeal, either open or secretly, to militarism, while this is at the root of fascist and Hitlerite theories. The American experiment is of quite a different character, whatever may be the outcome. It asks for voluntary sacrifice, which will be temporary. It leaves the parliamentary system untouched, controlled only by the electorate. It has not abolished the democratic conception of law. It does not infringe on the workers' rights." [18]

Largo Caballero, Minister of Labor in the Spanish Republican Cabinet, characterized the New Deal as "merely restricted capitalism." [19]

Sir Arthur Steel-Maitland, former Minister of Labor, after a tour in the United States, saw nothing in the American scene suggesting the slightest trend toward socialism.[20] The Comintern shared this view and attacked British Labor for seeing a "piece of Socialism" in Roosevelt's program. The official communist view on the President was: ". . . He never thinks of socialism, not even of replacing the capitalist system with an organized economy. As the government representative of the great financial bourgeoisie, Roosevelt wants simply to take resolute measures to mitigate the economic crisis. . . . His policy has resulted in an even deeper disorganization of the capitalist economy." [21]

Roosevelt's family background caused a French author to conclude that he had nothing in common with dictators, like Stalin, Hitler, or Mussolini. ". . . he is a typical representative of the traditional elite of America, an elite that . . . has had traditions for a century and a half and a sense of the State. . . . This class, small in number but cultivated and financially at ease, can afford to be disinterested in the struggle for the dollar and remains the only stable element. It has supplied America with almost all her statesmen." [22]

Many observers held that his emergency measures did not offer a reliable basis for judging the President's true political leanings. Some insisted that soon far-reaching reforms of the economy would be in order and the character of the reforms as well as the ways the President intended to carry them through might give evidence of where he stood.

The inevitable reform would have to be a structural one, in the opinion of a French author. "That will be the greatest revolution of our time. Whether Roosevelt will undertake it or it will go beyond him, he remains a great historical figure . . . who gave his people . . . a magnificent example of energy."[23]

An Indian thought that the President might be compelled to radical solutions. ". . . it is not beyond the realm of possibility that the President may be obliged to go to the logical conclusion of his present policies—a complete nationalization of the means of production and distribution in the public interest. The transition from haphazard, uncoordinated organization, to a planned economy, is, of course, not easy, especially in a country with the traditions and ideals of the United States. In the absence of a Revolution—like the Russian or the German—the process is bound to be slow. But whatever the eventual outcome, the courage, foresight, and genuine sympathy and understanding of the real situation of the authors of these policies, cannot be denied. The world needs a new social order; and they in America have already begun a 'New Deal.'"[24]

Lloyd George called the President's policies a great liberal program of reconstruction that did not go farther than the program his own Liberal Party had put forward in 1929.[25] However, a French conservative paper feared that the President might be pushed toward the extreme. "Mr. Roosevelt is expected to perform one miracle after the other. Having attacked the monetary problem, he noticed that it was not sufficient to decree higher prices in order to attain them. He was obliged to go to the basis of the problem, which is labor and production, and over them he has established a vast system of regulation. Thus directed economy at last appears in its true light. In the place of private enterprise and individual initiative which have proved their worth by test, this theory of complete state direction is substituted. This socialist malady has infected many countries, ravaged Russia, is threatening Germany and is ripe in the United States."[26]

A French magazine conceded that "Roosevelt believed in private property and in the institutions based on private property," but warned that events in the coming years might lead him to question whether economic planning was possible in a capitalist regime. A negative answer might induce him to reform the system itself.[27]

This might mean a revolution, but in the view of a German it would be an authoritative revolution, boldly planned by a single, half-crippled man, rather than an institutional one. This authoritative trait proved the American "revolution" in his eyes to be related essentially to the German Revolution. In many details the two new orders showed surprising similarities. While conceding that if the President believed the economic system to be bankrupt he would try another one, the writer found the bourgeois social system in America safer than anywhere in the world.[28]

"The Roosevelt government is treading the path towards fascism with iron heels," wrote a Leftist magazine in England. "Unemployment, which was to be solved by 'New Deal' magic, by grandiose paper schemes, by suave radio speeches, by the winning smiles of Mr. Roosevelt . . . today is barely below its highest point. . . . The New Deal, at first through inflation and other methods, helped to force production out of its deepest slough, and is now tending to maintain or even increase the present level of industrial output, but with a rapidly declining number of workers" [29]

A learned Frenchman acknowledged the failure of the NRA. He attributed it to the lack of "a superior authority equipped with real power to intervene. However, this could not have been done without a political revolution that would have wrecked the federal system, the perennial obstacle of great reforms." [30]

Visitors to America like Sir Samuel Herbert would pass no definite opinion on NRA, but called it the boldest and vastest economic experiment ever made by a government—with the single exception of Soviet Russia. According to him, the American people were aware that the alternative was certain disaster.[31]

H. G. Wells visited Washington and Moscow, "the twin centers of reconstruction effort," and found "a parallel refusal to recognize the nature of . . . the common drive toward a new life for all men. Either President Roosevelt or Mr. Stalin do not see the objective plainly or they dare not risk detaching themselves from the general body of their supporters by going too far ahead of them. . . . It is interesting to compare the President's recent book, *On Our Way,* with Stalin's latest report upon his past year's activities. The one insists that all he has done is in strict accordance with the American Constitution; the other is equally emphatic that the teachings of Marx, Engels, and Lenin have been rigorously followed. In reality, both, driven by practically parallel necessities, are feeling their way . . . towards a state capitalism which is already so far cosmopolitan that it is inaggressive and pacifist. These two systems . . . far the most advanced in the world drift towards a human life replanned on a world scale upon collectivist lines. The most interesting for the visitor to Washington at the present time is to hear what is said against the President. Hardly anything is said for him except that he is charming, brave, and a perfectly honest man. And then 'But'—. The summation for all that is said against him is in the mind of a disinterested observer a conviction that for a statesman he is quite exceptionally the right man in the right place. . . . The exciting thing about him, as about Stalin, is that he, too, has more of the appearance of having modern objectives, however incompletely apprehended, than anyone else in the world. The New Deal may change many things in America, and still will be no more than the last card played in an old game. . . ." [32]

Stalin, in December, 1933, called the President "a decided and courageous leader." When Walter Duranty reminded Stalin that he had insisted in 1929 that the crash was not the final crisis of capitalism, as the defeatist capitalists themselves had believed, the Soviet dictator, recognizing the compliment, shrewdly remarked that "the lowest point of depression is already past." [33]

The German press envisaged America as a companion in social adventure and assumed "that Roosevelt like the 'New Germany' has recognized that liberal capitalism is discredited and finished. Roosevelt is prepared to hasten the advent of the new era of nationalized economy." [34] "When he took office, Roosevelt was confronted with a United States neither loved, respected nor admired in Europe, Asia or South America. All this is now changed." [35] "In America, significantly enough, the structural change takes its initiative from the economic side, while in Germany the reorganization of the economy followed transformation of the political structure. At any rate the events in America show that the upheaval in Germany may become the trumpet signal for the world." [36] "Between the lines these commentators are already hailing President Roosevelt as the first Nazi Fuehrer of America." [37]

But even in the face of Nazi praise for Roosevelt, public opinion in Western Europe increasingly considered him a moderate and a reformer.

"The aspirations he was elected to satisfy were not of the order a Mussolini or a Hitler have chosen, negative, abstract and bewitching like the crushing of the internal enemy, the exaltation of a political mysticism, the regimentation of the masses, the filing by in uniform and great parades." No attempt has been made on the rights of the citizen, the freedom of the press and thought. The right of association and freedom of assembly have remained intact. . . . Mr. Roosevelt has confidence in democracy. . . . Never has the United States or any other country been as well informed about what the government is doing or intends to do. On the other hand, the President can study the slightest reaction of the public, and accordingly modify his attitude or direct his propaganda. As Mr. Lindley said, the regime of the ancient Athenian Agora has been restored this way [through the press conferences and the President's fireside chats] on a continental scope. . . . a people is reborn without having to be nourished with the mystique of violence." [38]

"Mr. Roosevelt is no dictator . . . he cannot be placed on the side of Stalin, Hitler and Mussolini. . . . Let us not judge [him] by our French standards and not complain of the incoherence of his policies, which do not derive from Descartes but from the empirical traditions of the pioneers," another French author pointed out, and asserted what his nation shared in common with the Americans. "No matter how we may change our regime we are not going to stifle in the brawl that passion for freedom that has animated us all the time, that is part of our blood and of our spirit and that, in a different form, has been and is one of the deepest passions of the Americans." [39]

The *Survey of International Affairs of* 1933 included the President along with Mahatma Ghandi among those "who achieved success in political or religious leadership without resorting to the dictators' violent methods." But it found that both had something in common with the dictators: "that genius for propaganda which perhaps, even more than physical force, is the ultimate basis of the dictators' power." However, the French say: "Dieu lui-meme a besoin de cloches (Even God needs bells)." If the President's direct approach to the public proved a great success, one should not forget that his opposition was also free to express itself and did so lavishly.

A man, who years later became his great friend, was irritated by those who mentioned Roosevelt's name in the same breath with the dictators. Winston Churchill wrote in 1934: "To compare Roosevelt's efforts with that of Hitler is to insult, not Roosevelt but civilization. The petty persecutors and Old World assertions of brutality in which the German idol has indulged only show their smallness and squalor compared to the renaissance of creative effort with which the name of Roosevelt will always be associated . . . in truth Roosevelt is an explorer who has embarked on a voyage as uncertain as that of Columbus, and upon a quest which might conceivably be as important as the discovery of the New World." [40]

Die-hard businessmen abroad, like Walter Runciman, President of the Board of Trade in Britain, continued to insist that Roosevelt was "the greatest autocrat in the world." [41] The owner of a great Holland conservative newspaper on tour with thirty business and professional men in the United States, put him in the same category with Hitler and Mussolini, but only in one respect. "They are men who are doing something, and that is certainly a need. It remains to be seen which of them is right. And when one is proved to be right then the world must follow." [42] It is not without significance that at the time of this statement the Dutch publisher gave democracy no chance.

But other observers came to the conclusion that the President had saved democracy in the United States. Sir Robert Horne praised him for "averting a collapse of America's whole social order." [43] *Le Temps* of Paris, looking back on Roosevelt's first year in office, wrote that "he has prevented the American masses from letting themselves drift . . . he has profoundly changed the atmosphere on the other side of the Atlantic. . . . For peoples as for men, confidence in themselves is the principal lever for all recovery and that is what Mr. Roosevelt has given to his fellow countrymen." [44]

The *Manchester Guardian* characterized the New Deal as "Roosevelt's controlled capitalism . . . and those who first hailed it as a step to socialism have invited their own disappointment. The capitalism will remain; but so will the control." [45]

Lord Camrose, publisher of the London *Morning Telegraph* and other newspapers, stated in Philadelphia: "President Roosevelt . . . has started a new wave of feeling in this country. Whether the policies are right or not I am not prepared to say. The English people have a great deal of admiration for the President's courage. Where there is an orthodox school of economists who do not believe in his policies, the great bulk of public opinion over there believes the President will pull it off." [46]

However, even conservative economists as the Belgian Prime Minister, Paul Van Zeeland, believed that "Roosevelt has saved his country at the moment of a great crisis and has obtained such absolutely essential results as will permit his country to go on living in peace and good order." [47] The Midland Bank *Review* of London, on September 2nd, went even further, acknowledging that the President had been right in 1933 when he had refused to agree to stabilize the dollar and had broken up the Economic Conference. The *Review* said Roosevelt "seized the right end of the stick" at that time. It warned: ". . . at the present stage of the world crisis the vital need is for much greater attention flowing from consistent ignoring of stability in terms of purchasing power over commodities" than the monetary stability of the exchange rates.

John Maynard Keynes called the President's achievement "colossal." [48] He said that the American recovery had started from a much lower point than the British, but whereas British employment had increased ten per cent from January, 1933 to June, 1934, the improvement in the United States was more than twenty-five per cent. He surmised that the national income in America also had risen, in the same period, about twelve to fifteen per cent. The country was not in a revolutionary stage, but the existing order of society would have become discredited had the main problems not been solved. The President's experimental and empirical method was the only alternative to inaction, since there was no one who could give infallible advice. The older generation of living Americans had accomplished the great task of learning to produce abundantly. But the problem now was to introduce central controls so as to make certain that a sufficient demand would be forthcoming. The individual firm sees the earth as flat, but for the man in charge of the central control the globe of economic life is round. One man's costs are another man's income. One man's spending is another man's sales. Keynes said that he envied the opportunity of the young men in the Administration in Washington, although they were surrounded by an impatient public which hoped much but understood little, and by politicians sensitive to a thousand influences in the atmosphere "which did not all come from heaven."

Much of the New Deal was taken from Keynes' books, but the President had not read them. He had no flair for theories, only for detecting the needs of the situation.[49]

A public opinion survey in England found a school of thought convinced that the President's activities had saved America from an "upheaval which would have been a real social revolution." Some people commended his courageous attitude which permitted him to enact drastic measures "without incurring the odium of a real dictatorship." But many in England acclaimed him precisely because they believed that he was a dictator.[50] Sir Josiah Stamp took a different tack. He was not impressed with the President's accomplishment. "The United States was like a big vessel," the economist stated, "which even when poorly navigated might ride out a storm that would sink smaller ones." [51]

A Frenchman visiting America in 1934 observed that "each and every measure of the Administration is criticized more or less severely; many see the future uncertain and somber. But there is no discordant voice concerning the improvement of the situation, the return of courage and hope if not unlimited confidence.

It is true, however, that no program has been offered in opposition to that of the government."[52]

If Roosevelt still intended to continue keeping both wolves and lambs in the same fold, a blow that struck down the basic statutes of the New Deal must have dissolved his illusions. The Supreme Court, in the spring of 1935, obliterated the National Recovery Act and Agricultural Adjustment Administration as unconstitutional. The majority of that august institution annulled all substantial government intervention in economic affairs. It denied such right not only to the federal government, but by declaring the New York State minimum wage law unconstitutional made it impossible for either federal or state governments to cope with any economic emergency. The Court was acting in its capacity of being a brake on democracy.

"America Stunned," "The Consequences Incalculable," "The Constitution Has Triumphed," ran the headlines abroad.

The world waited breathlessly for the President's reaction to this body blow dealt to his great legislative program. However, the President was not in a hurry. Writers and politicians abroad tried to explain to their public the veneration in which the Constitution was held by Americans. A British publication stated that "the Court is the most sacred institution of American life . . . it continued to enjoy immunity even while it was shattering the whole fabric of the New Deal. . . . A foreign observer could feel this sense of sanctity, though he might not fathom it."[53] A young American studying in Heidelberg, Germany, had a few beautiful words to say in his doctoral thesis about the significance of the Constitution for Americans: "The early comers panted for something else than easy bread-winning. They sought escape from the confinement of crusted-over societies. . . . The clingers abided at home, but the stalwarts came for freedom's sake and when, even here, society began to close about them and to crystallize they pushed farther into the wilderness . . ." This "impatience of restraint" was, according to the author, deeply anchored in the American spirit. It was the main reason why the United States would probably keep to the original Constitution, he predicted.[54]

But a Mexican who had studied in the United States, and had become concerned with the fate of America, exhorted the Americans, after the NRA had been invalidated, to change their Constitution. He quoted Lincoln's message to Congress in December, 1862:

"The dogmas of the quiet past are inadequate to the stormy present. The occasion is piled high with difficulty and we must rise to the occasion. As our case is new, so we must think anew and act anew. We must disenthrall ourselves and thus we shall save our country." The Constitution itself provided, of course, for its amendment. "Almost immediately the first ten amendments were adopted, limiting the power of the Federal government, in order to protect in a better form the interest of the individual. . . . The American people should not, therefore, be afraid of not being able to make proper changes in it in accord with the changing conditions."[55]

Whatever his intentions were, the President did not reveal them. With the elections approaching, he may have decided to wait for an overwhelming vote of confidence before taking any steps to preserve a broader conception of government by removing the obstacle to his program.

4

TOWARD THE SECOND TERM

In his first fireside chat after the 1934 election, the President interpreted the Democratic gains as "the recovery of confidence in our democratic process and institutions." But the savage attacks on him by the Liberty League convinced Roosevelt of the hopelessness of his appeal to the enlightened self-interest of businessmen and decided to protect capitalism from its beneficiaries.

Once resolved to submit a new reform program to Congress, the President had to strengthen his hold on the support of large masses of the people, especially organized workers. They must have been disappointed by Roosevelt's startling concessions to big business and his lukewarm support for genuine collective bargaining. But the bulk of them continued to trust him, as a true friend of the common people. The attacks of the Liberty League and the intense hostility of the bankers and businessmen only helped him to retain his position as a popular leader.

But the President faced mounting hostility from the Left as well as the Right. Delays in instituting thoroughgoing reforms might destroy him and also constitutional government. The "share the wealth" movements were swelling and it was not certain whether the President's own turn to the Left might not open the gates to irresponsible programs supported by discontented masses. Huey Long had constituted a threat to constitutional government, but he was killed in 1935. A Swiss paper called Long "the mouthpiece of the dissatisfied primitive America, a Crusader who wanted to realize the great American dream." [1] A rabble-rousing Protestant pastor, Gerald L. K. Smith, took his place, joining the radio priest, C. E. Coughlin, whose listeners were estimated to number thirty million. They found an ally in

Dr. Townsend and his pension movement which was popular in California, the paradise of the aged. Eventually they merged into a "Union Party." They blasted the timidity of Roosevelt's reforms and later accused him of betraying the people.

However, the President put his faith in the new reform legislation being drawn up to keep American radicalism at its traditionally low level.

The Wagner Labor Relations Act and the Fair Labor Relations Act laid down firmly the principle of collective bargaining through the elected representatives of the workers. The Works Progress Administration put millions of unemployed to work on projects selected for public usefulness, at minimum but livable wages. The Rural Electrification Administration gave loans and labor to extend power lines to farmers. The Housing Act accorded federal aid for wiping out slums and building low-rent houses.

The most substantial Act the President initiated in 1935 was the Social Security Act, which provided the financial foundation for the subsistence of the aged and disabled.

The principle aim of the Second New Deal was to increase directly the purchasing power of the consumer and thus to stimulate production. Previously aid had been given to industry to expand production and so provide the work and wages to guarantee more purchasing power.

A French historian, Bernard Fay, who was interpreting France to America as well as the latter to the former, re-visited America and considered it a sign of stability that such slogans of the nineteenth century as "small against big business" were dominating the election campaign. Moving around among middle class people, he was startled to find how unpopular Roosevelt had become. "People approve of the Supreme Court, respect it as the guardian angel of the country for having destroyed the 'Roosevelt revolution.'" Remembering the initial months of the President's first term, Fay mused: "As long as people were unhappy they clung to him as to a last hope. The entire country sang hosanna to him. Today, when he has apparently reached his goal and one feels safe again, he is attacked from all sides." [2]

However, many thought that the Supreme Court had done

Roosevelt a favor by wiping out the NRA. "Like Prohibition, the NRA was a 'noble experiment,' but its conception was too hasty and its problems too large to allow for its success," was the view of an Englishman.[3] "The power which selfish interests were able to manifest in and through the codes was an indication that many of the important capitalists had no intention of sending their economic institutions to the reform school. The inherent stubbornness and self-righteousness of big business interests which became evident with growing clarity in the early NRA foreshadowed a grim future.

"In spite of the limitations of certain aspects of the agricultural program, there is little doubt that the American farmer on the whole is a great deal more secure, a great deal happier than he was under the Old Deal. . . . the major features of the agricultural program will undoubtedly continue along present lines for some time to come. . . . The Supreme Court invalidation of the NRA was not as severe on labor as might have been expected, partly because most of the headway which the workers had made was their own making and partly because Congress in 1935 passed the Wagner Act. The significance of the Wagner Act in labor's struggle for power cannot be overestimated. . . . Labor has made greater progress in five years than in all the one hundred and fifty years previous." The writer drew a balance of the New Deal in stating that it might turn out as a social success and an economic failure. If it failed, however, it would do so because Roosevelt, in the opinion of another English writer, had attempted a task "beyond the achievement of any human being—the task of sustaining an economic system which has outlived its day." [4]

The author compared Roosevelt with other contemporary leaders, with this result: "When the history of this period comes to be written, four men will be immortalized as typifying its drama. Lenin will be regarded as the embodiment of the forces which are making the Socialist revolution. Ghandi will be regarded as the embodiment of a mystic mediaevelism challenging in vain the advance of the machine age. Mussolini (or perhaps Hitler) will be regarded as the embodiment of the Fascist alternative for competitive Capitalism. President Roosevelt will be regarded as the undaunted adventurer who challenged Destiny by attempting to rebuild a system that was crashing about him." Yet the author saw no indication that Roosevelt would succeed in equalizing production and consumption. Short of that he feared another economic crisis to come a few years later, in which power would be given to a strong President and to a few industrialist leaders. That President, he wrote, might be Roosevelt or someone else.

A comparison by a French liberal of Roosevelt with Stalin, Hitler, and Mussolini turned out to the favor of the American president.[5] His aim, like that of Stalin, is "the common good, but Roosevelt's organized economy is more flexible and clever, not removed from human factors, from the daily stimulant of private initiative, from human personality, which at so many times constitutes a decisive factor. Roosevelt's pragmaticism points to the spiritual source of the Yankee with his tendency to unite the real with the ideal."

While some critics considered the New Deal a total failure, others did not deny that there had been improvement, especially in industrial recovery. They stated, however, that this had happened in spite of the New Deal. "America's capitalistic system," a German expounded, "even though it produced abuses that the New Deal successfully attacked, was so healthy that it contributed more to the recovery of the country than Roosevelt's attempts." [6] One writer ascribed the success of the New Deal to the immigrants, who had readily submitted themselves to regimentation, as against the intrepid pioneer Americans, who had braved previous crises unbending.[7]

A pamphlet, written shortly before Stalin changed the party line to a popular front, summed up the results of the New Deal, stating: "There is nothing the New Deal has so far done that could not have been done better by an earthquake." [8]

Many non-Communists doubted capitalism could survive the New Deal. "Can the national income be distributed for the public welfare, can the public be saved from exploitation by the Stock Exchange and the banks, can labor receive a fair share of business profits, can the masses be given relief and protection and security through government aid, and can all these things occur without taking away from business the freedom to exploit and control which in the past has been its life blood?" an author heard many people in America asking.[9] A South American weighed the question from the political angle. Might not the New Deal end in fascism? He came to the conclusion that "the middle class in America, far from being the promoter of Fascism, as it has been elsewhere, seems destined to be a cushion in this crisis. In fact, although it does not harbor great faith in either of the two parties, it keeps them alternatively in power." [10]

Fascist type demagogery at home ceased to be a danger after Huey Long's death, but the growing aggressiveness of fascist powers abroad increased the danger of a new general war in which America could not help becoming involved. At least, this was the conviction of the internationalists, of whom Roosevelt was one, while the great majority of the people wanted no such involvement and believed that by vigilance and limitation of the powers of the President as well as of Congress it could be prevented.

Roosevelt's internationalism went back many years. As Assistant Secretary of the Navy in the Wilson Administration he had been for intervention in the First World War; in 1920, he had run for the office of Vice-President on the Democratic ticket, risking and meeting defeat by advocating America's joining the League of Nations. This gave him an early warning as to the strength of isolationist feeling across the country, which attitude prevailed during the first term of his Administration. The savage hatred for the bankers made the Congressional investigation of Pierpont Morgan a fascinating news item, and, in unveiling the business connections of American finance with British war goods suppliers, ripened a general conviction that America had entered the war as a result of the machinations of American bankers and British politicians to save the investments of the former and win the war for the imperialist ambitions of the latter. The strong adverse current made Roosevent cautious, but he could not desert his convictions. In his inaugural address as Governor of the State of

New York in 1929, he objected to his policies being called humanitarian. "It is far more than that," he said. "It is the recognition that our civilization cannot endure unless we, as individuals, realize our personal responsibility to a dependence on the rest of the world." [11]

An anti-imperialist Indian, Takaknath Das, hailed Roosevelt for his new approach to American foreign policy. He felt the President had broken with the European colonial powers and returned to the guidance of the Founding Fathers. ". . . the New Deal in America," he wrote, "has brought with it a new outlook —if not a revolution—in American foreign relations. This revolution is not a change of outlook or of fundamental principles in American diplomacy and international relations, but a new method of approach towards the fulfillment of the ideals of the founders of the republic." [12] The author enumerated the facts on which he based his opinion: recognition of the Soviet Union; the rejection of entangling alliances. With respect to the latter, he said Norman Davis, United States Ambassador-at-Large, had affirmed the fact that America would not make a special understanding or agreement with Britain in advance regarding the naval conference planned for 1935. The author also pointed out that Roosevelt had decided to build up the American navy to the strength allowed by the treaties of Washington and London. Roosevelt had asked Congress to approve the principle that the United States Navy was to be second to none in strength. The resolution of Congress, in 1934, prohibiting loans to countries which had defaulted on previous loans, was a further step toward breaking with the West European powers.

The Good Neighbor Policy, in Latin America, inaugurated by Roosevelt, was, in the Indian author's opinion, the corollary of an American foreign policy independent of the imperialist European powers. He took great pains to prove that the President and Cordell Hull meant what they said. Secretary Hull had given a solemn assurance in 1933, at the Conference of the American States in Montevideo, that in the future the United States would not impose armed intervention in any of the Latin American countries, even in case of chaos, but would seek the cooperation of all other American countries to promote peace and stability in the whole of the Western Hemisphere.

Roosevelt in 1934 renounced the right to police Cuba, which had been guaranteed to the United States by the treaty of 1903. In giving Cuba complete independence, the President stated: "I have publicly declared that the definite policy of the United States from now on is one opposed to armed intervention. In this new treaty with Cuba, the contractual right to intervene in Cuba . . . is abolished." The Argentine government promptly hailed the implementation of the Good Neighbor Policy, stating: "The abrogation of the Platt amendment in the treaty with Cuba justifies the opinion which we formed in Montevideo that the policy of the Government of President Roosevelt would mark a transcendental era in the development of closer relations and in the moral prestige of the United States with the whole of America." [13]

The President also ordered marine and naval forces withdrawn from Haiti, where they had been stationed for 20 years. And he initiated an act providing for a Commonwealth Government for the Philippines as preparation for complete independence, to be accomplished in ten years.

The Indian political writer may have been mistaken, however, in his interpretation of Roosevelt's foreign policy. It was in 1934 that the President stabilized the dollar in order to enter into international agreements on monetary stabilization, and he asked Congress for authority, granted for three years, to conclude trade agreements and to modify customs tariffs to 50 per cent of existing rates. In economic policies, Roosevelt proposed international solutions as soon as the national emergency was over. He was stopped by Congress, however, from taking steps in the direction of an internationalist foreign policy. In January, 1935, the Senate voted against his recommendation to adhere to the World Court.

A majority of Senate members were for freer foreign trade, but not for collective security agreements or cooperation with the League of Nations. The instance of a conflict between Bolivia and Paraguay stirred Congress to lay down a principle of strict neutrality, even if it benefitted the aggressor, and even though it deprived the President of the means to bring pressure to bear on the aggressor to desist. Congress authorized the President, in May, 1935, to declare an embargo on both warring parties.

This policy encouraged the European dictators, who did not wait long to commit aggressive acts; 1935 was a year of disquieting events abroad. In Austria, Chancellor Dollfuss, who had tried to stem the Nazi onslaught, was killed. So was the Jugoslav King, Alexander, together with a French Foreign Minister who had taken effective steps toward a genuine collective security against aggression. In the same year, Japan declared her own Monroe Doctrine with respect to China.

In August, 1935, the very month in which he signed the Neutrality Act, the President warned that its inflexible provisions might drag the country into war instead of keeping her out. Just at that time Italian troops were pouring through the Suez Canal under orders to invade Ethiopia.

This act of aggression became a test case for the League. Its task appeared to be the easier because French and British positions in Africa were threatened and because Mussolini's Italy, despite all bragging by the Duce, was incapable of surviving economic sanctions. And in this particular war America's Neutrality Act harmed only the aggressor, since primitive Ethiopia had no use for modern weapons. The Soviet Union was then the most fervent champion of collective security. The League proclaimed an embargo on weapons to Italy, but it was soon apparent that an embargo on materials that could be turned into weapons also was needed to make the sanctions effective before Mussolini brought his conquest to fruition. Roosevelt tried hard to avoid cooperating with the League, since it was considered a leper by the isolationists, contaminating those who came in touch with it. But when it became obvious that only an embargo on oil could stop the aggression, Roosevelt proclaimed a moral embargo on materials that might be useful in waging war. Such a moral embargo had little effect, however, because of the competition among the oil companies. British oil interests feared that they might lose the Italian market. Instead of an oil embargo, the infamous Hoare-Laval plan came to pass, yielding Ethiopia to the aggressor.

Its demoralizing effect on the democracies could never be undone. In America it gave the isolationists a powerful boost and disillusioned the already decreasing ranks of believers in the League and collective security.

The President was in a difficult position, according to a British author. He "has been caught in the midst of three fires: his own basic international sympathies, his duties as a politician to reflect the popular mind, and his loyalties to the self-contained internal economies of the New Deal." [14] His message to Congress on January 3, 1936 provoked stormy reactions in Europe, especially this part of the Presidential communication:

"I suggested in 1933 that 85 or 90 per cent of all the people in the world were content with the territorial limits of their respective nations and were willing further to reduce their armed forces if every other nation in the world would agree to do likewise. That is equally true today, and it is even more true today that world peace and world good will are blocked by only 10 or 15 per cent of the world's population. . . . Peace is jeopardized by the few and not by the many. The world has witnessed similar eras. . . . we hope that we are not again at the threshold of such an era. But if face it we must, then the United States and the rest of the Americas can play but one role: through well-ordered neutrality to do naught to encourage the contest . . . through example and all legitimate encouragement and assistance to persuade other nations to return to the ways of peace and good will."

A British Liberal M.P. severely criticized the President. He said: ". . . it is a direct encouragement to Italy to proceed with her war of aggression against Ethiopia by proclaiming to the world that in such an event the United States intends to remain neutral." [15] He took special exception to the embargo because it had been declared before an act of war had actually been committed. The British blamed United States neutrality for their own reluctance to take a stronger stand against the aggression.

In England opponents of sanctions against Italy warned that the United States Neutrality Act might treat Britain as a belligerent if she became involved in hostilities as a consequence of the sanctions.

The French press attacked America bitterly. "The aggressor and his victim are to be treated with equal severity. This policy of isolation and indifference to good and evil is evidently not that on which one counted formerly to make peace reign in the world. Its application will make the Kellogg Pact a mockery. It will be very advantageous to those States that make war their principal industry and in peace time subordinate everything to preparations for acts of aggression." [16] Another French paper thought that United States neutrality would compel every country to autarchy. "Whether one wishes it or not, that Act must modify profoundly the conditions of all wars, whether offensive or defensive," the paper argued. "All nations will be led by the force of circumstances to organize themselves industrially in such a manner as to be able to do without what in the past they expected the Americans to supply." [17]

The Italians wondered whether Roosevelt's message was intended to extend the embargo also to oil. Their press reacted with indignation: "The mania of neutrality at any price will push America towards injustice and to sacrifice a great deal of her best traditions, for example freedom of the seas. She may become the instrument of international slavery without even receiving the acknowledgement of the League. Roosevelt may harm the nation to which America thanks her discovery but in that case he ought to cover the Statue of Liberty in New York with a black veil." [18]

However, when the Senate Foreign Relations Committee resolved a week later that an embargo could be declared only in defense of American neutrality, the Italian press showed great relief. They still did not like the passage in Roosevelt's message pointing unmistakably to the fascist governments as those who disturb the peace wanted by the rest of the world. Thus, *Giornale d'Italia* drew quite an interesting conclusion from the message: ". . . this attempt by Roosevelt to interfere with the affairs of

Europe and the League creates a precedent for intervention by Europe on another continent in American affairs." [19]

Mussolini himself lauded America's example when he told a reporter from the *London Daily Mail* that other nations should follow the United States in order to preserve general peace.[20] German official circles were rather pleased with the message and the press expressed pleasure. But they blamed America for the continental dictatorships by saying that it was Wilson who, through the peace treaties, had made the rise of dictatorships inevitable. After that, "America, through high tariffs, the export of cheap mass products, and rigid collection of debts, had further narrowed the Old World's living space." [21] "America sees the many who desire peace but she will cooperate with nobody to curb the few who want war," an English paper said, scoring Roosevelt for his inconsistency.[22] A French paper remarked that, "If the ninety per cent keep their hands in their pockets and do not help each other, then the ten per cent, which believes in the Bismarckian ideal of expansion, will soon devour those who do not want war. It takes only ten wolves to devour ninety sheep." [23]

Moscow was highly pleased with the message. *Izvestia* stated that it was reminiscent of the tone and manner of Woodrow Wilson.[24]

The Latin Americans were jubilant. "The present government of the United States is really respecting the right of all countries to work out their destinies. . . . Roosevelt's reference to the American republics is not merely a gesture of courtesy but the expression of sincere friendship and good will toward all countries of our continent. The policy of the good neighbor is an accomplished fact." [25]

Bernard Shaw, on a cruise in the Caribbean, took a defiant stand on the Ethiopian question. He said that any man must be on the side of Italy in that conflict, calling it a campaign of civilization against savagery. He cited Great Britain's empire building and said that Italy was presently doing the same. He praised Roosevelt, stating that the United States had a good president but a bad constitution, probably alluding to the

Supreme Court's annulment of a substantial part of the New Deal legislation.[26]

Roosevelt's own respect for the Neutrality Act and for isolationist sentiment in the country reached surprising lengths. Joseph Aloysius Lyons, Premier of Australia, disclosed to Pierrepont Moffat, United States Consul General in Australia, that the President had told him that "never again would the United States be drawn into a European war, regardless of circumstances." The Australian Premier also revealed that he had expressed his doubts as to the President's making any agreement with the Japanese as long as Japan continued to violate the treaties in Manchukuo. The President had replied: "That's going too far; there is a lot we might be able to overlook if we could really help achieve lasting peace." [27]

The Germans noted with satisfaction the great changes in American foreign policy from Theodore to Franklin Roosevelt. They praised Roosevelt's stand on neutrality especially "because it ran counter to a disquieting minority of large segments of the American people, who abominate the present Germany. [Roosevelt's policy] assures Germany not yet America's friendship, but at least her neutrality." [28]

However, the sophisticated Austrians did not believe America would remain neutral if vital American interests were at stake. "President Roosevelt's policy of neutrality will be punctured the moment armed and saber-rattling Japan makes her appearance on the world-stage. . . . Roosevelt's message undoubtedly was a product of compromise. As everything which is done halfheartedly, it answers nothing, but on the contrary brings up new questions. This message does not mean equal rights, but only equal injustice for all. For this reason it leaves a bitter taste, despite its pacifist keynote." [29]

The British expected no leadership from America in the Far East even though Japan had threatened both by breaking the Naval Agreement of 1931, stating that she wanted parity with the British and American navies. "The current popular feeling," the Survey of International Affairs (1936) wrote, "is in favor of shunning commitments outside their own territories." No championship was expected for international morality either, since the lesson received in the Abyssinian affair, the Survey commented. "But deep in the American consciousness there *is* a feeling that America's stake in the East will be one day a vital American interest. It was no accident that the United States developed Transpacific airlines at a time when as yet no Transatlantic service had been organized."

André Siegfried, thoroughgoing student of the United States, revisiting the country, remarked: "Unrecognizable as they were three years ago, the Americans have become again what they have always been—optimists and interested only in their own affairs." [30] But he pointed to the paradoxical character of American foreign policy: "The Americans as a world power have interests all over the world. But the people remain attached with dogged tenacity to their old creed of isolationism. This double point of view explains the foreign policy of the country since the war. The Government intervenes everywhere, impelled by its interests, but always afraid of public opinion, and it does not admit the contradiction." [31]

In March, 1936, Hitler made a bold move: he occupied the Rhineland despite the prohibition of the Versailles treaty. It was a clear blow to the security of France and thus to Western Europe. Hitler, as was revealed later, was ready to withdraw at any resolute step by the Allies. He did not have to retreat. A few months later a revolt against the Spanish Republic broke out in Spanish Morocco under the leadership of General Franco. The Spanish Civil War began.

The disquieting international situation had no effect on the tumultous 1936 campaign for political control in the United States. The Presidential elections usually dominate public life and the country lives in suspense until the day the voters cast their vote. More than ever the people were making a momentous decision in 1936 for or against the new beginning in American political, economic, and social life that the New Deal represented.

The Supreme Court had greatly sharpened the controversy.

In June the Court declared the New York minimum wage law unconstitutional. It denied to government the power to cope with emergency situations.

Suddenly reviving, the Republican Party launched a crusade-like offensive against the New Deal. It was a bold decision, made in the heat of the campaign after a rather timid start. They had a formidable problem; they needed votes from the beneficiaries of the New Deal, whose memories were still haunted by the despair of the Great Depression. Compared with the desolation before Roosevelt entered the White House, there was no doubt that living conditions had strikingly improved.

The Republicans furiously attacked the New Deal. The editors of the *Economist*,[32] explaining the bitterness of the opposition, noted that "Hostility to Roosevelt is many times stronger than opposition to his policies. . . . his enactments are those of very moderate Liberalism, his statements, particularly in denunciation of the rich, are often extreme." Another English magazine saw little substance for the hatred. "It seems to be true . . . of the Roosevelt policy as a whole, that it is not so much what has been done, or what has happened, as what people fear will be done, or think will happen, which is behind the opposition to the President."[33] But a Frenchman put his finger on the sore spot, the source of hatred more venomous than the loss of income or of influence. He said that the unpardonable sin of Roosevelt was that he had dissociated the concept of wealth from the concept of virtue and by that exploded one of the most popular myths.[34]

Though it might have lost prestige, big business still possessed power. It had turned the NRA to its advantage. Reading only the editorials in the papers, an echo of their own voices, big business and the Republicans misread the mood of the public. Cautious at the start when they nominated Alf M. Landon, Governor of Kansas, a rather liberal businessman, they became emboldened in the course of the campaign, removed Herbert Hoover from oblivion, and eventually engineered an attack against the one New Deal institution that appealed most to most of the people, the great promise of security from unemployment, old age, and even illness: Social Security.

Roosevelt was well aware he was the target, and managed his campaign accordingly. The election was to be his personal vindication and his personal victory.

"Never before," Roosevelt said in his campaign speech in New York, "have these forces been so united against one candidate as they stand today. They are unanimous in their hate for me—and I welcome their hatred."

Reflecting on his chances and on the significance of the election, some British magazines drew a balance sheet on the New Deal again. One ascribed to its credit, or more precisely to Roosevelt's credit, that American public life now contained an atmosphere of creative endeavor which "is the most stimulating and hopeful feature of the New Deal." [35] But as an attempt to regulate capitalism "by drastic, coercive legislation it has wilted in the face of the realities of American life. The balance of power lies with property, however the electors may vote." [36] A conservative estimate expressed admiration, however, "for the amazing rapidity with which a large organization was improvised and for the imaginative humanity with which it has been administered." [37] A Latin American found a permanent feature in the New Deal: "Whether it has brought relief or not, it occurs to me that the principle will ripen in this country that some intervention, not occasional but permanent, of the State in the economic life of the nation will be necessary." [38]

"The decisive vote which will re-elect Roosevelt," an English weekly foretold, "will be cast by the millions who now have vested interest in the least constructive aspect of the New Deal"[39] —meaning in the immediate relief it brought.

Roosevelt stood on his record. He made the people remember and compare. His New York speech was the most eloquent reminder:

"Tonight I call the roll—the roll of honor of those who stood with us in 1932 and still stand with us today.

We still lead that army in 1936. They stood with us then

because in 1932 they believed. They stand with us today because in 1936 they know. And with them stand millions of new recruits who have come to know.

Their hopes have become our record.

We have not come this far without a struggle and I assure you we cannot go further without a struggle.

For twelve years this nation was afflicted with a hear-nothing, see-nothing, do-nothing Government. The Nation looked to government but government looked away. Nine mocking years with the golden calf and three long years of the scourge! Nine crazy years at the ticker and three long years in the breadlines! Nine mad years of mirage and three long years of despair! Powerful influences strive today to restore that kind of government with its doctrine that that government is best which is most indifferent.

For nearly four years you have had an Administration which instead of twirling its thumbs has rolled up its sleeves. We will keep our sleeves rolled up.

We had to struggle with the old enemies of peace—business and financial monopoly, speculation, reckless banking, class antagonism, sectionalism, war profiteering.

They had begun to consider the Government of the United States as a mere appendage to their own affairs. We know now that government by organized money is just as dangerous as government by organized mob."

In a campaign address in Chicago Roosevelt flatly stated: "It was this Administration which saved the system of private profit and free enterprise." He reversed the charges of dictatorship, autocracy, and un-Americanism levelled against him and hurled them at big business:

"Our job was to preserve the American ideal of economic as well as political democracy against the concentration of economic power. . . . Independent business was not allowed to exist, only by sufferance. [This situation] has been a menace to the social system as well as to the economic system which we call American democracy." Roosevelt described monopolies as representing "private government, a power unto itself—a regimentation of other people's money and other people's lives."

Foreign relations were not an issue in the campaign. Yet Roosevelt, in Philadelphia on June 27, 1936, reminded the nation what American democracy meant in a world threatened by aggressive autocracies:

"In this world of ours, in other lands, there are some people, who, in times past, have lived and fought for freedom, and seem to have grown too weary to carry on the fight. They have sold their heritage of freedom for the illusion of a living. They have yielded their democracy. I believe in my heart that only our success can stir their ancient hope. They begin to know that here in America we are waging a great and successful war. It is not alone a war against want and destitution and economic demoralization. It is more than that; it is a war for the survival of democracy. We are fighting to save a great and precious form of government for ourselves and the world."

The elections gave Roosevelt the greatest plurality in history. He carried every state but Maine and Vermont. Only seventeen Republicans were left in the Senate and the Democratic majority in the House of Representatives was increased.

"Roosevelt Towers in the Imagination of Europe"—under this title the *New York Times* described the strange relation of Europe to President Roosevelt on the day after the election. "Each country in its exaggerated nationalism pictured the triumphant President as one of its own heroes. . . . To the dictatorships of Europe his election was proof that swift, courageous leadership pays. To the democracies it brought a renewal of faith in popular government. . . .

> The wonder is not that Europe should have queer conceptions of President Roosevelt, but that it should feel so universally friendly toward him. In the past four years he has used cutting words about Nazi Germany; he recognized Soviet Russia but proceeded to quarrel with her; he angered the British Government and the

City of London in 1933 by torpedoing the world economic conference, and he affronted Italy by keeping a step ahead of the League of Nations in the sanctions controversy last Autumn.

But Europe thinks of none of these things today when it appraises Mr. Roosevelt. Its dictatorships and its democracies alike remember he has preached at them less than any American President since the war. His policy of the "good neighbor" has impressed even those countries that do not know what neighborliness means. His reciprocal trade treaties have given promise of breaking those trade barriers that until a few months ago threatened to strangle world trade. And his neutrality legislation has been accepted with good grace even here in Britain, which still hopes deep down in its heart that the United States will not stand aloof if another world war should endanger the empire.

Somehow the President's personality has crossed the ocean, leaped all Europe's barriers of language and tradition and made the common man here believe in him. He is liked by millions who are utterly ignorant of the things he has done or the policies he stands for.

President Roosevelt towers in the popular imagination today as a voluntarily chosen dictator over 125,000,000 people. If the election has given him vast responsibilities and colossal power for good or evil in the United States, it also has given him prestige in Europe such as no President has enjoyed since Woodrow Wilson landed on his peace mission seventeen years ago.

Serious students of American affairs are not underestimating his personal power when they think at the same time of the principles and philosophy behind President Roosevelt's New Deal. In Britain, France, the Netherlands and Scandinavia, America is seen to be passing through a long overdue revolution, from which she will emerge stronger and better able to survive.

The President's great opportunity, as all parties in

> Britain and Western Europe see it, is to purify and modify and thus strengthen American capitalism. If he achieves this task in the next four years he will tower even higher in the popular imagination than he does today.

Relief and enthusiasm hailed the overwhelming victory of President Roosevelt and the Democratic Party at the polls. Western Europe considered it a victory for the principles of democracy.

"The verdict of November 3 was resounding proof of the extraordinary firmness of the popular will which, once it is free, can revenge itself with devastating effect against either demagogues or doctrinaires. Some people accused Roosevelt of being possessed with a messianic spirit. Indeed, Roosevelt these days is, whether right or wrong, deeply convinced that humanity is the sole master of its destiny and that there is no difficulty that one cannot overcome by will, faith or cleverness, possibly with a combination of all three," was a French magazine's resumé of the significance of the election.[40]

It was at this time that important men in Europe first hailed the President as the spiritual leader of the democracies.[41]

However, an English magazine labelled the election "A Class Election" and to prove its point told this story:

"In a fashionable New York hotel, on election night, only dance music relieved the gloom, as results flashed on an improvised screen. The elegantly dressed clientele grew more and more morose. But when the news flashed that Governor Landon had conceded the election, a waltz was in progress, and it was not interrupted. At one table sat a party of New Dealers, two of them high officials in Washington, one an eminent woman in public affairs. After the election had been conceded the woman arose, lifted her glass and proposed for the entire room a toast to the President of the United States. The companions at her table promptly stood and lifted their glasses. But though a painful silence fell over the assemblage not another person stirred, not another glass was raised. And the New Dealers, with one accord, gathered up their things and stole away.

"The scene depicts to what extent the election was fought, and certainly felt, on class lines. A scattered handful of men above a given income level voted for Roosevelt, and a similar scattered handful below that level were for Landon. But on the whole, the poor won the election from the well-to-do." [42]

A French observer flatly contradicted this assertion:

"One of the most interesting aspects of the November 3 election is that Roosevelt was re-elected by no particular class but by all classes. Any of the groups could have passed entirely to the camp of his opponent without changing in any way the final result." This was so in the view of the observer because the victory was due to principles rather than to the personality of the President. "In 1932, the Americans elected a Savior, a bit blindly. This year they affirmed a sum of principles that were upheld by the man and his philosophy but surpassed them by far. After four years of trial and experience the Americans simply recognized that Roosevelt represented better than anyone else around the great currents of their national destiny." [43]

An Englishman also believed that the result of the election was first of all a victory for the New Deal, but he added:

"Partly, of course, it was a vote for Roosevelt, the man. His courage, his infectious gaiety, his capacity for intimate personal contacts, his consummate political strategy, his dynamic democratic leadership, the unquestionable sincerity of his belief in social reform and that it is the duty of the state to help the victims of depression have rallied every progressive mind to his support." [44]

The writer claimed to recognize a deeper note in Roosevelt's appeal: "In future, the vast economic machine must, like the political machine, be made to function for the benefit of all the people and not mainly for the privileged classes, the owners of rent and interest."

The Nazi press was looking forward to the President's next term with great expectations:

"He will have to discard the main obstacle to the New Deal, the Supreme Court. The most important question that arises from the election is whether the American Constitution will be amended. With a strengthened majority in both Houses, Roosevelt now has a free hand to reform a Constitution of which he himself had said that it belongs to the age of oxcarts," was a typical German reaction.[45] Even the official Nazi newspaper commented sympathetically on Roosevelt's re-election:[46]

"Germany has been watching the development of the peace policy in the United States under Roosevelt's leadership with the interest due to a great friendly nation. Roosevelt worked out in his first term a broad reform program, encompassing all areas of national life. This program broke in many respects with previous practice. Through control of economy and progressive social legislation he set an ideal of order against the concept of laissez-faire and he ran into opposition from many directions. The election proved that the nation has a growing understanding of the 'new course' and its methods, which have shown unmistakeable signs of leading to an economic upswing."

The paper believed, mistakenly, that there was a law in America prohibiting a third term and trusted that as a consequence Roosevelt "will not henceforth be concerned with elections and will dedicate himself entirely to the reconstruction program that so eminently bears the mark of his personality."

A Frenchman shared in this expectation. Unlike the Germans, however, his hope for the President's undisturbed dedication to his reform program was not fed by an implied wish that Roosevelt would care even less than he did for happenings beyond the borders of the United States. "They say in America," he explained to the French readers,[47] "that the President spends his first four years in office arranging his re-election, and his second four years making a place for himself in history. His deep knowledge of the past of his country and his love of history may now compel Roosevelt to give greater attention to posterity. His feeling for the dramatic will serve him in future even more than in the past. His grandeur resides in his feeling for the grand as well as his political acumen or his sincere humanitarianism. Like most of his compatriots, he loves life, his own and that of others, the life of America itself."

An English voice rose in warning against the general optimism abroad. Pointing to the pitfalls of a too great victory, it showed a remarkable insight into the workings of the Congress.

"Not since the Civil War have the Republicans fallen to such low representation, and only once, just after the war, were the Democrats reduced to so pitiful a handful. The danger of this result is obvious. The majority is too large for efficient service. It is bound to deteriorate into factionalism. And as the Solid South sent 101 representatives to the lower house, most of whom cannot by wild exaggeration be described as New Dealers, they will constitute an immediate conservative influence. . . . The public so far has not paid much of a price for the new doctrine of unionization. If strikes and riots, and, later on, gross inconvenience to the public become the order of the day, Mr. Roosevelt may topple from his place as labour's Messiah. He may have to treat labour more 'objectively' than he did on occasion during the last four years. And once he has chilled the enthusiasm of his labour following, his second honeymoon will have ended. President Roosevelt is more enviable to-day than he is likely to be a year hence." [48]

The Italian press hailed Roosevelt, the isolationist. Japan expected from him a policy of moderation in the Pacific by refraining from naval armament.

From Moscow, *Izvestia* wrote off the Republican Party for good. But it predicted that if Roosevelt failed "the toiling masses" a third party would rise to assume the role of the British Labour Party in Congress, opposing the Party which, Democratic by name, was actually uniting all conservative elements.[49]

Paul Claudel, the French-Ambassador had this to say of Roosevelt's re-election:

"It is a consoling and comfortable spectacle to see the triumph of good sense, courage and honesty and that thing which is so fine and rare in this epoch of mediocrity and charlatanism—a great man at the head of a great people." [50]

5

A PYRRHIC VICTORY

In his campaign speeches the President had painstakingly avoided the issue of the Supreme Court. He had failed even to hint at what he intended to propose to eliminate the threat to his legislative program that the Court represented. But he had assured his audience that he had only just begun to fight for the aims of the New Deal, implying that he meant to make that august institution yield to the demands of the age and to the will of the people as expressed through the elections.

Any action he planned was to be a joint effort of the administrative and legislative branches of the government against the judiciary. Since it was Congress that had passed the laws the Court had erased from the books, it was expected to be in the front line of the battle against the Court.

Yet, as it happened, Congress, though dominated by the President's own party, and though in a honeymoon mood after Roosevelt's victory, reacted to his desire to reform the Court with thinly veiled revulsion. The boldness of the Congressional Democrats stemmed from their strength in numbers. It made it unnecessary for them to court the President who, being in his second term, was, according to all tradition, on his way out of office. Many had been swept into lesser offices by the tide of sentiment which opposed the President's new radical course, some even being enemies of the New Deal itself. Now, each for his own reason, they joined forces to frustrate the President who had called upon them to help overcome the obstacle to the laws passed by them and approved so enthusiastically by the voters.

This was a remarkable development, particularly since it came so soon after the victory of the President, but if Congress wanted to reassert its independence the opportunity was well chosen.

Instead of attacking the Supreme Court head on, Roosevelt chose apparent subterfuges, pretending to be impelled by the overcrowding of the courts and by the advanced age of the justices who were allegedly incapable of understanding new social philosophies. He asked for power to appoint another justice for each one who, having reached the age of seventy, did not resign.

This time the President was unusually secretive with the Congressional leaders of his party. He did not ask them for advice—he presented them with the finished draft of the bill. He thus gave them plenty of cause for resentment, and provided substance for the suspicions of his enemies who insisted that ultimately he would aim for dictatorship. The strange procedure he chose and his lack of sincerity generated distrust to the extent that his enemies deemed it possible that suspicion might contaminate even the masses of the people. If so, the Supreme Court issue could become a rallying point of those who believed that the great scare of the depression had permitted Roosevelt to corrupt the spirit that had made America rich and powerful.

The world abroad was still feeling the impact of Roosevelt's victory at the polls when the puzzling developments in America began to take shape. It gave commentators ample opportunity to make varied appraisals of the President's personality and political creed.

A German writer attributed Roosevelt's success to his instinctive knowledge of men and his ability to win the favor and the vote of the little man. In all this Roosevelt had acted like a sportsman rather than a soldier or a man of principles. With this went an outspoken readiness to serve, the noblesse oblige of a wealthy man, ambition combined with a sense of justice, a desire to better distribute the goods of life without uprooting society. In his spiritual make-up, religion, philosophy, and art played a subordinate role. He had no interest in music, painting or the theatre, but he loved American history and read biographies widely. He had never read Karl Marx, but should he have read him, John Stuart Mill would soon have gained the upper hand on him. "The American people want their Presidents not too distant from their own average. They don't expect them to be brilliant or deep thinkers, but rather to be of firm character, honest trustees embodying common sense, capable of practical, healthy human understanding. If one of them on top of this possessed a 'magnetic personality' then he had everything his nation loved to see in the White House." [1]

A Frenchman observed that "for Roosevelt, democracy and civilization mean the same thing. He can think of only one lasting progressive regime: the democratic government which has functioned in his country for a century and a half and which has made the United States what it is . . . His great achievement has consisted in the fact that the mass of workers lived on the margin of the society before he allowed them to enter the State and become its integral part." [2]

Mussolini in February, 1937 still admired Roosevelt and told Anne O'Hare McCormick why: "I admire him because he is so bold, because he also is something of a dictator, though not in the sense that I am a dictator. He is what I should describe as a social dictator. He concentrates in his hands all the power possible under your system in order to dictate social justice. Thereby he has averted great dangers in the United States." As to democracy and its future, the Duce remained pessimistic. "I tell you," he said, "democracy is only a mask for capitalism [and] . . . the era of capitalism is over. . . . Bear in mind that in the future it will be recognized that we were the first to face and adapt government to the facts of modern life." [3]

The Nazis continued to praise Roosevelt also. A *New York Times* report from Berlin noted: "The German argument contends that democracies like Britain, France, and the United States are inherently weak through lack of ideology. . . . [However] President Roosevelt in German eyes already is well ahead of world democratic leaders in his perception of the importance of ideology as a factor in national politics. . . . He is believed to be more keenly alive to the post-war necessity of imbuing even democratic formulas with new, even radical spiritual values—less violent and robust maybe than those incorporated in the Fascist and National Socialist decalogues." [4]

Although resenting the President's open attack on the dictatorships in his speech on the 150th anniversary of the Constitution, the dictators continued to hope secretly that eventually he would join their ranks. It was the same speech that brought this comment from an Englishman: ". . . I heard it in my study at lunchtime on that September day. The eloquent phrases, like shafts of sunlight, streamed from the radio-box into the room, bringing the warmth of hope and encouragement. The cold world outside, so full of bitterness and strife, needed such a message. The words must have found an echo in many hearts." [5]

The same author contrasted his reaction to the speech with a German comment, which ran: "Germany for some time has been watching with astonishment the President's methods, especially in view of his predecessor's endeavor to smooth the political ways. The wholly different attitude of President Roosevelt leads us to draw very grave conclusions regarding the internal crisis through which the United States has been passing for some time under the Roosevelt regime. Here we find the causes for President's repeated attacks. President Roosevelt has no cause to criticize dictatorial government measures! Mr. Roosevelt seemingly employs his attacks on foreign dictatorships only to divert his people's attention from his own dictatorial aspirations. We may well understand that a dictatorial will is needed in the confusion existing in the United States, but we fail to understand the dishonesty which attacks third persons in order to defend itself."

A Belgian, like the still hopeful Nazis, saw Roosevelt's worth in the way he inculcated "ideology" into democracy, rather than in such accomplishments as the Tennessee Valley Authority or his social legislation, from which millions benefitted. "After a century and a half, the ideal of American democracy seemed to have lost its vitality and fertility," he wrote.[6] "Roosevelt restored it by giving it for a foundation, not laws or constitutions which would become obsolete and moldy, but the only eternally young force: the people."

In the view of a Frenchman, however, the significance of the "Roosevelt experience" consisted in consolidating the United States as a nation. "The depression in America," he asserted, "was a national crisis which unified the nation, while the only other grave crisis the Union had undergone since its formation, the Civil War, divided Americans rather than united them. The remedies applied to the crisis have now enlarged enormously the jurisdiction of the government: control over employer-employee relations; an active part in the fight against unemployment; restoration of the balance of incomes through monetary measures; protection of savings; the control of holding companies: these all indicate that America is vigorously engaged in moving toward a unified state." [7]

Other observers refrained from making generalizations, preferring to note the unexpected events that followed on the heels of Roosevelt's second inauguration.

A dramatic chain of events had turned Roosevelt's fight for reform of the Supreme Court into a struggle for power between the President and his party in Congress. Conservative Democrats found ready allies in Republican Congressmen; cooperation between them was extended to agreement that both would oppose the President's program for extension of the New Deal. The Republicans could hardly believe their ears when so soon after their crushing defeat at the polls the call for their support sounded. Besides the enemies of the New Deal, some liberals in the Democratic party and Progressives among the Republicans took the side of the Court, since they disapproved of the President's tactics in planning a "packing" of the Court instead of seeking to amend the Constitution.

The President still held a trump card—the people. He felt he could rouse them for support and by so doing keep Congress in line. The situation in the spring of 1937 provided arguments for foreign opinion weighing Roosevelt's alleged inclination to dictatorship against his respect for the Constitution.

"[His] reelection was so striking a testimony," an Englishman wrote, "to the man and his ideals that the only wonder is that he did not overcome all opposition and enforce his will. . . . In Great Britain such a vote of confidence would have made all opposition ineffective. . . . the country was still behind him, and it is from this angle that we can see that the United States at that time was in a condition amounting to civil war. . . . [The question is] . . . whether the President will be forced, by the very tenacity and idealism of his character, into the virtual role of a dictator. That he has no inclination to play that part he has repeatedly made plain. But it must not be forgotten that there was a time when he had no idea of becoming President of his country; yet when the moment for decision came, he shouldered the responsibility, in spite of all contrary arguments. . . . Therefore it is natural for people to ask, if it came to the point of assuming dictatorial powers or renouncing the cardinal points of the New Deal, whether he would not again undertake a role to which he believed himself to be called, however much it might go against the grain. In a world where the unexpected happens almost as frequently as the expected, such a question as the above is bound to be considered, even by those who have followed Franklin Roosevelt throughout his career and have an unshakable faith in the man's quality. . . .

"The question that I have raised regarding a dictatorship in America cannot be answered by anyone, not even by President Roosevelt himself. It is wise, however, to bear in mind that in America as elsewhere the ordinary man, that disillusioned soul, is apt at the present time to consent to any form of strong government in order to be saved from the responsibility of independent thought and action in the face of apparent chaos. It is wise to recognize the possibility of dictatorship in some form or other being thrust upon the present administration in America. If such a thing came to pass within the next few years, I believe that the American people could count themselves blessed that it happened when Franklin Roosevelt, and not another, was President." [8]

But an Indian saw no reason to fear that Roosevelt would become a dictator. "Roosevelt's powers," he wrote "are autocratic; but he never uses them autocratically. Ever since he attained authority, he has taken every opportunity to act with constitutional propriety. . . . Both by instinct and by choice he is a thorough democrat—and America need never fear that he will blossom forth into a Hitler or Stalin. . . . America's Roosevelt in fact is, and will remain, on the one hand, a genial gentleman, and, on the other, a determined friend of the poor." [9]

The President also feared a dictatorship if the Court had paralyzed the government, but felt such a threat came from sources other than himself. Looking back on it years later, Roosevelt wrote: "That year was a definite turning point in the history of the United States. It was the year which determined whether the kind of government which the people of the United States had voted for in 1932, 1934 and 1936, was to be permitted by the Supreme Court to function." If it had not been permitted to function as a democracy, Roosevelt continued, there would have been a great danger that some alien form of government might have come into power, in the vain hope that it could give the people the protection and cooperative assistance they had a right to expect. "The question at issue in 1937 was," in the President's words, "whether or not a majority of the Supreme Court were to be a super-legislature, leaving the people powerless to insist on Congress' handling of national affairs. Were the personal predilections of a few men to hold up all the Government wished to do for the unemployed, the workers, the old, the disabled, the children, and the great industries?" A writer underscored Roosevelt's words in adding: "All the Democrats elected were not New Dealers; but on the other hand all Republicans were not opposed to the New Deal; and that workers, small traders, and most professional classes wanted it to continue was shown by the record-breaking election figures, when 46 million voted and gave Roosevelt an 11 million majority with vast majorities in the Senate and House of Representatives." [10]

In March the issue appeared to be solved by an unexpected event; the Court suddenly reversed its former decisions. It recognized the constitutional power of the States to pass mimimum wage laws, upheld the Railway Labor Act providing for collective bargaining, in fact was ready to admit the New Deal into the constitutional framework of the country. Moreover, the most exposed ultra-conservative justices prepared to resign.

Roosevelt could have made a face-saving compromise with Congress then, but the issue of power that had grown out of the Court proposal had been built up too much. Either the President or his party in Congress had to yield.

It happened that the arguments of his opponents, hammered incessantly into the minds of the people, broke the solid popular support the President had enjoyed. Like Congress, many people began to see in such proposals as the reorganization of the administration, a quest for more power. In June the Senate Judiciary Committee delivered a terrific blow to the President's influence over Congress by defeating his Supreme Court proposals.

The sweeping victory at the polls veiled the real significance of the election. The huge majority of the Democratic Party rode into Congress on the groundswell of a counter-revolution. Its impulses came from wide-spread roots of traditionalism and from the hurt feelings of injured status; the Republican Party was too much discredited to be made their agent. Yet much of Roosevelt's party did not ascribe to his politics.

But the President could count on his personal popularity with the majority of the people. He might be frustrated by the Supreme Court or Congress or both but not subverted. The Constitution was sophisticated enough and the Democratic Party heterogeneous enough to allow different attitudes to be expressed in a vote for a single party and its leader. What many people abroad feared or expected was the reverse—Roosevelt's assuming exceptional powers in order to accomplish his program. The President was entitled to believe his program had been approved by those who had voted for him. But he was wise enough not to force issues against a strong adverse current. His deep respect for the institutions of democracy prevented him from ever seriously considering overstepping his constitutional powers. His confidence that the majority stood unswervingly for his reforms made self-restraint easy. The politician in him retreated to move more forcefully later.

It was not easy to explain to the public abroad the sudden turn of his party and of a decisive segment of public opinion against the President. A Frenchman put it this way: "This case demonstrates most clearly how conservative American democracy is, or more precisely, how faithful it is to its traditions of freedom. Traditionally, the Supreme Court gave judicial, thus legal, protection against the excesses of the legislative power, i.e., actually against the tyranny of the majority. Nothing but the complete independence of the justices vouchsafed for this protection. To injure this independence would cause the whole system to collapse. Therefore, the respect for the Supreme Court is deeply rooted in the minds and hearts of the American people. . . . Roosevelt was defeated because he injured a symbol, and in such cases popular wisdom is right, since the force of symbols issues from their representation of lasting principles in the life of the nation, and this is enough to make them indestructible." [11]

An English visitor to the United States was perplexed by the hatred that the Court issue had stirred against Roosevelt. "I arrived in New York," he reported, "at the very moment that Mr. Roosevelt was making his Supreme Court proposals. But what amazed me was the virulence and, I think, lack of judgment which even Mr. Roosevelt's most serious opponents show in their attacks. In the morning, for instance, I read Dorothy Thompson's article in the *Herald Tribune*—a very responsible and influential paper. She is an able woman and an excellent journalist. Yet she compared the President with Hitler and Mussolini and wrote two columns about his bid for dictatorship. In the evening, I went to see the dramatic version of her husband's book, *It Can't Happen Here.* In this play Sinclair Lewis has magnificently succeeded in showing how Fascist dictatorship might come to the United States. It was staged with government help as part of the Administration's scheme of nation theatre production. As I watched it, I wondered. If instead of enabling anti-Fascist propaganda to be staged at public expense, Mr.

Roosevelt had been, in fact, doing all the things portrayed in this play, if the President had things organized in every village to beat up those who opposed him, if his gangsters were installed in the offices of the *Herald Tribune* and Dorothy Thompson herself threatened with concentration camp, her criticism could scarcely have been stronger. . . . In fact, the whole attack upon Mr. Roosevelt as a dictator, or indeed anything but a very astute liberal politician, is altogether unconvincing. His calm, persuasive voice on the radio dispels the delusion in five minutes." [12]

Another article drew "an irresistible inference from the barren record of Congress that has just come to an end. With a tactical adroitness, irritating because of its very ingenuity, the President had assailed the legend that is the nucleus of the whole American myth. The Supreme Court plays the role of the Father in Freudian psychology to the timid, conservative, average man of the United States. It is what the Monarch is for England and the inspired Fuehrer for contemporary Germany. To assail this myth, when Roosevelt launched his long delayed attack after his triumph in November, seemed as necessary as it was audacious. But no sooner had he hurled his challenge than the necessity vanished, for in judgment after judgment, the intimidated Court reversed itself and swung into line with modern thought. In this situation it was easy for conservative Democrats to join the revolt against the President. . . . Under the specious arguments lay an intention to destroy the President's leadership and with it the New Deal." [13]

Some commentators tried to predict the President's next step. An attempt to turn the Democratic Party into a truly liberal, or progressive party, appeared to be in order. Should he fail to rid it of the conservatives, Roosevelt might form a third party. His uncle, Theodore Roosevelt, had done it, and his nephew in many respects had consciously followed the trustbuster's footsteps. Those who believed that Roosevelt was set to form a New Deal party logically concluded that he would also seek a third term since an outgoing President would not have the prestige and power for such a bold, far-reaching undertaking.

Prominent among them was *The Economist:* "The magic spell

of President Roosevelt over Congress is pretty well ended," the magazine stated.[14] "The Supreme Court fight was the means by which it came to an end, but not the cause, for the cause was the too great victory of the Democrats at the polls last November. Overwhelming majorities are beyond discipline, as every democracy knows, and the one formula for maintaining leadership over them—to undertake as little as possible—works only for a time. Mr. Roosevelt has not aimed at being inactive. He has not even kept to the middle of the road, the natural impulse in leading a party with Right and Left wings. He has led the Left, in his attack on the Supreme Court, in his proposal for the reorganization of the Government, and in his sympathy for the Lewis movement in organized labor. This has not, however, been Liberalism as his liberal followers understand it.

"In each instance, the President was reaching out for more personal and/or executive power. In attacking the Supreme Court this feature estranged many liberal Democrats. And the harmony between the Administration and Congress of Industrial Organization is giving rise to suspicions that the President s playing with the idea of a third term. . . . What is more likely is that the President may be weighing the wisdom of letting his party split, to make of 1940 a rallying of liberal forces on the Democratic side, the Conservatives being left to coalesce with the Republicans. This is no new idea in Washington, and Europeans will not understand the hesitancy of Americans to shape party politics on a clear division between Conservativism and Liberalism. . . ." The magazine forecast that Congress' revolt would continue, since Roosevelt's plans for reorganization of the administration would enormously reduce political patronage. As a counter move, the President might purge the party at the interim elections in 1938, emphasizing his determination to continue the New Deal.

A Swiss magazine reported that the question of a third term for Roosevelt had popped up immediately after his triumphal re-election, although it was without precedent in the history of the United States. But the magazine had information that the President "had told friends that he had given no thought to the idea. At the same time he said that he deemed the future very dark and feared grave world conflict in 1939, or 1941 at the latest. Therefore, his successor must be energetic and definitely younger than sixty." [15]

Roosevelt's position in his struggle with Congress became weaker when in the second half of 1937, for the first time since 1933, a recession developed suddenly and the economic situation began to deteriorate at a frightening pace.

The Economist in July, 1937 stated that although unemployment figures were being withheld, undoubtedly there was now little industrial unemployment. Summing up the results of the New Deal, the magazine commented: "The first term of shock tactics in handling the urgent problem of the depression is over; the New Deal in essence was the pursuit of reform so that recovery might appear; now that recovery is here, what is to happen to reform?

"American recovery is now an established fact. A revival of some consumers goods industries, based in part on Federal disbursements for relief, in part on the vastly improved position of the farmers' income in relation to costs of goods he pays, in part on what are termed natural causes, has spread to some durable consumers goods and producers goods. . . . There has been a substantial rise in national income."

But after the economic activity had almost returned to its 1929 level, "it suddenly began a downward trend from the month of August on and lost in a few months all the gains achieved in the last two years," a French paper commented in 1938.[16] "Wall Street lost more in six months than in the whole year following the 1929 crash. . . . Five years after assuming power, President Roosevelt faces the same difficulties he met then and thought he had definitely surmounted."

"No wonder that he is considering employing the same measures he did then," the magazine reported in another issue. It reminded its readers that the downturn might be the consequence of the Government's fiscal policy in 1936 and in the first half of 1937 when its principal concern was to prevent the development of a boom by balancing the budget.

The Government immediately lowered the obligatory reserves of the banks, voted a billion and a half to the Reconstruction Finance Corporation to lend for investment purposes, and began new public works. This time, however, the humility of the businessmen was gone. On the contrary, they blamed the crisis on the Government's interference with business. Recovery depended on the return of confidence, but a French magazine, relating information garnered from Wall Street, wondered whether it would come forth: "The new measures of the Government again contain governmental controls and interventions; they don't promote the return of confidence. Business circles are tempted to conclude from this situation that the President has learned nothing and forgotten nothing. One might say that confidence can be reborn only to the extent Roosevelt suffers setbacks. The Stock Exchange improved in the last days of April, 1938, only because of Congressional opposition to the President. . . . The American crisis is political rather than economic." [17]

Since the crisis began with a general price rise and was followed immediately by the fall of raw materials prices, it showed the same symptoms as the great depression. "Could not the same symptoms imply the same consequences?" asked a French author. And he added: "Fear of a new depression is disquieting the circle around the Presirent." [18]

It was not until the summer of 1938 that the economic situation showed definite signs of improvement. A German author drew a poor balance from the effect of the New Deal on the American economy. "When all is said," he wrote,[19] "the fact remains that the initial recovery in the United States has not lasted. . . . The richest and most powerful country in the world cuts a poor figure in the family of industrial states. The statistical bulletin of the League of Nations compares the American recovery with twenty countries, putting the production in 1937 against that of the year of 1929. The United States is in sixteenth place. For this the Roosevelt administration cannot deny responsibility."

A Swiss paper, however, gave more credit to American recovery efforts than those in Europe. "Although emergency measures still constitute an important factor in the economy and unemployment persists—the economic situation in America is in essence healthier than that in Europe, since her prosperity is far less based on unproductive armament production than most European countries, including Britain." [20]

Another observer insisted that the real problem was a technological one and it could not be solved without dictatorial measures. "The President disguises the crisis," he wrote; "he is bridging the abyss; but when the state is finally exhausted in sustaining an artificial prosperity by expending billions one will note that nothing has been done to solve the problems, first of all the unemployment which no prosperity is able to absorb. . . . The directed economy presupposes certain means of action which not even the most powerful democratic leader can afford. In plain language: they demand a dictatorship of a single man, of a party or of a class; a dictatorship alone is able to overcome the inevitable resistance. Thus, the Roosevelt experience, like all experiences, was interesting but it got stuck halfway. But he still has a long way to go, he may perfect his work. The experience continues." [21]

A leftist magazine in Britain was rather pessimistic as to the future of the New Deal when it stated: "American psychology in 1933 was sufficiently frightened to be willing to accept a dictator who preached social justice but saved Wall Street from financial disintegration . . . Because he remains a Liberal, clinging pathetically to the belief that social justice and capitalism are compatible, he will lead no revolutionary assault against the system of production for profit. This being so, his surrender to the entrenched financial interests may be gradual, but it will be as certain as the post-war capitulation of Mr. Lloyd George, with whose political make-up he has so much in common. The President is not the man to die for causes which have lost their popularity. With industrial 'shut downs' looming ahead and Congress openly rebellious, the New Deal, it is to be feared, is destined to go the same way as the Land fit for Heroes. Mr. Roosevelt's empirical Liberalism, when it comes to the test of the class issue, is not enduring stuff. . . . Mr. Roosevelt is unprepared to take up the challenge which Big Business has flung down." [22]

Another British writer was also skeptical. "He is trying to break down the purely artificial party barriers of Democratic and Republican in order to set a new criterion for political allegiance conservative vs. liberal, or if you prefer, reactionary vs. radical. But what does this liberal-radical banner signify? If Roosevelt has not changed his 'liberalism' since 1933, the only future in sight is a dismal one: a continuation of the present muddle program towards economic chaos. If on the other hand the President means and is prepared to march with his followers down the rocky road to the left, the chances are that American capitalism in the near future will undergo a drastic transformation." [23]

H. G. Wells, however, held the economic experts and the social scientists responsible for the President's mistakes and inconsistencies. He said before a distinguished audience in London: "President Roosevelt is one of the most interesting figures in all history, because he really did make an appeal for such knowledge and understanding as existed to come to his aid. America in an astounding state of meekness was ready to be told and shown. There were the universities, great schools and galaxies of authorities, learned men, experts and teachers. Out of this mass of knowledge there have since come many very trenchant criticisms of the President's mistakes. But at the time this higher brain . . . of America was so entirely uncoordinated . . . The President had to experiment, and attempt this and that, to turn from one promising adviser to another because there was nothing ready for him. He did not pretend to be a divinity. He was a politician of exceptional good will. He was none of your dictator-Gods. He showed himself extremely open and receptive to the organized information and guidance that was not there." [24]

Roosevelt had succeeded in making the people realize the crying need for more economic democracy, when in his second inaugural address he conveyed a startling vision of the state of the nation. "I see one-third of the Nation ill-housed, ill-clad, ill-nourished" was his shocking revelation; but it did not break the opponents to his reform policy in Congress. Congress passed only two important laws in 1937, one helping tenants to buy land, the other a slum clearance law that promoted the building of low-rent houses by government loans to local authorities.

The new recession moved Congress to adopt legislation which the President had urged in his special message to Congress and again in a fireside chat in the spring of 1938. It passed the so-called second AAA and a law setting minimum wages and maximum working hours.

Prosperity was restored within a year by three billion federal dollars pumped into the productive process and by the Federal Reserve Bank's lowering reserve requirements for banks. Yet the President was reluctant to resort to the same recovery measures that he had successfully tried in 1935 until the recession worsened, since this proved that short of them the New Deal was unable to insure sustained prosperity.

Finally, however, he chose not to emulate Hoover. He did not remain passive or hesitate to return to drastic government intervention.

During the resulting gradual recovery, a new factor played a part. A series of sinister events in Europe had made the President aware of the danger to America in a further expansion of the dictators' power and further demoralization of the democracies. His preoccupation was the graver since he realized how unprepared American public opinion was to shoulder the responsibilities involved in cooperative action to fend off the menace before it reached the Western Hemisphere. He began to concentrate on building the country's defense psychologically by a significant appeal for Americans to cease partisan activity in time of national emergency. This was after his abortive attempt, in 1938, to purge from the Democratic Party members hostile to him or to the New Deal. The attempt failed, and the Party itself suffered losses heavier than the government party usually receives at American interim elections.

An important factor in the new rise of prosperity was the growing confidence of businessmen, but new orders from a re-arming Western Europe also increasingly contributed to widening its scope. These orders enabled American industry to adjust to the manufacture of armaments, helping the nation shift quickly to a full-scale war economy later when America was forced into the war.

Under the impact of events abroad, and the failure of Roosevelt's purge, followed by Democratic defeat at the polls in 1938, observers began to speculate about the possibility that the President might run for a third term.

"To some, the political lesson of 1938's election is that the only New Dealer who can be elected in 1940 is Mr. Roosevelt himself," an English magazine asserted. "If that is true, he would presumably prefer to challenge the strong tradition than to let his program be put on the shelf. . . . The opposition can make a big fuss about it, but there is no evidence that the millions of 'common-man' voters . . . are greatly moved by such considerations. Rather they want a President who has their welfare at heart; who is their 'friend,' and Mr. Roosevelt still retains that title." [25]

But the European events in the fall of 1938 were causing Roosevelt to "put the New Deal on the shelf. Let us work for greater unity, for peace among the nations of the world, for restraint, for negotiation and for community of effort. Let us work for the same ideals within our own borders in our relations with each other, so that we may, if the test ever comes, have that unity of will with which alone a democracy can successfully meet its enemies," he exhorted the nation.

Indeed, Roosevelt had introduced a new course, the English magazine commented. "He could have taken one of two widely different courses. He could have donned his shining armor again and gone forth to battle against what he calls the fortress of privilege. He could have plunged again into the temper of the Supreme Court fight, which, alongside with the sit-down strikes, were the atmospheric prelude to the 1937-38 slump. He could have gone on the war-path. But instead of choosing this course, he began to stress pacification and national unity. He spoke with new patience and resignation of 'the American way' of achieving reforms slowly and painfully. He was, in short, in a mood which American observers had never seen in him before." [26]

A French correspondent familiar with the American scene who knew the President and his circle well, wrote a long article on the crisis of democracy in America and gave an illuminating analysis of the President's personality. "Since a few months, in fact since his re-election," the writer asserted, "the President is inclined to think that democracy and Rooseveltism are one and the same, which means that democracy cannot survive unless it evolves continually. . . . [But] only if it surpasses the dynamics, destructive but real, of the dictators will it avoid being swept away by them." [27]

Speaking of the President, the writer reported that even in America where everybody lives in the present with an intensity unknown in Europe, people were astounded at the President's vitality. He wrote: "The truth is that President Roosevelt spends much less time and energy in his efforts to reach the aims he has set himself than in satisfying the prodigious personal pleasure that he feels in accomplishing a task. The Promised Land toward which he carries his nation is perhaps but a mirage, but his optimism, his good humour and ease have their source in the very simple fact that Franklin Roosevelt is enchanted with being President. The job of chief of state appears not at all heavy for him, nor tedious or tragic. He is perfectly conscious of the immense responsibility that weighs on his shoulders but this does not incite him to adopt the attitude of a Hamlet or a Napoleon. He does not believe that fate has assigned him the task of saving his country; on the other hand he thinks that nothing is impossible. Like all real Americans, he has an inalienable faith in the perfectibility of man's intelligence and in the progress of his nation. He is not interested in metaphysical messianism. His philosophy is essentially humanitarian. He believes in the ultimate triumph of men of 'good will'. . . ."

The same writer had his own explanation for Roosevelt's alleged lack of sensitivity and seriousness: "This is the normal attitude of a well-born, well-raised man whose mind is sufficiently polished and supple to prefer irony or a burst of laughter, which is not always frank, however, in replying to a brutal attack. Roosevelt has a sense of humor and belongs to a circle in which good manners demand that one shows courtesy at all times, receives with a good mien even people whom one detests; which does not prevent him from detesting, even taking revenge on them. Men of the world learn to be hypocritical, and President Roosevelt is essentially a man of the world. The truth of the matter is that at the center of the personality of President Roosevelt is an energy, a force that is his but at the same time identical with something that surpasses him, the spirit of a people who want to feel that they are on the march toward a better world."

6

PRE-WAR RUMBLINGS

In the last months of 1938, after the slump that so ominously recalled the beginnings of the Great Depression had been checked, the prompt recovery made it manifest that American democracy was able to cope with the most invidious economic crises. President Roosevelt did not resort to dictatorial powers to reinstitute his New Deal, even though it had to a large extent been destroyed by the great assault of the Supreme Court. By renewing America's self-confidence while preserving her freedom intact, Roosevelt demolished the primary totalitarian argument against democracy. Indeed, he saved democracy as an alternative to two totalitarianisms, Fascism and Communism, at a time when democracy in Europe, panicked by the world economic depression, was voluntarily professing bankruptcy.

America was also the living denial of the second totalitarian argument, which purported that the democracies were decadent. The third argument, that the democracies lacked the moral fiber to defend themselves, could not however be dismissed by a simple denial so long as isolationism in America compelled her to abandon positions of vital interest.

Retreat and demoralization had started in 1931 when the British had refused to take part in an American naval demonstration against Japanese aggression. Then "even a Republican administration was willing to initiate collective action. A great opportunity for linking American policy to the system of collective security on an occasion when American interests and sentiments were strongly engaged was lost, perhaps irretrievably." [1]

However, fascist conquest by demoralization would not have succeeded in Europe had not the Great Depression sapped the self-confidence of the middle classes. The fascist dictators had risen due to that demoralization, and all they had to do was to deepen it by divisive tactics and intimidation. Each new aggressive step increased the prestige of the dictators and lowered the morale of the peoples threatened by them, until their ultimate success appeared as inevitable as their propaganda pretended. Still, it would require more than demoralization to conquer Russia and America; they would have to be defeated by external force. The fascist master-plan called for an invasion of Russia, while America was to be kept in self-isolation until the totalitarian conquests had isolated her to the point that she would forfeit her chances to unfold her latent forces.

When the British sacrificed Ethiopia to appease Mussolini, they deserted a host of small nations who had followed her lead in voting economic sanctions against Italy. They had been enthused over the possibility of collective action that might guarantee their security in the future; now they were duly demoralized. Meanwhile the Germans not only increased their trade with Italy, but also replaced the Italians in the East European markets while Mussolini kept industry and people busy in the Ethiopian war. To complete Hitler's success, the result of the war had disgusted the American public and disappointed President Roosevelt who, without openly cooperating with it, had kept pace with the sanctions imposed by the League.

In the spring of 1936, Hitler defied the stipulations of the Peace Treaty and sent his troops into the Rhineland. France made no military effort to defend her security, nor did England seem perturbed by Hitler's clear-cut breach of the Treaty. After that, it was obvious to Hitler that they would not take up arms against Germany if he went on to conquer countries less vital to their security.

However, on the westernmost peninsula of the Continent, a military revolt led by General Franco had unleashed a civil war against the legal government of the Spanish republic. The revolt would soon have collapsed without full-scale military intervention by Italy. Spain became the field on which the first battles of an ideological war were fought, but Germany, Russia and the two great West European powers did not join the lists. The civil war was still raging when, in 1937, Japan openly attacked China. A year later, Hitler annexed Austria and persuaded England and France to surrender the rights of the Czechoslovak Republic at Munich.

A French magazine described the state of mind of the middle classes as foreshadowing the moral and military collapse of their country. The description was valid for other Continental countries as well. "It was no unconscious submission on the part of the French bourgeoisie. They began to admire fascism, though hypocritically hiding their admiration. They admired power and success. They shuddered with pleasure at the dictators' brutal manner. The pomp and the parades, the superb production of a mystical comedian, drove them into a frenzy. Above all, being alarmed over their property, they saw their protectors in the rows of goose-stepping soldiers, in the police who intruded into the innermost sanctums of private life. This iron order would save them from communism."[2]

Meanwhile, from 1937 on the situation in America showed disturbing signs of a different order. "The restlessness of the American scene in recent years had puzzled all visitors, and most Americans as well," the Survey of International Affairs later wrote. "Every institution of the American nation, the whole superstructure of the people's life, seemed to be slipping slowly but irresistibly away from its accustomed moorings . . . Internally, the appearance of distress and unemployment since the depression, and the almost universal economic insecurity, brought about an enormously intensified awareness of the nation's social problems." The passions they generated were of such intensity that a visiting French author was frightened. "Yesterday night," he reported, "at a dinner party, my neighbor, an agreeable, even cultured old lady was telling me of her love for France with apparent sincerity, when she suddenly remarked: 'But of course, even though I love your country I am a savage isolationist.' When I admitted that I could not understand the contradiction, she asked, 'Don't you see, that if we should go to your support Roosevelt might have a strong chance of being elected for a third term.' 'Would you sacrifice, Madame,' I answered, 'my country and probably yours as well to such resentments?' But she stated with passion: 'I would rather see the planet blown up than to give a third term to that man. . . .'"[3]

Her bitterness was due to the change in what Mr. Roosevelt called the "moral climate" of the United States, as a reporter visiting the country after a long absence sensed. "The slump and the pressure from below have awakened a social conscience in the United States. . . . The great majority of Americans have elected as President a man who has uttered sentiments that were sometimes enough to send a man to jail during the fanatical anti-Red fervor after the war. It has become impossible to argue that the poor are only poor by their own fault and that any good worker can become a Mr. Rockefeller, if he only tries hard enough."[4]

However, the new moral climate had produced no essential change in foreign policy. Some European observers deemed it contradictory when they compared "American intervention and unsparing effort in the General War of 1914-1918 and her subsequent defection and unhelpfulness in the organizing of world peace. . . . But that intervention can be regarded as an interlude, a break in a continuous tradition of isolation, a departure from that tradition, made—as in 1812—precisely in order to assert America's right to remain neutral. The United States stressed this point when she entered the war in 1917 as an Associated Power fighting for certain general rights and not as an Allied Power fighting for special cause."[5]

Roosevelt had followed this inveterate tradition when, in the spring of 1933, he had asked from Congress powers to prohibit the sending of war supplies to any state guilty of aggression. But the Senate had insisted that any embargo be put on the export of arms to all belligerents. It feared that the President, by favoring one side, might involve the country in a foreign war. In 1937, the new Neutrality Law gave a little more elbow room to the President, empowering him to state whether war existed, which implied his right not to make such statement if he deemed the embargo would injure American interests. Moreover, if the peace and neutrality of the United States were endangered, he was entitled to allow the selling of arms on a cash and carry basis. This freedom to maneuver came in handy when Japan attacked China. Roosevelt, by not declaring that war existed in Asia, could supply China with war materials. The cash and carry provision was to help western Europe, once it was engaged in war with the dictators.

Some writers warned that isolationism might be in the American tradition as far as Europe was concerned, but the history of American policy in the Far East consisted in "an uninterrupted succession of interventions. True, Roosevelt repudiated dollar diplomacy, commercial imperialism, in words as well as in actions, but in the Far East America remained the champion of the open door policy and a member of the Nine Power Treaty that guaranteed the territorial integrity of China. Japan has made no secret of her intention of abolishing the 'open door,' the international settlements and other privileges of foreigners in China and that, in case of a Japanese victory, China would fall into an exclusively Japanese sphere of interest. Roosevelt prepared American public opinion to resist Japanese ambitions and to defend American interests, in tacit understanding with Great Britain." [6]

In contrast to his policy of defending the status quo in the Far East, Roosevelt was ready to abstain from disturbing Prime Minister Chamberlain's appeasement of the dictators on the European continent. American foreign policy had usually been hampered by American public opinion, which was essentially isolationist. But when issues of international morality appeared to be involved in a conflict, Americans were roused to sympathy or anger, only to withdraw into indignant isolation again when eventually both parties struck a deal smacking of cynicism or double-talk.

Spain proved to be another area of Anglo-American cooperation. The British had decided on a policy of non-intervention unless Germany or Russia intervened on a large scale. Italian intervention would be overlooked.

The Neutrality Law, in its original form, did not apply to civil wars, but Roosevelt extended an embargo on arms to both parties. In practice, it deprived the legal government of supplies while the Italians openly supported the rebels with troops, equipment, and ammunition.

"This situation was the result of a convergency of desires, that of the President to collaborate with Britain and France as he had done in the Ethiopian conflict, and that of Congress to avoid an entanglement that might implicate the U.S. in war. . . . At the same time, the pacifists in the country were anti-fascists who had, like Faust, two souls in their breast, the one wanting to part from the other during the long, bloody Spanish civil war." [7]

"It was the end of illusions," a Swiss paper commented, at the time when the Spanish rebellion had broken out.[8] Following the Ethiopian war, "the world entered an armament race humanity had perhaps never experienced. Then the Spanish bomb crashed. From a halfway misfired provincial riot, as people mistakenly held Franco's rising, the bloodiest and biggest civil war unfolded that the history of Europe has known. It started with fights in the streets of Barcelona, Madrid, Malaga, Sevilla, proceeded to the ruthless conquest of Bajadoz and took on its final feature in the big battle at Irun: that of an embittered, implacable fratricidal war in which Spain made up for the losses she had been spared by staying out of World War I . . . The Spanish War is the most brutal international military manoeuvre since 1918. Perhaps this is not bad after all. Afterwards the poor, discarded little word peace will be cherished anew."

"This is a peculiar war," the Conservative *London Daily Telegraph* characterized the Spanish fratricide. "One side has no men; the other side has no arms." [9]

"The day when the U.S. Senate voted in January, 1937, the embargo on arms to Spain—81 to 0 with 12 abstentions—General Franco exclaimed: 'President Roosevelt behaved like a real gentleman.'" [10]

It was a humiliating spectacle. The democracies contributed to the fall of the Loyalists by their passivity in the face of open intervention by Italy. The Spanish supporters of legality and of democratic government faced strangulation and slow exhaustion.

But the Survey of International Affairs of 1938 exonerated Roosevelt from the bulk of responsibility. "It is true that isolation continued to be the base of [his foreign policy], and that the U.S. refrained from taking any direct action in connection with the incidents. In this, however, she was no more passive than the Western powers, and in the matter of the Spanish conflict far less passive, for she had to pass special legislation and break with a strong tradition in order to follow the example of the Western Powers. For the rest, the U.S. was more forward than the other democratic states in the use of the two instruments of foreign policy. . . . the U.S. was the most determined of all the Powers in diplomatic, as well as in economic action. Indeed, she gave the lead in both. . . . there was in the declarations of French and English statesmen nothing to compare with the major utterances of President Roosevelt and Secretary Hull, either for the firmness with which they stated the liberal point of view or the unequivocal manner in which they pointed the finger of accusation at the dictators."

In general, others abroad were much less understanding of Roosevelt's foreign policy. "It was irritating," a French magazine wrote, "to hear the Americans ceaselessly preaching morals to the rest of the world without ever coming to a resolution to do something so that morality might triumph." The article found the cause of this dichotomy in the fact that Roosevelt was incapable of convincing his people that the dictators were a potential danger to their own country.

"In vain the Americans approve of Roosevelt when he denounces the Japanese, the Germans, and the Italians as dangerous to general peace, since it is difficult for them to construct a concrete image of that danger. They know that their country is too distant and too powerful to be invaded. They may admit that in the more or less distant future and under certain circumstances (in case of Britain's defeat, for instance) the relation of powers might change and Japan, Germany, and Italy might become an actual menace to the U.S. But this is only speculation and if Roosevelt is convinced of the necessity of taking measures of precaution to prevent such possibilities from happening, he is unable to say so openly. One can accuse him—as a matter of fact he is being accused—of sacrificing the security of the country, which lies in her isolation, to meet a hypothetical peril which is in any case not verifiable today. . . . Hence the official silence when it comes to defining the perils menacing national security." [10]

If it was true, as the Survey of International Affairs of 1937 stressed, that "From the message to Congress on disarmament in 1934 down to the famous quarantine speech in Chicago at the end of 1937, the President and the Secretary of State literally set themselves the task of re-educating American opinion in the need for an active international policy," the effect of the Chicago speech on public opinion proved that they failed.

Roosevelt made that speech on October 5, 1937 under the direct impact of Japanese bombardment of Nanking and other Chinese cities. He was aware that the public was more sensitive to Japanese aggression against China than to the European dictators' sharp games with England and France. The President had said in Chicago, among other things, that the interdependence of nations "makes it impossible for any nation completely to isolate itself from economic and political upheaval in the rest of the world. . . . It is, therefore, a matter of vital interest and concern to the people of the United States that he sanctity of international treaties and the maintenance of international morality be restored. . . . It seems to be unfortunately true that the epidemic of world lawlessness is spreading. When an epidemic of physical disease starts to spread, the community approves, and joins in a quarantine of the patients in order to protect the health of the community against the spread of the disease. . . . There must be positive measures to preserve peace. America hates war, America hopes for peace. Therefore, America actively engages in the search of peace."

The *Survey* of 1937 summed up the reaction to the quarantine speech this way: ". . . such sparks as Mr. Roosevelt had struck went out without kindling the tinder, and the final effect was to reveal the measure of the distance by which popular feeling in the United States was still lagging behind the opinion of the better instructed minority. . . . There were other . . . and perhaps wider, though assuredly less intelligent, circles in the U.S. that yielded to the common human impulse to flinch from a danger instead of grappling with it; and in these circles the panacea of isolation has been recommended all the more vehemently the nearer the peril of international anarchy approached towards American shores."

The adverse effect of the speech made the President more cautious. "A visitor of repute asked the President a few days after the speech whether he believed that the United States might take part in economic sanctions against the aggressors. Mr. Roosevelt replied: 'You read page 252 of the book; I am still no further than page two.' "[11]

On the other hand, the dictators were heartened. The Japanese reaction to the quarantine speech conformed to that of the Germans. Their press stated that President Roosevelt's "attitude was in contrast to those Americans who would have America keep out of all complications in the Far East. . . . The unusual speech by President Roosevelt that virtually out of the clear sky assailed the 'aggressor' nations of the world was . . . an attempt to distract American public opinion from the Administration measures that had failed to effect an improvement in the country's economic conditions."[12]

The official answer to the quarantine speech was the announcement of the Anti-Comintern alliance of Japan, Germany, and Italy.

The emboldened Japanese created an incident that suddenly brought war near to America. In December, 1937, Japanese planes pursuing the Chinese along the Yangtze River near Nanking, bombed and sank the American gunboat *Panay*. They also sank tankers of Standard Oil, which the gunboat was escorting. The President sent a note to the Japanese that was resolute, calm, dignified, and forceful. To dramatize the issue, "hardly was the confidential note transmitted when the White House produced to the press the original of the Presidential instructions to the State Department concerning the note. It carried the corrections, alterations and cuts by the President's hand . . . and the public greatly appreciated the publication. It had the impression of having been in contact hour by hour with the government and, so to say, taking part in their decisions: this was no more secret diplomacy. The public also admired the dignity, moderation, firmness of the Presidential message. The fact that he asked the Japanese government to present the document to the Emperor himself, indicated that the President would not be satisfied with the excuses of the civilian authorities alone." [13]

The Japanese apologized and paid for the damages. Congress voted money for naval rearmament, but almost adopted a proposition for the amendment of the Constitution to the effect that the right of Congress to declare war would be restricted by a prior referendum. "International incidents were crowding upon each other, and causing the various currents of American opinion to flow strongly," the Survey of International Affairs of 1938 commented. "With every new act of violence the American people were roused into giving expression to their strong condemnation of Nazi and Fascist methods. At the same time and on every fresh occasion the American people failed to discover a possible point of contact with the policy of those West European countries with which, on the whole, they sympathized. The conviction grew that the Old World was beyond hope, not for military inadequacy but for the lack of moral stamina. It was not the difficulties of the position or even the possible risks involved which created this state of mind, but above all the dour conviction that, in spite of all their democratic professions, the English and French Governments would prefer to see the Fascists rather than their opponents in power. For this was a conviction which disheartened and disarmed those very liberals and believers in international cooperation who otherwise might have stemmed and perhaps turned the tide of isolation."

This conviction was, however, only too well substantiated by the West European governments. British Conservative reaction to the President's annual message to Congress in January, 1938, in which he assured that "there are many methods short of war, but stronger and more effective than mere words," revealed that the British government had decided on a consistent policy of appeasing the dictators.

Thus, the *New York Times* correspondent in London quoted a British official as saying that "official British opinion . . . does not entirely agree with President Roosevelt's sharp distinction between democracies and dictatorships. Turkey, for example, has a powerfully entrenched dictatorship, yet it is felt here that no country in the world is such a 'good neighbor.' Similarly it is argued that Russia wants peace and is an influence for peace in spite of its ruthless dictatorial regime. For these reasons the British feel that President Roosevelt made a more truthful distinction in his earlier speeches when he contrasted the 90 per cent of the world's people who want peace with the 10 per cent who want war."

The same newspaper registered a similar conservative reaction in Paris: President Roosevelt's words "are thought to be the pronouncements of a partisan of an ideological war against fascism. . . . It is thought rather that it tends to widen the gulf between dictatorships and democracies, thus rendering the ideological conflict, which is largely responsible for the present unrest, even more bitter and insoluble." [14]

In February of 1938, Foreign Secretary Anthony Eden resigned. It was an open secret that he had advocated a policy of collective security, using the League, as against the policy of appeasement of the Prime Minister. In April, an Anglo Italian agreement was made public that not only recognized the Italian conquest of Ethiopia, but also implied that the British government took for granted that the Spanish civil war would end with the victory of the rebels.

This act, which demoralized the liberal and democratic world public, roused many Americans. Those who had followed the President's support of the Committee of Non-Intervention with sympathy, demanded now that America should make her foreign policy independent of the British and French. Since this was also the demand of the isolationists, the Administration was buffeted on both sides. Anti-Fascists urged that the embargo on arms ot Spain be lifted.

"One of the worst effects of the Eden crisis has now been to deprive us of the remnant of confidence and good-will which we possessed abroad," an English magazine complained. "Our hard-headed businessmen . . . are lightheartedly ready to throw to the winds all the 'goodwill' of our national business. They forget that . . . individual freedom and . . . democratic institutions . . . as Mr. Eden once said, is not a halfway house between Communism and Fascism but is in another street altogether. . . . In the last resort, we should be ready to fight for them. . . , for it is the only faith that will ever avail to hold the British Commonwealth together and gain for us the support of the United States."[15]

"The moral leadership of the world may pass from Europe to the United States," an English M.P. warned. "Already my constituents in lonely farms . . . take the trouble to tune in to Mr. Roosevelt. . . . It may be that the mass resistance of the Chinese and the almost incredible pertinacy of the Spaniards have won the sympathy of an American people who are nevertheless unwilling to be entangled in the tortuous procedure of a Geneva controlled by the Hoares, the Lavals, the Simons of Europe. If the United States were to modify their neutrality policy in favor of the Spanish republic, the grim foreboding of the uses to which a victory for General Franco would be put by his principals in Berlin and Rome may never come to pass."[16]

Indeed, it appeared that a decisive turn had taken place in public opinion in America, with the possibility of far-reaching consequences for the world. The arch-isolationist, Senator Nye, suddenly advocated an exception to the Neutrality Law be made in the case of the Spanish Civil War. The opposite measure had been accepted, inspired by the endeavor to conform to the procedures of the British sponsored Committee of Non-Intervention of the European powers. Since the Committee had ceased to be neutral by openly recognizing violations that it had been called to suppress, collaboration with it had to stop and the embargo lifted.

"Since Mr. Chamberlain saw fit to bargain with the dictators, to grant a certificate of good behavior to Mussolini, to surrender to him the fate of the Spanish Loyalists . . . a great number of Americans who hitherto were favorable to Roosevelt's policy resolved that the time has arrived for the United States to resume her liberty of action," a survey described the political effects of the Anglo-Italian agreement.[17] A French magazine warned, however, that it was a mistake to believe that the isolationists had turned into internationalists. The opposite was true. Those who six months earlier had been the most ardent partisans of cooperation of the three democracies had gone over to the isolationist camp, disgusted with the British appeasement policy.[18]

In fact, lifting of the embargo now would have been an isolationist gesture, an open break with the West European powers. "Three factors contributed in the main to this development," the Survey stated, "horror caused by the bombing by the Nationalists of open towns; evidence that the Fascist countries were taking an open part in the conflict; and increasing suspicion of the real intentions behind the British policy of non-intervention. . . . It was realized . . . that another Fascist victory in Europe must be prevented before it was too late. And the blatant evidence of Fascist participation on the Nationalist side in Spain made the embargo appear still more unpardonable in the eyes of American liberals. . . ." Many conservatives, almost all the liberals, and apparently many Senators close to the Administration, agreed on the action so that for a few days it seemed that the resolution would pass easily.

Secretary of State Hull would have gladly seized the opportunity to get rid of the Neutrality Law that had hampered his foreign policy. Sumner Welles was, however, against raising the embargo. The President was on vacation. When he returned, the President decided against it. An observer noted: "The Catholic hierarchy and laity were exercising great pressure upon the Administration, which was warned that it might risk losing the Catholic vote." [19] Other sources also emphasized that the President would have looked to regain his freedom of action, but "a new factor intervened: domestic policy. The Congressional leaders dissuaded Roosevelt from supporting the Nye proposition. It threatened to alienate the Catholic vote." [20]

Roosevelt was also influenced by "the argument that the Government needed all their authority and prestige to lessen tensions in Congress and in the country, whereas the Nye resolution, if passed, was likely to have the opposite effect, besides creating serious embarrassment for Chamberlain whose Spanish policy was at that very time being assailed in the House of Commons. The President declared he was powerless to lift the embargo. . . . The Nye resolution was eventually blocked in Committee." [21]

The President was afraid that Chamberlain's appeasement policy was only feeding the dictators' ambitions and increasing their prestige and power. They might ultimately force the democracies to a showdown at a time when the dictators would have grown stronger than they. But, with an isolationist public at home he had no power to commit his country to independent action.

The intelligent public in Europe understood the predicament of the American President from the time when Wilson had been repudiated by the Senate, but it meant only that they blamed America and not the President. ". . . the President of the United States," a Belgian magazine explained to its readers,[22] "enjoys extremely large constitutional powers which can take on, under certain circumstances, quasi-dictatorial forms, but he never makes use of them before he has concluded that public opinion will support him. He may start a fight with the Senate or the Supreme Court but he always has to make sure that public opinion stands behind him. Thus, the American people will have to speak out before President Roosevelt has a chance to quit his official aloofness and enter into international collaboration with the democracies."

The Survey of International Affairs of 1938 believed that the current American isolationism was different from that previous to World War I. ". . . before the war of 1914-1918 people had been isolationist because they knew little and cared little about Europe. After the War they felt that they knew rather too much; the earlier state of mind was an indifferent and passive isolationism, the later was an isolationism of disillusionment which found expression in the neutrality laws and the embargo against war."

But disillusionment only prevented cooperation with the European powers in foreign policy. Economically the bulk of the public remained internationalist, but not enough to fight for their investments or trading rights, whether in China or in Mexico. A French author thought that "American opinion is isolationist only to the extent it is dominated by its instinct. Otherwise, a profound evolution has been going on among the policy-making people, in the minds of the active elite and even in the depths of public opinion. They know that their country, as a great power, cannot be disinterested in conflicts that may upset the world equilibrium, especially since they may compromise that liberalism which is the basis of Anglo-Saxon civilization and which has for a century inspired the economic life of the world." [23]

Actually, the American people felt deeply their community with the West European peoples, but had come to distrust their governments. The sequence of events only confirmed their distrust. The public did not realize that their refusal to take part in a combined defense of common principles was an element in the Europeans' betrayal of those principles. ". . . the American public is profoundly hostile to totalitarian regimes," a French author expounded, "but it desires the victory of the Russians over the Japanese; it is resolved not to participate in the struggle in Europe, but criticizes England and France sharply for their inclination to compromise with Hitler's Reich; it implores these countries to resist, convinced that they would win, but gives them no more than moral support. The President and the nation's natural tendencies are unanimously hostile to the Nazi regime but are not in favor of armed intervention. At most, they are willing to sell Britain and France goods and materials, but not to give out loans. Cash and carry." [24]

Soon after Eden quit, in March, 1938, Hitler invaded Austria. Western Europe once again made no move against this new breach of the peace treaties. Indeed, for the moment it dealt a straight blow to Mussolini, who had been instrumental in setting up a Fascist regime in this little country as a safeguard against its incorporation into the Reich. Some pale hopes existed that there would be an estrangement between the two dictators, but with the pacification of Ethiopia and the Spanish Civil War still occupying Italy, Mussolini could not afford the enmity of the Nazi chief. By acquiescing, the Duce accepted the fact that he was second fiddle in the totalitarian orchestra.

But the invasion of Austria had a much farther reaching effect on the power distribution in Europe. With the possession of Austria, the Reich practically encircled Czechoslovakia, the last firm and strong bastion of the French alliance system that had preserved peace on the Continent until Hitler had marched into the Rhineland.

Hitler did not rest on his laurels, but launched a propaganda campaign against Czechoslovakia for "tyrannizing" its three million German minority.

Portentous events were also taking place in the Far East. The Japanese apparently were trying to find out how the Russians would react to frontier incidents and intended to act later according to the indications of the initial experience. Frontier skirmishes began to develop into serious armed clashes on the Manchurian and Korean borders. The President soon acquired evidence that Chamberlain also meant to appease the Japanese aggressors, leaving America alone to defend the status quo in the Pacific.

The President occupied himself with building up the navy and strengthening the defenses of the Western hemisphere. Fortunately, this area was exempt from the isolationist mood, especially since Nazi and Fascist influence in Latin America had become alarmingly evident. In the words of the *Survey of International Affairs:* "At the very time when Americans were blessing the fate which had put three thousand miles of water between them and Europe, Germany and Italy were rash enough to begin to tamper with the Western Hemisphere. . . . As frequently happens, the manner of . . . German and Italian activities proved more irritating than their substance. Taken together with certain similar manifestations in the U.S. itself—trivial attempts at espionage, and the naïve demeanor of a relatively small group of pro-Nazi Germans, who strutted about in uniform and displayed the swastika—these activities had the effect of a revelation upon the American outlook. . . . they went a long way towards redressing the balance of popular feeling."

The President's Good Neighbor Policy now began to bear fruit. In particular, his presence at the Pan-American Conference in Buenos Aires right after his triumphal re-election in 1936 had left a deep impression on all Latin America. "Up to Roosevelt's assuming power," a French comment asserted,[25] "the United States was incapable of accepting the equality of the 21 American republics. . . . President Roosevelt's entire sincerity, perseverance, all Secretary Hull's loyalty and tact were needed in Montevideo, then in Buenos Aires, and finally in Lima, to surmount this difficulty and create the indispensable atmosphere for the unfolding of Pan-Americanism."

When the League of Nations was breaking down and proving unable to either prevent or punish aggression, Latin America found itself in the danger zone and began "to look to Washington for insurance coverage against possible aggression," an English magazine stated in explaining the success of the policy of the Good Neighbor, and added, ". . . it is no secret that many of the Latin States lined themselves up with the Geneva collective system for purposes of internal prestige and to remind Uncle Sam that they would obtain protection elsewhere on the basis of equality and without the support of the Monroe Doctrine whose unilateral genesis was held to be humiliating for them. But with . . . recent historical lessons before them, the South Americans are realizing that the Monroe Doctrine, in any form whatsoever, is a very desirable thing to have. Fortunately at this time Washington is not disposed to take any mean advantage. It is sincere in its good neighborliness and President Roosevelt and his Secretary of State Hull, between them, have built up a huge fund of friendship and good faith, which, however, as they have been careful to insist on with their Latin colleagues, depends on mutual respect for the practice of democracy."[26]

The personal factor played a great part in the Latin American outlook, the British *Survey of International Affairs* asserted. Their trust in President Roosevelt accelerated the process of "transformation of the Monroe doctrine from a unilateral doctrine into a multilateral and collective policy. On the other hand, Hitler and Mussolini impressed the Latin American public, while the statesmen of the European democracies stood low in prestige. The rulers of the United States fortunately redressed the balance of that democratic deficiency . . . and forged a strong momentary link for Pan-American solidarity."

The greatest success of the Pan-American Conference in Buenos Aires in 1938 was that it had not ended in a complete success of the United States. The Latin governments did not accept the principle of the American Neutrality Law that would have required, even in case of war between two American countries, that the non-belligerents declare an embargo on both with no regard to the fact that the one was the aggressor and the other its victim. In this respect the Latin states stuck to the principles of the League. But the fact that the United States did not use undue pressure on the sister republics to conform made them feel they had reached the equality they had so ardently desired in their relations with the United States. This feeling made possible the Declaration issued on the next Conference in Lima reaffirming international morality as an all-American principle.[27]

A Swiss report from Latin America also stressed the deep roots Pan-Americanism had struck there. Speaking of public sentiments, he said that "they believe that they have built an institution in Pan-Americanism that will stand up to all possible dangers. More than that, they are convinced that this close collaboration of all American states will enable their spiritual leader, President Roosevelt, to wage a campaign for peace with more authority and success, not only in America, but throughout the whole world." [28]

The President was compelled to consolidate hemispheric solidarity in the face of expected expansion of totalitarian might abroad. To resist the onslaught, however, America had first of all to gather moral strength. President Roosevelt commissioned those people whose vocation was to educate the youth to strengthen democracy at home in the face of the barbarism inundating more and more countries abroad. ". . . when the clock of civilization can be turned back," the President warned, "by burning libraries, by exiling scientists, artists, musicians, writers and teachers, by dispensing universities, and by censoring news and literature and arts, an added burden is placed upon those countries where the torch of free thought and free learning still burn bright. If the fires of freedom and civil liberties burn low in other lands, they must be made brighter in our own. If in other lands the press and books and literature of all kinds are censored, we must redouble our efforts to keep it free. If in other lands the eternal truths of the past are threatened by intolerance, we must provide a safe place here for their perpetuation . . . The ultimate victory of tomorrow is with democracy, with education, for no people can be kept eternally ignorant or eternally enslaved."

To which the *Popolo d'Italia* replied on July 4th, 1938: "It is clear that democracy is at war and in an ideological camp, against whom Mr. Roosevelt does not specify; but if our perception does not betray us, it might be Fascism. . . . Moreover, he speaks of ultimate victory which means victory to come . . . we shall see."

7

THE DRIFT TO MUNICH

"Whatever destiny is reserved for Franklin Roosevelt," an Englishman's review of the President's six years in office ran, "this one thing is clear. His term is epoch-making: it divides the older America from the new and unpredictable. At the close of his sixth year the President occupies a position of challenge and peril to which there has been no parallel in the experience of any predecessor." The writer discovered a "central irony" in both international and domestic policies of the President. His "instincts and convictions . . . in normal times would have made him a progressive Conservative, and an active internationalist," but he has "been forced by implacable circumstances, and by a political system remote from present-day realities, to remain outside the orbit of world affairs; and in view of some millions of his fellow-countrymen, to appear as an enemy of that American system which, commanding his own entire allegiance, can have nothing to fear from any policies that he could initiate or support." [1]

Roosevelt made a desperate final attempt to save the New Deal by having a liberal Democratic majority returned in the election of 1938. The cooperation between anti-New Dealers and isolationists in both parties had paralyzed his policies. The most solid opposition to his domestic reforms came from the Southern Democrats, although they supported his international policy. Roosevelt discarded traditional Presidential neutrality at primary time and took an open stand against candidates of his own party whom he considered stalwarts of reaction in Congress.

Since a President's influence usually wanes during his final term, Roosevelt's failure was not surprising, but failure at this time took on unusual significance. The dictators may have misread the President's difficulty in advancing his international program, and drafted a fatally misconceived plan of future actions based upon the assumption that they need not fear American interference. As the international situation rapidly deteriorated, the President had no other choice than to surrender his policy for domestic reforms in order to face the dictators abroad with a Congressional majority willing to support vital measures for defending the country's position and interests.

The end of the New Deal began to open the way for a more determined stand in the international field. "It was during this time," one of his American biographers [2] wrote, ". . . that the politician began his rise to the status of statesmanship indifferent to self; above the level, finally, even of national concerns. . . . He would emerge into the world at war a different man from the one who had fought so clever an electoral campaign in 1936, who had sought to enhance the presidency in 1937 at the expense of the Supreme Court. . . . In the end he would belong to all humanity, not to America alone, much less to any faction, class or sect in the nation."

The change was also noted by some foreign observers. "Without renouncing his policy," one of them commented, "the President has decided to play a new card . . . He began by standing up to big industry, today he appeals for its cooperation. Roosevelt has let it be known through his authorized mouthpieces that the era of reform is now terminated. A new Roosevelt era may thus be beginning. His domestic reforms may be restricted to the suppression of certain holding companies . . . and the corporations may refrain from contesting his legislation before the Supreme Court. There is talk also of the revision of the anti-trust laws. Yet, many still fear that the declaration of peace by Washington may be but temporary." [3]

Another reason given for Roosevelt's renunciation of further reform legislation was: "Had Roosevelt continued his great work from 1933 and 1937, he would have turned into a revolutionary. But tradition won over reforms. The New Deal experiment has changed nothing essential in American thought. Roosevelt foundered on this obstacle. Refusing to become a revolutionary, he wanted to be a reform President. He failed, but he may preside over the counter-reform of the entire western world." [4]

Hitler's overrunning of Austria cast evil portents for the future since he has insisted on applying force even though the Austrian Chancellor had offered a plebiscite. This should have discouraged those politicians and their large following in the West who would have been satisfied with a thin smoke screen of legality behind which they could yield to Hitler's demands in order to save peace. Actually, nothing did discourage those who hailed Hitler for his promise to make no further claim on the Continent now that German-inhabited Austria had joined the Reich, even if he had defied the prohibition of the Versailles Treaty.

But the same event had a profound effect on American opinion. "Whether it would add the United States as a reserve of strength to the democratic front," the *Survey of International Affairs* wondered, "depended on the firmness of Anglo-French policy." The test of that firmness came about very soon. Hitler and his propaganda orchestra took no rest to consolidate the conquest of Austria, but started a campaign against the Czechoslovak Republic, the only democratic country among the successors of the late Hapsburg empire. The Nazis, in whipping up disurbances among the Germans living in Czechoslovakia, and inciting riots, were creating a European problem.

The question being discussed throughout the world, namely, whether appeasement of the dictators would lead to peace or war, received an undisputable answer in the following months.

During this agonizing time, writers and politicians on both sides of the fence tried to size up the President of the United States, upon whose personality, character, ambitions, and capacity for leadership the fate of the world appeared to depend.

"It is fortunate," liberal opinion held, "that there is such an eloquent and authoritative champion for the cause of freedom and decency in a world where every guilty conscience unloads its spleen on the ideals of democracy. There is a very true sense in which Roosevelt has the moral leadership of the world for his asking. Whether he can take it depends entirely upon the degree of confidence he enjoys from his countrymen."[5]

For German interpreters of contemporary history his leadership meant something very different: a "grand attempt to set up a world dictatorship of American democracy. . . . This aim is in line with the unbounded personal ambition of Franklin Roosevelt to become the total arbiter of civilized humanity who lays down the laws of peace and freedom as he understands them. This aim corresponds also to the Anglo-Saxon claim of introducing a 'just world order' through democracy."[6]

"It is not beyond the bounds of possibility that Franklin Roosevelt will succeed where Woodrow Wilson failed, and that he will lead America to the redemption of the world," a British magazine wrote.[7] Its expectations were derived from the change of economic outlook of the country during his administration. "His economic concept is a direct repudiation of American beliefs, cherished for generations; but today the most bitter of his political opponents would not dare to touch the foundations of the President's domestic policy. It seems, on the face of it, to be incredible to guide the United States into the main traffic of international politics. But President Roosevelt has already achieved other miracles."

The President had no greater admirer than the Canadian Prime Minister, Mackenzie King. Under the leadership of these two men, the two countries came closer to one another than ever before. Indeed, Canada became the link tying neutral America to Britain, which was being swept by the inexorable compulsion of continental dictatorship into the danger zone of war. "In President Roosevelt [Mackenzie King] saw the champion of all that he held most dear in the field of social reform," an American envoy to Canada asserted.[8] "The President had the art of putting into telling phrases, which carried conviction to the most despondent, the injustices being suffered by the underprivileged, and the duty which had passed from the hands of capital into the hands of government to remedy them. Mr. King was a big enough man not to resent the success of the President in preempting the field, in which above all others he would most have liked to shine. Instead, he became a hero-worshipper and dedicated to Mr. Roosevelt a friendship, wherein the personal and the official are curiously blended."

A French visitor was astounded at the extent to which Roosevelt dominated the American sciene.[9] "Fifty-seven years old, he is at the height of his power. He has been in the battle for eighteen years . . . and still in the lead role, exalted, adored by some, criticized, abused and at times calumnied in the lowest fashion by others. There is no day in which his portrait or caricature does not appear in the press, or in which magazines do not print articles about his person. The public is vividly interested in his actions and even in his gestures. 'What do you think about the things he said on the press conference? . . . Did you hear his speech?' . . . Roosevelt is an obsession."

"Some time ago," an English journalist wrote, "in the popular heyday of Freud, a game was being played by arm-chair psychoanalysts. They suddenly shouted a word at you, and you had to tell them, truthfully and quickly, exactly what emotion the sound of the word created in you. If 'Roosevelt' were suddenly shouted at an average American, assuming him not to be a Republican who believed Roosevelt should be impeached, the sound would be likely to stir the memory of an emotion which might be roughly rendered as Hope. An alternative word for it might be Relief, the sensation which comes from the alleviation of pain, or fear, or worry. For in many American minds there is the memory of a time when Roosevelt, his face, his voice or his recorded words, brought personally, to the remembering American, the warm and grateful feeling that fear was passing and all would be well." [10]

The writer also recalled that awful period of waiting for the President to make his appearance. It was the moment when the Anglo-American Trade Treaty was about to be signed. In the high-ceilinged East Room . . . several hundred people were sitting on semi-circular rows of frail gilt chairs. Crystal chandeliers were glittering overhead; there was a golden piano in one corner of the room; there was a central table, the Cabinet table of Abraham Lincoln, where Secretary of State Hull, the British Ambassador, Prime Minister Mackenzie King of Canada and Mr. Arnold Overton of the Board of Trade were sitting, waiting for the President. Then a door at the back opened and the guests rose and the President on the arm of his Military Aide began to cross the room. You remember how long it took, how the silence lasted while a tap . . . tap . . . moved over the polished floor, down the aisle between the standing people. You were humbled by the thought of how little the President had made this disability mean." [10]

"If the public's love for a statesman, respect for his achievements and his reputation could be expressed in figures," a German wrote before Munich, "then the United States has never had a greater President in the White House than Franklin Roosevelt. . . . What has impressed the public most is the change he introduced at the moment of assuming office in dealing with governmental affairs.[11] The public has the feeling, as in Wilson's first Presidential years, that there is a man in the White House who is something new in American politics."

A French writer elaborated on the "change" that his German colleague credited Roosevelt with introducing into the White House.[12] "Life in the White House under Roosevelt has meant a new epoch. He has brought into the mansion the cordial manners of a private person and created an atmosphere entirely in harmony with that simple residence, which ignores the pretentiousness of ornament, marble staircases and lackeys in grand regalia. Yet, the innovations have been sensational. To the stupefaction of the public, the Roosevelts, exactly like other good bourgeois families, give a day off to the domestic personnel on Sunday evenings and serve dinner with the help of their guests. The same simplicity applies at White House concerts. Previously, the invited guests had been ushered with great pomp into the large salon. They would solemnly rise upon the entry of the President who, amidst dead silence, would take his place in the first row with great dignity. Now Roosevelt and his family came to the door to receive the guests. . . . Roosevelt likes to surround himself with young people and this attitude conforms very much to the national temperament. Entering the White House one hears laughter from all sides; good humor prevails on all levels from the typist girl to the first secretary. A caricature on the wall dispays the President's famous smile, which is known to everybody from the screen and the pictorial magazines, but which has nothing in common with the forced smile of the publicity stereotype. It is the reflection of his profound nature. One can say that he is one of the rare people who resemble their portraits, because he is able to preserve the source of his youth, faith in productive efforts and in the future. To no one is the famous formula more applicable than to him: 'The loss of youth wrinkles the face; the loss of enthusiasm wrinkles the soul.'"

His dominant principle was, according to a French observer who liked to put spiritual things in economic terms: [13] "The human budget is as important as the financial budget."

However, a lady writer more perspicaciously grasped the atmosphere in the White House when, in relating her impressions of a press conference, she wrote: "In a delightfully spacious room with tall windows looking out on sunny green lawns, and bright walls covered with colored prints of early America, at a long desk, behind which the Stars and Stripes was draped, sat a man of middle age, well-groomed, broad-shouldered, with an air of great physical fitness, a bold curve to his shapely head, and a clean-shaven, handsome, sensitive, intelligent, and complicated face. Immediately I remembered other rulers of equal significance: the theatrical truculent ugliness of Mussolini, the bawling bully; the sneering brutality and granite-like heaviness of Stalin, the ruthless peasant; the fanatical, stupid, banal countenance of neurotic Hitler, with his nauseating expression of deeply embedded fear. The face in front of me was of a different essence: it was one of the most remarkably civilized faces I have ever seen. The eyes, set rather close together, quick, keen, perceptive; the celebrated smile, now distinctly fixed and automatic, . . . but very attractive and persuasive; the clear, alert, beautifully modulated voice; the easy, courteous manners and the genial forms of address—all these things had an instant effect of indefatigable vitality, of tremendous resiliency, of capacity sharp-edged and very diverse. They were stimulating to the imagination, and the senses also became excited by the exhilarating vigor which this dynamic man exuded. It was impossible not to be captivated at once." [14]

"But it was impossible, too, not to grow perturbed as the conference proceeded. I never lost the impression of charm, but slowly a feeling of disquiet began to rival my enjoyment. It is very difficult to analyze why. It had nothing to do with criticisms I had heard of the President: it was a personal intuition." the author thought the rapidity and fluidity of the President's mind was abnormal.[11] The crowd of journalists, grouped opposite him, pressing against his table, questioned him on whatever they wished. He caught the questions, he flashed back the answers, exactly like a tennis champion striking the twisting, hurtling balls on a court. Sometimes he did not choose to reply, and then the dexterity with which the interrogations were evaded, or diverted, was astounding. It was evident that he was impulsive, but his impetuosity was so controlled, he was so agile and so wary, so slick, so watchful and decisive, that in fact he directed the conversation as he pleased. The more I looked at him and listened to him the more firmly my conviction took root that this magnetic individual, who assembled in himself so many complex factulties, was above all a player performing superbly, but in a game." [14]

An Englishman who stayed in the White House as well as in the Roosevelt country home at Hyde Park, painted a more reassuring portrait of the President.

"One Sunday afternoon I was sitting with the President in his room at the White House talking in a general way about the relations between Great Britain and the United States. The conversation was interrupted by the President's grandchildren who had come to say 'Good-bye' and to thank him for giving them a happy time. 'For the President, too,' would have been the thought of anyone who could have watched his genial and natural way with these children to whom he was just Grandfather and nothing else. Not that he had changed his manner specially for them. Both at the White House and a few days later at Hyde Park, important, clever, ordinary intelligent and plain stupid, bold and shy, talkers and silent people, friends, acquaintances, neutral observers, members of the family and servants never knew him to be anything but spontaneous and wholly natural.

"To explain his power as a leader no better reason need be sought than his complete naturalness. That is his secret. His influence is essentially personal and depends upon personal contact. . . . Whenever there have been signs of antagonism or waning popularity in any part of the country, President Roosevelt, with immense confidence in the force of his appeal, has taken thought as to how he could visit the region. If a visit could not be immediately planned, he has resorted to the radio. There is another secret of the far-reaching influence of his leadership. President Roosevelt is blessed with a good broadcasting voice, but he has also taken the trouble to master the technique of broadcasting."

In the author's view, it was this mastery that established his power all over the country. "His opponents . . . did not lose a chance of criticizing his disconcerting way of staging one surprise after another. They spoke of shock tactics and snap judgments. But even among those who were not prepared to follow the President all the way, there were some who admitted the value of his provocative methods. They could not but admire a man who . . . could challenge the country so effectively that the opposition was forced into the open. They had to admit that Franklin Roosevelt was an excellent showman and that for the President of the United States to excel in showmanship was no bad thing. Some were wise enough to realize that an ignorant public is a danger in itself, and were impartial enough to concede that since he had been President, Franklin Roosevelt had kept the public alive to every problem of the government. In that, above all else, he had shown how true a democrat he was.

". . . Originality, in fact, is the dominant note of everyday life at the White House, for no one needs to be reminded of the President's strong individuality. His force of character is felt in the first handshake. . . . It was to be a small, informal dinner party, the President and Mrs. Roosevelt, a young girl, another guest, and myself. We all went into the lift and went down to the dining room on the ground floor.

"At dinner, conversation was easy. The President had just returned from his tour of the West to find a huge mail awaiting him, chiefly as a result of his Chicago speech. He spoke of this and other matters freely and naturally, not as one who was bearing the burden of State, but as a single, normal member of the community. With zest he told me of his train passing through Chicago and how one of his companions called his attention to the office windows thronged with people. At many of the windows, he said, were clerks and stenographers shouting 'Hullo, Mr. President'; at others were the directors, silent and glum. With a sudden seriousness and a quick turn towards me, he added, 'You couldn't have a better picture of what things are like here at present.'

"During that week-end I saw the President from many angles and in touch with many sorts of people. My lasting impression is of a man who is essentially a real person. Moreover, to his people, whether opponents or supporters, he has made himself completely real; and if to the readers this should seem a simple achievement, let him reflect how rare it is for any public figure to remain a reality for long, and not become, even while he is in the public eye, a mere photograph or an unsubstantial silhouette." What this author meant by "real person" is revealed in this description. "Many pictures of Franklin Roosevelt are fixed in my mind, but none clearer than the memory of those occasions, when, as on one morning and before and after dinner, two or three of us stood beside him in the lift. His attitude was always the same, hands upon knees, fingers moving as if for a keyboard exercise, the fine head thrown back, a cigarette in its holder sticking up at a sharp angle from the mouth. During the few seconds while we were moving from one floor to the next he would make brief, good-humored inquiries of one or another of us. There was no waste of time or of words, yet I think of those interludes as being curiously intimate and revealing." [15]

The author found Roosevelt different in the family home at Hyde Park surrounded by the objects of his childhood. "In the big room at the southern end of the hall, I found Franklin Roosevelt sitting alone by a log fire and giving all his attention to his collection of foreign stamps. It was the same figure that I had so recently seen at the White House, but another man. Even the greeting he gave me told me so. He seemed relaxed, unexcited. He was wearing country clothes and was sitting there quite calm and content. . . . My impression was that while he was turning over the leaves of his stamp-books, looking at old stamps, putting in new ones, he was waiting for all this environment of his boyhood to take possession of him."

At the informal dinner, the author had an insight to Roosevelt's relationship with his wife. Politics had casually crept into the conversation. "In such a friendly gathering I did not expect to hear the subject of Japan discussed, but there were points in the President's [last foreign policy] speech which his wife had not fully grasped, and she began to question him, not in any argumentative mood but quietly, as though she were confident that he would be able to clear away her doubts. Her confidence was justified. With great care the President explained his approach to this thorny question showing how a problem which proved too stubborn as a whole might conceivably be solved by being divided into two separate parts."

In the late summer of 1938, however, the atmosphere of the White House became tense as reports from Europe stressed the mounting danger to peace stemming from Hitler's insistence that the situation of the three million Germans in Czechoslovakia had become unbearable.

In January President Roosevelt intimated to the British that he wanted to call an international conference to settle the outstanding issues disquieting the Continent. Chamberlain let him know that such a step might disturb the well-advanced negotiations he was conducting himself with the dictators.

"Subject to the proviso—to which Chamberlain attached paramount importance—that Germany's demands must be presented in a reasonable manner for consideration according to an orderly procedure . . . the British Government seems to have looked forward . . . to the prospect of readjustment in Germany's favor of the Paris peace settlement in Central Europe. . . . Though, in the process of readjustment, there were bound to be some awkward moments, the British Government felt that these could be faced with equanimity if there was a real prospect—as they believed there was—of arriving at a permanent settlement of Germany's claims"—this is how Arnold J. Toynbee read Chamberlain's mind.[16]

Czechoslovakia was an ideal object for demonstrating that appeasement of Hitler would work. By disposing of it as a military factor, Chamberlain would open the gate toward the east for German expansion and deter it from the west. He did not fear adverse reaction from the public since Hitler only demanded the right of self-determination for the three million Germans in Czechoslovakia, a right that had been proclaimed by an American President but had been denied by the peace conference. Who would expect Britain to go to war in order to prevent a late righting of a wrong? The West had done nothing to stop Hitler when he had annexed Austria; why should it rush to arms when other Germans wanted to do the same as their Austrian kin? Czechoslovakia had a treaty of mutual assistance with the Soviet Union; by stripping it of military significance without even consulting the Soviets the treaty would be invalidated and the Soviets excluded from the concert of European powers that was to direct the general readjustment to be made on the Continent.

Chamberlain had nothing against Hitler's claims. As a matter of fact, he was anxious to satisfy them, except that he wanted Hitler to learn that he must make an orderly presentation of them and refrain from threats of force or the actual use of force. Chamberlain thought he was taking exception only to the German dictator's methods and not to his objectives, because he could not admit that for Hitler terror and force were more essential than the territories he demanded. Each success increased Hitler's power and weakened resistance to him. The German dictator preferred to seize a chunk of Czechoslovakia by ruthless force to receiving the entire country on the strength of an agreement that would imply his dependence on factors other than his sheer might. Chamberlain learned this lesson when it was too late.

The British Prime Minister undertook his first pilgrimage to the Fuehrer on September 15, 1938. The talks were friendly and gentlemanlike. Chamberlain agreed to award Germany such Czech territories as were inhabited by a clear majority of Germans, although these lands had never been part of Germany. On his return to London, Chamberlain invited the French government to a conference at which Chamberlain's concession was approved. Great pressure had to be brought to bear, however, on the Czech government to force them to accept the mutilation of their country at the hands of their allies.

On September 22nd, Chamberlain took the plane to deliver what he had promised. But the Fuehrer did not share in the Englishman's enthusiasm. Instead, he presented him with a memorandum. In it, Hitler now demanded a huge piece of additional territory from Czechoslovakia, land once inhabited by German colonists. Chamberlain found the new claims exorbitant, stated that he could not advise the Czechs to accept them, and ordered the mobilization of the fleet. The Czech government, immensely relieved, ordered general mobilization, as did Hitler, whose army contained one and a half million men. On September 28 Europe hovered on the brink of a second world war.

It was a fearful bluff on Hitler's part, since the German army was not yet ready to wage war against the up-to-date Czech army, assisted by the Soviet Union in the east, and the French army, supported by the British in the west. Hitler knew it, and the German General Staff also knew it; they duly warned Hitler who, however, trusted on his ascending star.

Consternation was general in America. Leon Blum, former French Prime Minister, sent the President an impassioned appeal, calling him the greatest personality in the temporal world, and asking him to speak out and not wait further, to proclaim a truce and offer to act as umpire.[17]

The President sent an appeal to all heads of states involved in the Czech developments "not to break off negotiations looking to a peaceful, fair, and constructive settlement of the question at issue."

In a second message, two days later, the President addressed Hitler alone, reminding him that "resort to force in the Great War failed to bring tranquility. Victory and defeat were alike sterile. That lesson the world should have learned."

The President proposed a conference of the interested governments, to be held in a neutral country. Hitler's answer was that the decision for war or peace now rested exclusively with the Czech government.

At this point, Mussolini entered the drama. He established his place at the conference by calling on France, Britain, and Germany to convene with him to decide on the Czech issue. Mussolini thus rose from the low ebb of his prestige that he had reached when Hitler had overrun Austria without even consulting him. A Japanese newspaper had then written him off as a statesman of consequence, commenting: "A few years ago he openly proclaimed it his purpose to keep Germany out of Austria and he failed to win Abyssinia while still losing Austria. Further, he hoped that Austro-German unity would be achieved in circumstances of his own choosing, whereas on March 14 Hitler took him by surprise, showing that he set no great store upon Mussolini's benevolence." [18]

But in the role of the savior of peace, the last two days of September were his since Hitler had set September 30 as the day when his new claims would have to be accepted. In fact, he saved Hitler since the German General Staff, as we now know, was resolved to liquidate him in case he proved to be wrong and England and France refused to yield.

Thus the conference at Munich came to pass, empowering Hitler to occupy immediately the Czech territories he had first claimed. His second claim was left to a mixed commission to determine.

The Czech government sent a last, desperate appeal to Roosevelt on September 30, asking him to mediate in case the Munich conference failed to produce an acceptable settlement. But her allies compelled the Czechs to accept an unacceptable settlement.

"One pound was demanded at pistol point. When it was given, two pounds were demanded at pistol point. Finally, the dictator consented to take £1 17s. 6d. and the rest in promises of good will for the future," Winston Churchill summed up the results of Munich and he established his reputation for prophetic foresight when he warned the House of Commons on October 5: "It must now be expected that all the countries of Central and Eastern Europe will make the best terms they can with the triumphant Nazi power. The system of alliances in Central Europe upon which France had relied for her safety has been swept away, and I can see no means by which it can be reconstituted. The road down the Danube valley to the Black Sea, the road which leads as far as Turkey, has been opened. In fact, if not in form, it seems to me that all those countries of Middle Europe, all those Danubian countries, will, one after the other, be drawn into this vast system of power politics—not only power military politics but power economic politics—radiating from Berlin." Yet an English magazine, although it shared Churchill's portentous views, did not believe the public would unconditionally oppose further appeasement. "We must recognize that were Germany wise enough to proceed slowly with the exploitation of her conquest, to lull us meanwhile into a sense of false security, the British public would as a man, and above all as a woman, adhere to the appeasement theory." [19]

In the days prior to the Munich conference, when it seemed that the West European democracies would resist Hitler's demands, the American public was aroused. At least, this was the impression on the Continent. Even such cautious papers as the Swiss *Neue Zurcher Zeitung* [20] drew this conclusion from the President's message. To the Swiss paper it was significant that Roosevelt had stressed that he spoke for 130 million Americans. It meant that there must be a change in American isolationist sentiment, since he would not otherwise have used this unusual reminder that he was President of all the people.

But if the public was aroused, Munich ended it. The public was "astounded to learn that Hitler had been able to lay down the law at Munich and compel the Western powers to allow him to break up the integrity of a State and invade it in the midst of peace." [21]

In his first speech after Munich, the President warned: "There can be no peace if the reign of law is to be replaced by a recurrent satisfaction of sheer force. There can be no peace if national policy adopts as a deliberate instrument the threat of war."

Soon after, Hitler invaded those Czech territories whose fate was supposed to be decided on by a mixed commission.

"War has been averted," the President said in January, 1939, "peace is not assured. Events abroad threaten American traditions in religion, democracy, and international good faith. The world is so small and attack so swift that no nation is safe while some nations refuse to negotiate disputes. Acts of agression abroad should not be allowed to pass with nothing stronger than mere words to express American opinion." [22] His warning suggested that America was to re-arm in the midst of spreading lawlessness. Secretary of State Cordell Hull spelled this out more clearly by stressing that the crossroads had been reached: was it to be the rule of force, with regimentation and lowering of the standards of life in America, or were peaceful processes to be used and the nation's resources to be devoted to things of peace? The choice, he said, was still open. The choice of negotiation or force, as we know now, was not open to any but the aggressors.[23]

The State Department deplored that "America is now ruled by a wave of isolationism, a reaction to the deep disappointment over the fact that the Nazi policy of violence succeeded in destroying a structure resting on the respect of treaties and international morality." But it discouraged criticism of the British and French governments as long as the Neutrality Law and an isolationist public left the President with nothing but words to support resistance to lawlessness.

The effect of Munich did not fail to influence the American public. "The feeling of danger from Germany very much increased after Munich. Prior to that catastrophic capitulation before Hitler, the Americans believed that the two strong West European democracies constituted a rampart between the United States and the totalitarian countries; after Munich the public in America considered that rampart as totally collapsed. The danger seemed to have crept into America itself. . . . In July, a Federal grand jury indicted eighteen suspects accused of espionage in favor of Germany. . . . Moreover, Nazi organizations engaged in feverish activities had been discovered in the country." [24]

As a consequence, "the public approved a policy of rearmament since the equilibrium of power had been upset and it was reasonable to expect a fresh Japanese push in China and an Italo-German penetration into South and Central America which might become dangerous if the equilibrium between the democratic and the totalitarian powers were not redressed." [25]

"Words may be futile, but war is not the only means of commanding the decent respect of the opinions of mankind. There are all the methods short of war, but stronger and more effective than mere words to bring home to aggressor governments are the aggregate sentiments of our own people," the President stated in January, 1939, in his annual message to Congress.

At the same time he had the American Ambassador to Tokyo hand a note to the Japanese government that cooled Japanese plans to invalidate existing treaties concerning China as a consequence of the changes in the power situation. Japan had argued: ". . . The East Asian situation today has entirely changed. The Nine Power Treaty must be immediately abolished at this time. The United States, when the South American countries were exposed to the pressure of Spain and other European countries, caused President Monroe in 1823 to reject those European nations' intervention there. . . . Japan must also declare the establishment of an Asiatic Monroe Doctrine, by abrogating the Nine Power Treaty which was devised on the initiative of some such European powers which hitherto treated China as their base of colonial operations." [26] The American note replied: "The State Department is prepared to enter into negotiations for changing treaties affecting China, but will not tolerate Japan's efforts to supersede the principles of equal opportunity and the open door in China."

The President wrote to a friend: "I am in the midst of a long process of education—and the process seems to be working slowly but surely."[27] This education had started with the President's message to Congress in 1934 on disarmament. He had followed this up with his "quarantine" speech in Chicago at the end of 1937. A French author surmised that Roosevelt "seemed to have had a clear vision of the events to come after 1936. The brutal remilitarization of the left bank of the Rhine and the total impotence of the British and French at that dramatic event had revealed to the President that the democratic leaders of the old world were incapable of resisting their opponents by their own force alone. The Austrian Anschluss confirmed him in this opinion and he took clear cognizance of the part he was to assume.

"But his first concern had to be public opinion. . . . Slowly he was to persuade America to back him, applying the method that Wilson himself had borrowed from Lincoln in changing the outlook of the nation towards the wider world. This demanded from Roosevelt a tenacity and prudence without precedent. . . . in the course of the year 1938, he repeatedly spoke of the identical destiny of the free countries, of their common ideals, of their inescapable interdependence, toughening the democratic fibre in all good Americans. Without furor, his ideas found their audience, and, when in January 1939, the President read his message to Congress, he was able, without scandalizing anyone this time, except some journalists and members of the opposition party, to announce that he was resolved to induce the aggressors to reflect upon employing methods other than war. At a confidential meeting before the Military Committee of the Senate, he declared that America's first defense lay on the Rhine. Of course, there was a leak and an uproar followed. This time it was no longer a question of platonic meddling in European affairs, but clearly of war. The next day an official denial was published. But on April 9, leaving the railroad station at Warm Springs, Roosevelt said, 'I will be back in the fall if we don't have a war.' . . . And now once more, except for some papers that reacted violently, the nation as a whole docilely acquiesced."[28]

The Nazis recognized the danger to them in Roosevelt's education of the nation, and they began to concentrate their attacks on the President. "His Chicago speech against the totalitarian powers pinned Roosevelt down before the world and his nation," a Nazi author wrote.[29] ". . . The combination of the personal ambitions of an extremely unscrupulous politician, of the depression in his country, and of inevitable events in Europe, produced serious consequences. His speech spelled out that North America, through her president, although not through her people, had become the enemy of peace and of the rational new order. . . . Roosevelt was afraid that if a solid bridge were built between Germany and the West European countries his international influence would suffer a tremendous blow. . . . In Chicago he employed only words but subsequently he resorted to premeditated action. Munich seemed to contain the nucleus of a European solution arrived at exclusively by European powers. . . . Yet, while the people of Europe struggled for peace, public opinion in America seemed to take pleasure in a vision of bloody war to come."

Many in Western Europe wanted to see Munich in the same light, but there were voices of warning, like this one from England: "We must face the fact that we have abandoned a great fortress of security in Central Europe. We must face the fact that the smaller powers may now be obliged to capitulate and that Germany will within a few weeks acquire an economic hold over South Eastern Europe such as will render her almost impervious to anything but the most protracted blockade. We must face the fact that our own authority upon the Continent has declined almost to the vanishing point."[30]

"Through their desire for peace and disarmament, the British and American nations allowed their armed strength to fall so low that in time they could not defend weaker nations from aggression. . . . The Americans refused to believe that policies in Europe might affect them, and that an attack on the United States would come from the Far East. Nothing but the facts would make them see themselves and the world in their true light." So did Churchill reason throughout the fearful year from Munich to Poland, but perhaps most eloquently when he told his people: "This is only the beginning of the reckoning. This is only the first sip, the first foretaste of a bitter cup which will be proffered to us year by year unless by a supreme recovery of moral health and martial vigour, we arise again and take our stand for freedom as in the olden time." [31]

And in America it was reasoned: ". . . the press of events was inexorable, bringing opinion to [the President's] side after Munich. The test was not what was said in Congress but what was done in Congress and that was a rapid melting away of opposition to rearmament and overwhelming votes for the military plans of the Executive. And so, after all, it would be events that would make policy and not Mr. Roosevelt." [32]

8

A WORLD MISSION

"The public excitement throughout America in the autumn of 1938 was an extraordinary phenomenon," a correspondent of an English magazine reported.[1] "It was created in great part through a continuous broadcast commentary upon the news from Prague and other Central European centres—the most complete radio build-up in connection with international events that has so far been achieved. The unbroken service of news and exposition had seemed to be preparing the American public for a collective stand by the democratic powers, when the news of Munich destroyed the immense illusion."

President Roosevelt approved of Chamberlain's attempts to redress the European balance of power in favor of the dictators through the orderly process of negotiations. He was much relieved, as were people all over the world, when Mussolini at the last minute succeeded in persuading Hitler to accept what he wanted from Czechoslovakia through a four power conference instead of by force of arms. It was a sham, but in a struggle in which psychological factors like prestige and propaganda played prominent parts, the sham influenced further developments. In this case the influence was in the opposite direction from the one that the democratic world had been hoping for.

By ignoring Soviet Russia, which had a treaty of mutual assistance with both Czechoslovakia and France, the Allies had excluded her from the decisions which re-distributed power in Europe. Thus, some substance was lent to the suspicion that the Western democracies wanted to demonstrate that they would not oppose Hitler's drive toward the east. Britain and

France had consented to take part in determining the fate of a small, East European state, the only democratic country in that region, without even admitting Russia's representatives to the deliberations. At least, this was the way Stalin explained the spirit of the Munich agreement when, in the following March, he addressed the Soviet Communist Congress. He said: "In the case of Germany, they let her have Austria, they added the Sudeten region, they left the Czechs to their own fate, urging the Germans to march further east, promising easy pickings, and prompting them, just you start a war against the Bolsheviks and then everything will proceed nicely."[2] Actually, the West had broken up the Little Entente by knocking out its westernmost bastion, Czechoslovakia, and thus undermined their strategic position in the face of Nazi Germany.

In his 1939 New Year's Message to Congress, President Roosevelt summed up the results of Munich: "A war which threatened to envelop the world in flames has been averted; but it has become increasingly clear that world peace is not assured. . . . There comes a time in the affairs of men when they must prepare to defend, not their homes alone but the tenets of faith and humanity on which their churches, their governments, and their very civilization are founded."

"Most Englishmen and women when they listened to President Roosevelt on the radio must have wished sadly that it was the head of their own Government who was saying those things," an English paper commented.[3] "They must have recalled with a little shame Mr. Chamberlain's naïve confession that, although Fascism might not do for us, he cannot get up much excitement over different systems of government, apart from particular action which may not necessarily be inherent in the system, and they must have regretted that it has been left to the American President to state the British (as it is also the American) way of life without apologizing for it."

"The British government, by misunderstanding the real aims of the Third Reich, is allowing the democratic case to go by default," was the reaction of Scandinavian public opinion, according to the London *Times.* "Great Britain is surrendering her leadership, on which the safety of Scandinavia largely depends, not only in Europe but in the world." [4]

A French magazine agreed with Roosevelt that a new capitulation by the West would mean a definite triumph for the dictators, who would compel the East to submit to them. "But," the magazine added, "they would triumph also in the rest of the world; in Latin America where the influence of the United States would fade before that of the totalitarian countries, in the Pacific where Japanese ambition would burst all limits; even in the territory of the United States itself where totalitarian activities would have an easy job in attacking unfortunate democratic ideals that had already been wiped out elsewhere in the world." [5]

There was a cleavage between Western European statesmen and America, as represented by President Roosevelt. As a French paper put it: "The points of view are at discord. . . . England and France tend to minimize the ideological peril. They may be ready to fight because they feel their independence threatened or because their empires appear to be endangered. America would fight for a different reason: for a certain concept of life, of civilization, for an ideal and a morality incarnated in 'democracy.' The word 'democracy' may be vague, but its meaning is entirely clear to the Americans." [6] The same article admitted that expediency had led Mr. Roosevelt to mount the same platform as the western Europeans when making efforts to persuade the country to accept and Congress to vote for increasing armaments. "Expediency impels him to use such arguments as France and England being advanced defense bases. We have to defend them, he says, because by doing so we defend America."

The German Nazis read Mr. Roosevelt's mind the other way around. They called the American foreign policy a new-fangled Americanism which "dresses itself in the bright garment of high principles to impress the world, but its actions reveal that it is bent on drawing the biggest benefits from England's difficulties and from the vicissitudes of Europe. Even the President—surely a man who loves England—stresses in his every speech that any American help serves the purpose of the defense of America." [7]

However, a conservative English magazine detected the President shifting toward political realism. It made a rather premature statement to the effect that Roosevelt had been successful in drawing the people away from an isolationist attitude as a consequence of Munich. "Practical, rather than ideological, considerations seem to have hastened the process," the magazine expounded. "There is a wide feeling in the United States that, unless a balance of power in Europe is maintained, a situation may result which may affect American security. In official circles in Washington one hears less about 'Fascism' and 'Democracy,' and more about American security." [8]

The people of Western Europe had been elated that war had been averted, but they soon sobered. The same political writers who in the Munich days had hoped that "realism" would prevent Roosevelt from opposing appeasement of Hitler, now began to appreciate the President's reaffirmation of democratic ideals as well as the American people's determination to sustain them. "Beginning with his Message to Congress of the new year [1939] the pronouncements [of the President] have come at frequent intervals . . . and in America . . . they have been all the more effective because there is no comparable European voice enunciating the same ideas and convictions. When speaking of all-important matters of government in relation to justice and human freedom, Mr. Roosevelt expresses the common thought and feeling of all democratic peoples. He cannot do other than make a straight moral appeal; and as more than one prominent American publicist has lately reminded us, the American nation is not able to remain unmoved whenever the central problem of world affairs appears as a moral issue." [9]

Would the cold shower of Munich strengthen isolationism in America or, on the contrary, compel Americans to support the tottering democracies in Europe? "Many close observers of the American scene forecast that Munich would lead to a renewed wave of disgusted isolationism. This view, however, was badly mistaken," the (*London*) *Economist* commented. "With Munich, the . . . buttress of isolationism disappeared. It was no longer possible to believe that the two democracies of Western Europe would always act as a shield between America and the dictators. For the first time the possibility dawned on the American consciousness that the consequence of standing aloof might be standing alone. A shrewd . . . and cynical Congressman in the early days of the last war remarked that England's best tactics to ensure American help would be to lose a few battles. The lost battle of Munich had exactly the predicted effect." [10]

Roosevelt's distaste for the Munich settlement irritated Germany and the appeasers abroad. Some of them attributed it to personal rancor. One disgruntled observer asserted: "His humiliating defeat in his struggle with Congress . . . threatened his control over the Democratic party, with the prospect that he might be unable to name his own successor in the next Presidential election. A stormy and dramatic foreign policy offered an excellent chance for an executive to recoup his losses." But Munich stole the show from him; he had planned to play the peacemaker. ". . . Washington learned with astonishment that the Munich conference had been decided upon. Needless to say, Mr. Roosevelt did not relish the spectacle of Mussolini being given the role of world peacemaker to which he himself aspired. Nor did he like the Four Power character of the meeting. It was, to say the least, humiliating, and no one who has followed the turns of Mr. Roosevelt's temperament can imagine that he will easily forget the incident." [11]

"Public opinion in America instinctively felt after Munich that Roosevelt was also to be counted among the statesmen defeated by Munich," a French correspondent in America reported,[12] since Roosevelt had apparently believed that a deal other than surrender to their claims could be made with the dictators.

In fact, he wrote, neither Roosevelt nor the State Department had faith in the Munich settlement and they were expecting "new manifestations of Hitlerite impatience in its wake. This accounted for Roosevelt's statement before he left Washington to join the navy maneuvres to the effect that he might shorten his absence should events in Europe develop in a direction his information pointed to." [13]

Hitler soon vindicated their pessimism. Before that took place, however, an incident in America stirred an uproar among the isolationists and indignation in the totalitarian countries. A new type of bomber crashed in California at the end of January, 1939, and the body of a French officer aboard was recovered. He obviously was a member of a military purchasing mission. "The Administration relied at first on the argument that it was an advantage to have the capacity of American factories occupied by foreign orders pending the coming program of expansion of the United States' own Air Force. But Mr. Roosevelt, with characteristic directness . . . summoned the investigating Senators to the White House and told them in secret that the United States' frontier was in France and the country must do everything short of actually declaring war and sending troops to support the democrats against the dictators. . . . There is a shout of protest from all isolationists and pacifists . . . but there can be no question that the President has a very large body of opinion, perhaps a majority, on his side." [14]

The President, at a press conference, denied that he had made the statement, but it was generally assumed that he had spoken to the Senators to that effect. At this point the German press began to paint Roosevelt as a warmonger, depicting his attitude as "being in contrast to the statesmen of Europe who are actually trying to avoid a conflagration. Mr. Roosevelt's help is not wanted by France or by Britain except by France's chauvinists and Bolshoviks and Britain's 'war agitators' like Mr. Churchill . . . and Mr. Eden. Even Mr. Chamberlain will be apprehensive about Mr. Roosevelt's help today. The peoples want peace and know that it is to be had if Germany and Italy have political, economic, and moral equality of rights throughout the world." [15]

A few weeks later, on March 14, 1939, Hitler invaded what was left of Czechoslovakia in a brazen breach of the Munich agreement, and in contrast to his public declaration that with the Sudetenland his territorial ambitions had been fulfilled. This undisguised agression was Hitler's satisfaction for the "concession" he had made at Munich.

This blunt step completed the reversal of public opinion in Western Europe, even among those who had hailed Munich and believed that a redress of the mistakes made at the Versailles peace treaties would make peaceful coexistence with the dictatorships possible. Prime Minister Chamberlain himself now reversed his field. The public was clamoring for him to curb the dictators. It bordered on the unbelievable to witness Chamberlain, who a few months ago had denied Czechoslovakia even moral support, offering unsolicited military assistance to such countries as Poland which had actively collaborated with Hitler in destroying the alliance system. Poland had been the first country to break with collective security and enter into a pact with Hitler. It was, indeed, so unbelievable that the countries approached by Chamberlain hesitated to accept his offers of help. For England, the spectacle was intensely humiliating.

In April, Mussolini made a further step toward empire-making, invading Albania as a stepping stone toward Greece.

In the same month, the State Department notified Germany that the United States Government did not recognize that any legal basis existed for the *de facto* administration of Bohemia and Moravia by German authorities. Such steps, repeatedly taken in the years to come, seemed futile, but they actually meant a great deal to the subjugated peoples, who felt that no matter how far the conflict might spread in space and time, America's word would weigh heaviest in any decision about their fate.

The President wanted Congress to revise the Neutrality Act, since its embargo on both warring parties favored the aggressor who had armed well ahead of the action. He proposed that it be amended with a provision for cash and carry sales, which would benefit England and France, since they ruled the seas between America and western Europe. The President also requested Congress to vote huge appropriations for an unprecedented quantity of arms.

The European events increased his prestige among the public. "By the end of 1938," an Englishman noted, "Mr. Roosevelt's loss of prestige with Congress seemed to be reflected in a similar decline in the country. Until the end of 1937 it would not have been difficult to argue that in foreign policy he was taking great risks. But since March 1939 the American public has wanted the President to speak out loud and clear—in reaffirmation of essential principles, and in judgment against the violation of treaties, the breaking of pledges and the rape of small peoples. His power of recovery is extraordinary, and today his pre-eminence is universally acknowledged." [16] But even a Democratic Congress was, in another Englishman's opinion, "determined to safeguard the United States as far as this could be done by legislation at Washington, from being involved in war again. . . . But these purposes in the minds of senators were cut across and confused by an anxiety not to enact anything—even in pursuit of these purposes—that would increase the President's prerogative by enlarging the field of his freedom to act on his own discretion. . . . Another point . . . that was having an effect in the international field by March 1939 was the expectation that the Roosevelt Administration would come to an end in 1940, and that its successor—whether that were a weak Democratic regime or a Republican one—would steer a new course in foreign policy" [17]

"President Roosevelt's control of foreign policy is somewhat dependent on his position in domestic politics," a correspondent reported, noting that Roosevelt "is no longer losing ground in the struggle with Congress, and the chances are that in the end he will secure much of his legislative programme. Congress has talked loudly of economy—and keeps on increasing appropriations. Congress first refused the President an additional 150 million dollars for relief, most of which it will probably appropriate in the end. Congress opposed many parts of the national defence programme in January, but by late March has enacted it all . . . Mr. Roosevelt has rather cynically left Congress largely to itself, on the rule of 'Give them enough rope and they'll' . . . etc. Congress has not disappointed him thus far. . . . Herr Hitler and Signor Mussolini are the President's greatest allies. The lavish praise their controlled press pour upon American isolationists and the equally generous abuse they hurl at Mr. Roosevelt are vastly helpful to him." [18]

The armament program sailed smoothly through Congress, but the Neutrality Bill made no progress. The truth seemed to be to *London Economist* [19] "that most Congressmen have not been thinking in international terms at all. They have seen in the Neutrality Bill an occasion for another round in the domestic political struggle between pro- and anti-Roosevelt political factors. . . . The foreign observer, conscious that his own fate is involved, is painfully reminded of the conflict between President Wilson and Congress in 1919, when the question of American membership in the League was likewise debated in domestic, and sometimes in sheerly personal terms." Indeed, the Senate wound up for the summer without the bill having been reported out of its Foreign Relations committee. They refused to be influenced by the highly charged atmosphere in Europe. "The Senate did not exactly want to rebuke Mr. Roosevelt's foreign policy, but it did not like to give him a new vote of confidence that might have been too wildly construed. So it kept him under a kind of check and balance by deferring action on neutrality until a European crisis or to next January's session—whichever comes first." [20] In return, Roosevelt declared that a coalition of Republicans and Democrats in Congress were playing with the security of 150 millions of human beings by encouraging Hitler, who was preparing for the fatal plunge.

While England was negotiating with Poland for a pact to block further aggression, the President, on April 15, 1939, appealed directly to the two dictators, Hitler and Mussolini, asking them to promise not to attack thirty-one nations, which he named one by one. If they would pledge themselves, Roosevelt asserted, the United States would then take measures for the general reduction of armaments and the opening of international trade freely to all nations. "Roosevelt was a difficult man to fool, and was certainly aware of much of their roguery, but he could only appeal to any honesty and good sense which might still exist in Berlin and Rome." [21]

The Nazi press reacted vehemently. Under the headline "Market Crier of Democracy," the official party paper ran: "It is a remarkable bit of work when the leader of a great nation debases himself to the extent of circulating a shabby propaganda pamphlet to the heads of other states in the form of a 'note'. . . .

President Roosevelt is a boundlessly ambitious party politician who has utterly failed as head of the government and has terribly disappointed his people." [22] But a French paper rejoiced that the dictators could not keep the note secret before their people, since "even dictators have to respect public opinion. It does not mean that peace will be saved, but if it is saved it will be through Roosevelt's intervention. It does not bring us firm hope this time, but encouragement. It confirms our conviction that we are right." [23] A Swiss weekly wondered whether the dictators would be able to yield. "Napoleon could hold his sway only as long as he was the exponent of the French Revolution storming across the Continent. Hitler can keep his reign only as an exponent of the imperialistic German revolution. Nobody can be static and dynamic at the same time. It is even difficult for one and the same person to change from one attitude to the other. Napoleon found this out when he wanted to appease the conservative powers by wedding the daughter of the Austrian emperor. Hitler has not taken such a step despite Chamberlain's invitation to do so at Munich. But even if the Fuehrer dares to try such a step he may be as unsuccessful as Napoleon was." [24]

Hitler replied to the President's note "in a public speech, in which he repeated the names of the countries whose frontiers Roosevelt had asked him to respect, and roused laughter as he uttered each name." [25] While he tried to ridicule the note he abrogated the British-German naval agreement and the Polish-German non-aggression pact.

Hitler's arrogance was disheartening. But to those who argued that Roosevelt should not make appeals to the dictators if he was not prepared to back up his principles, *The Economist* replied: "There may . . . be an impatient tendency to ask, why all the consultation, speech-making, the declaring of principle if nothing is to come of it? To which the answer is . . . that in an epoch in which the rule of law and the role of reason and objective truth have ceased to be accepted even in principle, their restatement at regular intervals by eminent persons is a matter of vital importance." [26]

While the Anglo-Polish negotiations proceeded, Hitler reviewed his military position as a result of his invasion of highly industrialized Czechoslovakia. He said: "We can consider the pre-conditions of waging war now as compared to the situation of September last year as favorable. The Czech army has been eliminated, its arsenals and weapon factories seized, our frontiers shortened by many hundred kilometers, our own army and air force strengthened, the civilian population to a large extent militarized and the production of war materials strongly increased so that Germany is still ahead of her opponents." [27]

Hitler's success did not slow down his dynamics. The Nazi press began to apply the pattern of conquest, so successful in the case of the Czechs, to Poland. The German ethnic group in Poland became restless and their situation was said to be increasingly unbearable. Also, the position of Danzig, the harbor declared a free city by the Versailles Treaty, was called outrageous. Poland was alarmed. However, any English-French military assistance pact with Poland would be effective only if Russia adhered to it, since the former countries had no direct access to the territory of Poland. But the Polish government would not consent to allow the Soviet army to enter her territory, even as a friend coming to her aid. Chamberlain declared that he was ready to negotiate with the Soviet Union for a mutual defense pact that would also guarantee Poland's territorial integrity against aggression. But the going would be rough, as the *New York Times* warned the British: [28] "It is difficult for Britons to realize the profound indignation felt in the Soviet Union during the so-called Munich crisis."

The British royal couple's visit to the United States was a success beyond expectations. "The friendly handshake with which the President welcomed the King of Britain in Washington is the beginning of a new era in the relations between the United States and Britain. At the same time it started a magnificent, in the history of both countries, unique profession of friendship by people of all walks of life of democratic America. . . . Those who know the country are convinced that the Government in Washington would never stand idly by the collapse of the European democracies, but would actively, perhaps decisively intervene. It is rightly noted that the hearty welcome tendered to the King and Queen was the biggest demonstration for peace of the last twenty years." [29]

But the visit also worked out to favor President Roosevelt, in the view of The *London Economist.* "The great and unexpected success of the British royal visit has perhaps contributed to the tide of American politics flowing for the moment in the President's favor, for the ceremonies—and still more the non-ceremonious private hospitality extended by the Roosevelt family—have shown Mr. Roosevelt as not merely by virtue of his office but also in his person the head of a great nation. Some messages from Washington report that the visit also had some bearing on the fact that the Administration's proposals for the amendment of the Neutrality Act . . . have made a first short step toward acceptance by Congress. They have been approved by the Foreign Affairs Committee of the House of Representatives and may well pass the whole House; but their real test is . . . in the Senate." [30]

The Senate was in no hurry, although the Anglo-French negotiations with the Soviet government were going disquietingly slowly. The reasons for Russia's reluctance were that the Russians insisted on Poland's permitting the entry of the Soviet army into her territory in case of a German attack on Poland, and also on the British-French guarantee being extended to the Baltic states, from where a direct attack on Russia by the Germans might have been expected. Rumor had it that there was a more ominous reason for Soviet delaying tactics, and this version made even the Japanese uneasy. Under the heading, "Soviet Ruse," Nichi Nichi wrote: "A well-known authority on Soviet questions, wiring from Warsaw May 8, says that a current rumor concerning a rapproachement between Soviet Russia and Germany emanates from Moscow. By spreading this sort of information, he says, the Soviet authorities hope to get a stronger bargaining position vis-à-vis Britain. . . . The real chances of the Soviet switching from the democracies to the totalitarian group, says the same correspondent, are daily getting more remote." [31]

However, a month later, A. H. Zdahnov, leader of the Leningrad

Communist party, attacked Britain and France in *Pravda.* He blamed them for endless procrastination in their negotiations with the Soviet for the conclusion of a pact of mutual assistance. "In the present situation this fact cannot but be of serious importance and it is strongly emphasized that such delays only incite aggressors for further acts of aggression. . . . I believe and I wish to prove it by fact that the British and French governments do not wish an equal treaty with the U.S.S.R. and an equal treaty is the only kind of a Pact to which a self-respecting state can agree."[32] Zdahnov then pointed out that Great Britain only a short time before had concluded a pact of mutual assistance with Turkey and Poland within a short space of time. He concluded: "They have been producing artificial difficulties so as to make it appear that serious differences exist between the negotiating parties."

Though the situation of Europe was fraught with imminent danger, the President could not slacken his attention to another aggressor whose ambitions kept growing—Japan. Britain, being now engaged on the Continent where she might be involved in war at any moment, tried to assure the safety of her possessions and dominions in the Pacific by appeasing Japan. She recognized, on July 24, 1939, "the special requirements of the Japanese forces in China." But the President, in a drastic step, warned Japan that the United States would not be deterred from her policy concerning China and the Pacific by British appeasement. He notified Japan that the Commercial Treaty existing between her and the United States would be terminated after six months, as provided for in the Treaty. At the same time he tried to bring strong pressure to bear on Japanese statesmen to keep a moderate government in power.

The Japanese press tried to mitigate the effect of the note by informing the public that the abrogation by Roosevelt was but a dramatic gesture to redeem the political defeat inflicted on him by the Senate, which had refused to enact the "Un-Neutrality Bill" proposed by the President, thus restraining the foreign policy of the Roosevelt administration.[33]

Meanwhile, Winston Churchill broadcast to America on August 9, 1939: "In Germany, on a mountain peak, there sits one man who, in a single day, can release the world from the fear that now oppresses it, or, in a single day, can plunge all that we have and are into a volcano of smoke and flame."

On August 23 the world was astounded to hear via Radio Moscow that Hitler and Stalin had concluded a non-aggression pact. A secret agreement provided for a partition of Poland.

Roosevelt made a personal appeal to the European governments and the King of Italy, asking for assurances that there would be no invasions, and offering negotiation as a means of settling disputes. In writing to the King he urged that Italy and the United States cooperate to advance the ideals of Christianity. "Unheard voices of countless millions," he pleaded, "ask that they shall not be vainly sacrificed again." He appealed to Hitler and the President of Poland to negotiate directly or arbitrate through a third power, and asked that no fighting should start. . . . Poland's reply to Roosevelt was in favor of negotiation. The President forwarded the reply to Hitler, saying: "Countless human lives can yet be saved, and hope may still be restored that the nations of the modern world may even now construct a foundation for a peaceful and happier relationship if you . . . will agree to the pacific means of settlement accepted by the Government of Poland."

Hitler gave no answer. Instead, his troops rushed forth on September 1 to invade Poland. On September 3 Britain and France honored their pledges to Poland and declared war on Germany. That evening Roosevelt spoke over the radio of the position of the United States toward the European war, while millions in Europe anxiously listened, wondering whether help would come from the world's wealthiest and most powerful nation. Events abroad, said the President, had been based on force or the threat of force. America should seek a peace which eliminated the use of force between nations. Peace, however, had been broken, and this fact endangered the peace of all countries everywhere. Americans might wish to remain detached from the war, but "every word that comes through the air, every ship that sails the sea, every battle that is fought" affects the American future. The United States, said Roosevelt, would remain neutral, but he could not ask that every American remain neutral in thought. He promised that as long as he could prevent it there would be no "blackout of peace" in the United States.

Even then the war, as a British writer later recalled it, differed greatly from World War I. "In 1914," he wrote, "war came to the man in the street as an almost complete surprise. Down to the ninth of the thirteen fateful days which shaped the catastrophe, he thought that the crisis was only a newspaper story. It would settle itself as the crises of 1911 and 1912-1913 had done; Britain would not be drawn in. . . . It was only the episode of Germany's attack on neutral Belgium that brought unity back . . . for a national struggle. In 1939, there was neither surprise nor disagreement. Both had spent their force a year earlier, during the days before and after the Munich negotiations. After that, and more particularly after the destruction of Czechoslovakia in the intervening March, the evidences multiplied that Herr Hitler's was not a limited ambition. The nation had begun to realize that Europe could not go about its business indefinitely with the Damocles-sword of German aggression suspended over it. The Government's decision to treat the Polish issue as a test case was clearly understood and fully supported by all parties; and such opposition as there was to it never grew to be more than a camarilla." [34]

But the Poles, under the political leadership of generals and colonels, prepared and trained their army for a repetition of the past war. When Hitler let loose his Panzer divisions on them while his Stukas poured fire and death indiscriminately to the tune of a deafening howl and rattle, the Polish army disintegrated. In two weeks the war against Poland was over. Then, Stalin declared that the Polish state had ceased to exist and that this fact conferred on him the duty to protect the White Russian and Ukrainian ethnic groups living in the east of Poland. The existence of the secret agreement dividing Poland was revealed by the coordinated action of the Germans and Russians when the Soviet army invaded East Poland and soon after incorporated it into the Soviet Union.

President Roosevelt proclaimed a "limited national emergency" on September 8. In his message to Congress two weeks later, Roosevelt affirmed that the government "personally, officially and without reservation is in favor of measures protecting the neutrality, security and integrity of the country, measures that, at the same time, keep the country from war." [35]

The European events may have put in jeopardy the security of the United States, but they only caused bewilderment among the aggressors in the Pacific. ". . . The Soviet-German Pact brought about a marked revulsion of feeling against Germany in Japan; apprehensive, no doubt, of increased trouble with Soviet Russia. The Japanese, while continuing the war in China, seemed ready to avoid trouble with Britain, France and the United States for the time being." [36]

Among the powers threatened by Japanese aggression, the United States was clearly cast in the role of leader. "Probably no result of the European war is more significant," a British magazine commented, ". . . than the increased importance it gives to American influence in the Pacific. To a much greater degree than ever before Japan will now be dependent upon the United States not only for war materials and machinery, but also for the export trade upon which depends the financing of her foreign purchase. There are increasing indications that the United States intends to take full advantage of this situation in order to enforce, if possible, a return to the twin principle upon which American policy in China has traditionally been based—observance of the Open Door as regards commercial opportunities and the maintenance of China's territorial and administrative integrity." [37] There were rumors that Britain considered making a deal with Japan, recognizing the special status of Japan, and ending all aid to China in exchange for a guarantee of Hong Kong, Singapore, Australia, etc. The same magazine quoted Mr. Grew, American Ambassador to Japan, in a sharp criticism of Japan. He said "the United States has no intention of abandoning its interests there, regardless of whatever other powers do. This country intends to live up to all treaty obligations and will not condone any contrary actions by any other power."

The Japanese press did not conceal their misgivings over the cooperation of the Nazis with the Soviet Union. It was shattering all their plans in the Pacific. "The Soviet Union will extend military and other aid to Germany to a certain extent," Nichi Nichi speculated in October, 1939, "but it is highly doubtful that the two countries will be closely united for their common victory. Germany now cannot act without being influenced by the Soviet Union. The German-Soviet pact is not only a menace to the Anglo-French bloc but to Germany herself. This amazing fact must be watched with the keenest interest, for the war between Germany and Britain may be manipulated by the Soviet Union."

The Japanese also warned Germany of the significance of America not recognizing her conquests. "With the extinction of Poland there has also gone the necessity of fighting, says a joint communiqué of Germany and Soviet Russia," Nichi Nichi recorded, but it pointed to Secretary Cordell Hull's statement to the effect that America would not recognize the partition of Poland and added: "The indication of such an attitude on the part of a major power like America will seriously affect the future political situation in Europe."

In the United States itself, as a Frenchman noted, even the most hard-headed isolationists were becoming uneasy. "In vain one tried hard not to be interested in the fate of the Ethiopians, of Hitler's entry into Vienna, of the Spanish Civil War and the bombardment of Guernica, of the dismemberment of Czechoslovakia and Hitler's march into Prague, of the invasion of Albania (and of Poland). . . . The simple accumulation of strange events gave birth to the confusing thought that these Ethiopians, Austrians, Spanish, Czechs, Albanians (and Poles) must have been brave people who had no other wish than to live in peace under a regime of their own choosing. On the other hand, the people who disturbed the established order have always been the same. One came to say to oneself that these Germans and Italians had passed beyond all limits and to wish that there would be someone to put an end to their vagaries. These thoughts have been suggested to them, without being conscious of it, by the attitude of the President." [38]

The President called Congress into a special session to vote on the amendment to the Neutrality Act cancelling the embargo on both warring parties and substituting it with the cash and carry provision for war materials. This time, in a changed mood in view of Hitler's blatant aggression against Poland, the Senate was in favor of the bill.

In the midst of an unfolding world catastrophe, foreigners watched the President's actions and words to see whether or not he had decided to run for the Presidency for the third time.

"Mr. Roosevelt is still head and shoulders, waist and thigh, above anybody else in political stature and in personal popularity, and has gained very considerably from the widespread approval of his conduct of foreign affairs since the outbreak of the war," *The (London) Economist* stated.[39] "What is driving him to run for a third term is not so much personal ambition as the knowledge that he is certainly the only candidate who would have a chance of holding the White House for the New Deal and probably the only one who could keep it for the Democrats."

Another English magazine, reflecting upon his personality and its main driving forces, noted: "Americans know their President as a man of impulses, as a dramatic and daring man. Many of them fear that his foreign policies may at any time become as unconventional and risky as his internal policies. This apprehension is true of a good many men-in-the-street, it is keen in those parts of the country most remote from the seaboards, and it is also intensified by partisan opposition. . . . There are still plenty of men-in-the-street who are prepared to trust President Roosevelt to any length. . . . Political observers have continually assumed that in the event of war Mr. Roosevelt would be elected for a third term. Some are reminded of a public speech of the President about George Washington's wish for retirement, followed by his patriotic decision to turn from the private life he loved and serve his country in a moment of crisis. The parable was pat. And as the parable continues to sink into public consciousness that in the event of war Mr. Roosevelt would 'of course' be re-elected, he gradually builds up a powerful political position without appearing to do so." [40]

"President Roosevent maintains complete poise and equanimity," was the view of another observer.[41] "The graver world developments become, the more likely he is to be nominated and elected for a third term. Such a result is by no means a probability. Far from it. But it is significant that politicians constantly agree that the only circumstances under which the President could be nominated and re-elected would be a war or a crisis threatening war. Mr. Roosevelt may therefore be enjoying a little cosmic jest. The reason for his easy inaction may be that he expects to walk in at the last moment, when 'Draft Roosevelt' has become inevitable." The writer praised him for his proposal to reorganize the government machinery, stating that "in achieving these practical and widely extended reforms towards the end of his present term in office, the President is setting up a real monument to himself. [These] . . . long overdue changes will modernize the federal plant, will 'keep the tools of American democracy up to date,' as Mr. Roosevelt said in an eloquent message to Congress. He was seeking, he said, to make democracy work—to strengthen the arms of democracy, in peace or war and to ensure the solid blessings of free government."

On the occasion of the publication of Roosevelt's Public Papers and Addresses, a commentator saw him in this light: [42] "These volumes give the reader a vivid impression of Mr. Roosevelt's unique capacity to visualize America, not like his predecessor, Mr. Hoover, in terms of statistics and blueprints, but in terms of individual men, women, and children, with their widely varying qualities, aspirations, problems and fears. They show equally his even more unique capacity to express himself on all occasions, in writing and in speech, in simple, lucid, fluent English which even the humblest citizen can understand. He is thus able to communicate his own keen personal interest in the problems of individual Americans to the man in the street, who is very often alienated by the lifeless, artificial verbiage of politicians and civil servants. He has travelled far more widely throughout the country before and since becoming President than any predecessor. . . . His intimate personal knowledge of the United States and 130 million individuals with special qualities and problems

. . . has given Mr. Roosevelt an impatience with the ordinary generalizations, evasions, and delays in politicians. The President is an opportunist in the sense that he is so conscious of things which America and Americans vitally need, and so determined that the Government shall produce these things, that he is impatient of advice that they cannot be done, or are not constitutional, or are contrary to precedent, or do not square with the party platform. . . . Mr. Roosevelt . . . is never prepared to admit that anything which seems to him worth doing cannot be done and done quickly. . . ."

A French correspondent in America summed up his observations and reflections upon the President's performance during the year of 1939: [43] "The events in the last months have raised the prestige of the President, thanks to the statesmanlike fashion with which he succeeded in impressing his leadership on the nation. He took over the foreign policy of his country in the face of a Europe at war. His prestige had dropped in June after the defeats inflicted on him by a rebellious Congress. Now, even his opponents acknowledge his clever maneuvering in the fight for the revision of the Neutrality Act and in setting himself above party quarrels. Roosevelt has been accused of dividing America for seven years, but he now finds himself in the privileged position of having created a national unity under extremely difficult and continually changing situations. In other words, Roosevelt is recognized today as being the only statesman in America who has enough authority and knowledge of world affairs to steer the United States clear of the hidden and visible rocks of the present and the future. . . . We believe that Roosevelt will accept office for a third time because he considers that he has a mission to accomplish in the world, a mission that does not spring from any mystical source, but from the conviction that events have proven him right, and that he has been on the right path not only as far as it concerns his own country but also the world. . . . Thus the reply to the question of a third inauguration for Roosevelt is not up to the President or even to the American nation. The reply to reserved for the future and the unforseeable developments of the war in Europe."

9

WORLD WAR BEGINS

The West was given a first glance at the timetable of mechanized warfare when Hitler wiped out the Polish army in a couple of weeks. After hostilities had subsided on the Eastern front, the Anglo-French armies, entrenched in fortified lines, gave only feeble signs of activity. This strange quiet on the western front was called the war of nerves at first and later the phony war, both very appropriately.

Both sides were eager to reduce hostilities to a token war, indicating a stalemate. The Germans made use of it to demoralize an idle mass of men through slow but penetrating propaganda; for the Allies it was a secondary field of action complementing the sea blockade which they believed would eventually force the Germans to accept a reasonable peace. Responsible authorities in Washington apparently approved of this strategy. Walter Lippman explained it by stressing that America's industrial power would suffice only to enable the Allies to wage a defensive war. The Allies would need to outnumber Hitler's armies by three to one in order to defeat them.[1] But Lippmann was not certain whether or not Hitler intended to probe the strength of his opponents' defenses before turning reasonable.

Although no offensive was expected in the winter, the Russians, Hitler's partners in the partition of Poland, provoked an incident that threatened to ignite a shooting war. The incident was the result of a new German-Russian agreement in September, 1939, delineating the spheres of influence between the partners. Russia had been awarded the Baltic states and Finland. On the strength of the agreement, Stalin demanded and obtained bases in the Baltic states, and he tried to impress similar demands on Finland.

These demands, which were to serve for the defense of Leningrad from the sea, were moderate; but the Finns felt that yielding to the Soviet might jeopardize their national independence, and they resolved to resist. Neither the advice of the Scandinavian countries nor that of Germany softened their stand, and the little country took up arms ready to fight the invading armies of huge Soviet Russia. The task of forcing Stalin's demands on the Finns by arms proved tougher than he and everybody else had expected; it developed into a regular war that was to last through the winter.

For the world it became a heart-lifting spectacle to witness a people of less than four million beating back the assault of one of the world's greatest powers, especially as it came after the surrender or ineffective resistance of much stronger victims of Nazi aggression. The enthusiasm stirred by the bravery of the Finns stood, in the words of an Englishman, in inverse proportion to the distance from the battlefield; but it was strong enough in the West and in America to create a situation that might have turned critical.

In America, strong isolationist forces became bellicose when not the Nazis but Communist Russia was the aggressor. On the other hand, the Nazi press appropriated Bolshevik semantics and began to call the Third Reich "National Socialist Reich" and "Socialist People's Reich of German Workers and Soldiers."

"The invasion of Finland," an English magazine wrote,[7] "made a tremendous difference in the American attitude toward the European situation. To many Americans the war between the Allies and Germany was the same old struggle, between two powerful groups, for empire, the old game of power politics. But the invasion of Finland was stark aggression, with the grisly ogre of Bolshevist imperialism behind it. President Roosevelt immediately extended his good offices in the hope of settling the conflict. Instantly, many Republicans and isolationists began to clamor for even stronger policies. They asked at once for severance of diplomatic relations with the Soviet Union, and various other measures 'short of war' which they had condemned when the United States sought to apply them to Germany. A great wave of national sentiment on behalf of Finland has swept the country. The Administration, concealing its satisfaction at this wide-open breach in the ranks of isolationism, at once set about devising stronger policies. . . . The important point in all this is the volte-face of the isolationists. Former President Hoover, who had been one of the most severe critics of the Administration's policies of 'measures short of war'—is now heading a vigorous Finnish relief agency. Other isolationists are splitting the heavens with their denunciations of Moscow. There is no longer a 'war party' and a 'peace party' in the United States, there are two 'war' parties! President Roosevelt knows how to make the most of the new 'national unity' which has come his way. . . . In preparation for a peace-making effort, the President needs to retain national unity, which will be difficult enough in the atmosphere of the election campaign. If a genuine mediation opportunity comes his way, President Roosevelt will probably forget about the third term and throw all his energies into the struggle for peace."

A French magazine also found the sudden unanimity in America baffling.[3] To see in the same camp such dissimilar personalities as Roosevelt, Hoover, Henry Ford, John L. Lewis, Dorothy Thompson, William Randolph Hearst, and Father Coughlin, with Roosevelt in the role of a moderator, appeared unbelievable. However, Roosevelt was careful enough not to be carried onto dangerous paths by conservative elements who wanted to present Stalin and Communism as the sole enemy and to underplay the peril of Hitlerism.

The British Left poked fun at the ambiguity of the isolationism of its foremost advocates. "Certainly Mr. Hoover's shock at the invasion of a small country seems a little sudden," one of their journals wrote. "The day Helsinki was bombed he proclaimed that civilization had reached a 'new low' and that Russia had carried us back to the morals and butchery of Ghengis Khan. It is odd that when Spain and China were bombed for three years civilization apparently didn't budge, or that the ghost of Ghengis Khan did not rise when the *Blitzkrieg* was visited upon Poland. . . . People who venture to suggest that a German victory over the Allies would threaten free American institutions are still called British propagandists and warmongers. But no one calls the propagandists of the Moscow menace warmongers." [4]

The contradiction in American thinking continued throughout the Finnish war. As an English paper put it, ". . . the Americans continued . . . to maintain their desired aloofness towards the main war while they indulged in an emotional orgy over the Baltic sideshow. . . . But the contradiction has been rendered more insupportable than ever; the day of greater participation in the struggle—if and when the need becomes acute—has become a great deal nearer. It is in this sense that the Soviet attack on Finland may be called one of the greatest historical 'accidents' of our time." The same writer stressed, however, that the President had not taken advantage of the changing mood to guide the public toward accepting the need for joining the Allies. He asserted that the President "is constantly and alertly watching for an opportunity to launch a peace intervention. His Christmastide effort to work with the Vatican has borne no direct fruit, and it is recognized that the time is not now propitious. . . . But Mr. Roosevelt remains as eager as ever to round out his historic career with a contribution to peace. Time draws short, too, for this is an election year and the President's authority may not be undiminished for long. Yet the President does not wish to have anything to do with a peace that would reward aggression, and he will not offer to mediate until he knows in advance that his offer will be acceptable . . . he, like other informed persons, knows that more grim drama must enroll in Europe before a peace based on freedom can be negotiated. . . . But it cannot be overemphasized that the White House is today all eyes and ears, watching for opportunity . . . preparing American public opinion for its contribution and seeking the chance for Mr. Roosevelt to use his leadership, his resources, his energy toward the solution of the greatest problem of the times." [5]

The President's direct message to Soviet President Kalinin before hostilities had actually started, in which he expressed the hope that Finland's independence and peace would be preserved, provoked a reply by Kalinin, reminding Roosevelt that the Soviet government had recognized Finland's independence "of its own free will." The aim of the negotiations was, according to the Soviet President, to strengthen cooperation by consolidating mutual security. Molotov, the Soviet Foreign Minister, sarcastically commented that Finland was in a better position in her relations with the Soviet Union than were the Philippines or Cuba in their relations with the United States.

The American government did not go further than to favor sending financial aid to Finland, but France and England set out to organize expeditionary forces, and negotiated with Norway and Sweden for allowing the transit of troops and equipment. Afraid of provoking not only Russia but also Germany into war, the Scandinavians remained adamant in their refusal, but the Allies continued to try to join the Finns even when they were already negotiating with the Russians for an honorable surrender.

During Christmas, 1939, Roosevelt decided to send two missions to wartorn Europe, a personal representative to the Vatican, and Sumner Welles, Under Secretary of State, to visit the heads of the governments of Germany, Italy, and the western countries. It appeared significant that the President had chosen Christmas for this step. People considered it an offer to mediate or a proclamation of principles behind which the spiritual power of the Church and the material power of the United States would try to force upon the warring parties a just and lasting peace.

Sumner Welles listened carefully to the statesmen he visited, but did not reveal the intent of his mission, which kept the public in a stir even when responsible men in the various governments deprecated its importance.

"What was his purpose?" asked a British magazine [6] after Welles had returned home. "It seemed formidably impartial for an American official to be hearing both sides . . . [but] the greatest care was taken in the announcements about Mr. Welles' disclaiming any intention to make peace efforts. With labored reiteration American official pronouncements protested that Mr. Welles was concerned not with the making of peace but with American participation in the work of reconstruction that would follow the making of peace. . . . Mr. Wilson sent Colonel House in 1915 to visit London, Paris, and Berlin with the frank and open intention of mediating for peace between the belligerents. . . . By contrast, it was believed in influential circles, both in and out of the United States, that Roosevelt was speaking the literal truth when he denied any intention to mediate for peace. . . . Mr. Roosevelt did not want to stop the war. Would it be fair to him to go further and say that he even wanted not to stop it: that is, wanted it to go on, at any rate till November 1940? Republican propagandists in their private propaganda did not hesitate to make so terrible a charge." Yet the magazine carefully listed all the arguments supporting the "terrible" charge.

"The New Deal had caused such havoc to the economic and financial welfare of the United States, that at all costs it was necessary for Mr. Roosevelt to sidetrack the attention of the electorate from that subject. Indeed, they went so far as to say that but for the war in Europe he could never had dared to stand for a third term. . . . If . . . Mr. Roosevelt could go on telling the American public that he was keeping them out of the war, but that the war and its issues were of profound interest and importance to America, then he would achieve the dual purpose of keeping their minds off the New Deal and cultivating his own reputation as benefactor and protector of the American people. It is always possible that human nature, even political human nature, cannot sink so low; and Mr. Roosevelt's public statements have certainly given ground for the belief that his own conception of political exigency has not deteriorated to anything like such a depth."

The article acquitted Roosevelt from the charge of refraining from mediating for peace, having his re-election in mind, but it argued that America's interest demanded the earliest possible end of the European war, since as a consequence of the war, she has been losing her export business.

American law required payments in advance, but Britain, fighting for her life, would obviously retain her reserves of gold and foreign exchanges to the bitter end and would cease to buy anything from the United States she could buy elsewhere under better conditions.

Thus it was against the interest of his country when Roosevelt failed to mediate for peace.

A French conservative attributed more good faith to Roosevelt and to America. "The Welles mission," he stated, "proves, if it was necessary to prove it, that the United States can neither morally nor materially be disinterested in the war and its issue. It hopes to model the new Europe according to its own idealism and to the requirements of its economy. The Allies will easily find a common basis upon these principles." [7] But the article warned: "The future world will bear the marks only of those who have taken the hammer to forge on the anvil."

Hitler was puzzled about the actual purpose of Welles' tour, but after the visit of the American diplomat he and Mussolini played the visit down. Mussolini was informed that: ". . . the visit of Sumner Welles to Berlin produced nothing new. In Germany people are asking what Roosevelt actually meant by that step. The Duce observed that it must principally be a question of an internal American matter." [8]

Responsible opinion in the West saw no prospects for peace other than on Hitler's terms, due to his strong position on the Continent. American mediation thus had little chance for success. Moreover, the American public was not ready to make sacrifices for the sake of European peace, and it appeared that American economic concessions might represent the only attraction for the Axis to accept a reasonable peace. But the eventless war in the West amazed people everywhere and made them ready to believe in the most surprising turn of events. An English magazine reported from Washington that the President's great ambition was to become the Peacemaker. "President Roosevelt," it asserted, "is following the policy of the Great Neutral who leans weightily toward the forces of order in the world, and seeks to create his role in history in peacemaking. . . . He may be expected to be eagerly alert for any future opportunity of assisting a balanced and sound peace. Whether or not he will be empowered to make a substantial American contribution to that peace depends upon the future evolution of his nation's public opinion. However, public opinion has a very long way to go if President Roosevelt is to make a genuine contribution which goes beyond the most trivial diplomatic errand-running. At present, there is no great disposition either to lower tariffs materially as a contribution to economic peace, or to accept political responsibilities in Europe. . . . The nation is in the very throes of disillusionment about the ability of Europe to make peace. . . ." [9]

The magazine made the American statesmen responsible for the public complacency. "No strong and responsible voices have yet been raised," it stated, "to tell the American people of their real stake in the war. President Roosevelt and Secretary Hull are probably privately convinced that a more actively cooperative policy is necessary. Some Republican leaders, like Henry L. Stimson and a few other isolated men of affairs, are equally convinced. . . . There are plenty of private citizens who will say, 'Would it not be better if we got into the war right away? Won't the job be harder later on?' But such convictions have little effect on the great mass of public opinion. The dam still holds. No important public man, at least no one who is running for office this year, dares to turn against the current, ventures to tell the American people what many of them secretly know to be the facts. We are in a time of grandiosely wishful thinking." [10]

European neutrals observed no inclination on the part of the Nazis to accept less than the legal consolidation of their conquests. Swedish papers were particularly aroused at the German press for approving of Russian aggression against Finland. "It is asserted in Berlin," a paper reported, "that the Russians have a just claim to recover what they lost in the Great War. Such pronouncements show that the demand for national self-determination which Berlin has been so fond of using is a mere mockery. Germany's present attitude raises once again the question as to how long the German-Russian cooperation is likely to remain solid. The stronger the strategic position of the Soviets becomes the more difficult it is for Germany to resist. It is therefore quite probable that there exists a plan to establish on the European continent a Russo-German domination." [11]

With such a prospect in mind, a French conservative magazine surveyed the political situation in America as it was developing during the election campaign, and it ventured some forecasts, pending a sudden flare-up on the western front. "The Republicans avoid making public statements concerning foreign policies. They affirm their pacifism, but want to preserve their freedom of action while launching a campaign that denounces President Roosevelt as a warmonger. . . . The opposition to Roosevelt is vast . . . and it appears that only a brutal event can dissipate the fog in the public mind and restore a national unity which will at the same time be a mental unity. Such an event would occur if Hitler launched a massive attack on England, or if he bombarded the great cities of western Europe, and this might result in a mass rally around Roosevelt. The feeling of immediate danger combined with a rousing indignation would override old antagonisms. The partisans of Mr. Roosevelt have been expecting such an event for a long time. . . . Short of a 'brutal event,' Roosevelt could rally the nation behind him only as a Peacemaker. He has one single means by which to silence his enemies: by becoming the center of a successful peace initiative. It is apparent that he is aware of this, but his desire not to harm the Allies restrains him from action, since he does not want to play into Hitler's hands. Hitler's war, Roosevelt's peace: these visions are floating over America, while the electoral campaign is getting under way and while fate is ripening in the fields of Europe, eventually to determine whether Roosevelt will become the arbiter of the universe or a politician in retirement." [12]

However, the French were prone to overlook the importance of another ambitious expansionist country, Japan. While the phony war in Europe and the Russo-German alliance had put a curb on further aggressive steps, Japanese leaders eagerly followed the unfolding of the Presidential campaign in America. In the view of a reporter, "the Japanese want to find out what positions the parties will take in the campaign concerning policies toward them. They expect a modification of the American attitude; indeed, this is what most interests them. Yet they are keeping an eye on the European war also, hoping that developments may benefit them in their latent struggle against the Russian's." [13]

The Japanese were hard put while Nazi-Soviet cooperation lasted. Hitler seemed to have lost interest in an alliance with them. For the moment, the Japanese were ready to accept the Nazi-Russian cooperation as a means to keep America from interference outside the Western Hemisphere. At the same time they offered Hitler a "common policy in Central and South America . . . directed against American interests." [14]

America then held a strong deterrent against further Japanese aggression, in the opinion of an English commentary. "It is the view in Washington that the decision to hold Japanese-American trade relations in suspense is the most important external action in the Pacific since Japan undertook to close Asia to the rest of the world. Now the United States can withhold decisive war materials believed to be essential to Japan's continuance of the war in China. At the same time the American Navy continues to be strengthened, strategic fortifications in the Pacific are under construction, the Chinese are still putting on a good show and the Japanese encounter continuing difficulties in setting up an amenable government in the areas they control." [15]

The writer's optimism may have been exaggerated, since isolationist protests hampered even defensive measures in the Pacific. Another English comment presented this balance sheet. "Public opinion in the United States has flinched from the further fortification of Guam, as recommended by the naval experts, on the ground that such a step would be a wanton provocation to Japan. But it can rest comfortably on the strength of the central point of American Pacific defense—Pearl Harbor, Hawaii, is one of the strongest naval bases in the world, and the works now being carried out there are intended to make it ample, if necessary, for the entire American fleet. So long as the American fleet is in being and Pearl Harbor is intact and adequately provisioned, the danger of attack upon the west coast of the American continent is inconsiderable." [16]

In April, 1940, Hitler dispersed the misty illusion of phony war. During the winter he had prepared for total war, while the French had mobilized young and old to man the fortified lines, trusting in her concrete rather than her men's determination.

Britain was doing business almost as usual. Hitler overran little Denmark. With the help of a fifth column he overpowered Norway, attacked Holland, and occupied it after his Stukas had poured down terror and death on Rotterdam. His tanks broke through the defenses of Belgium. King Leopold first called in the Allies to help, then capitulated, leaving the French and British armies trapped by Nazi tanks which broke through the French lines. The incredible was to happen: the German armies in a few weeks defeated the French and forced upon France a defeatist government, headed by Marshal Petain, who asked for an armistice. The British succeeded in saving the bulk of their expeditionary armies in France and also in returning their fighters and bombers to the British Isles, although they had to abandon weapons and equipment. Hitler, by July, 1940, had become the master of the Continent. Britain alone opposed him, protected only by a narrow moat, but its people were determined not to surrender.

What causes a great nation to surrender, a British writer wondered. "The most dangerous opinion that can afflict a country at any time, though most of all in time of war, is the opinion that the ordinary person will be no worse off under foreign rulers than under his own, so that it matters little (and is certainly not worth so much suffering and sacrifice) 'if the Germans win.' This opinion if sufficiently widespread will make defeat in war certain." [17] The writer found a striking similarity between two heroes, two Field Marshals who both had surrendered to the Nazis. He wrote: "Pétain bears a curious resemblance to Hindenburg. It is the second time in recent years that a senile Field Marshal, having helped to lose a war, has connived at surrendering to its deadliest foes the Republic he is pledged to serve. It is the second time, also, that a senile Field Marshal is the accomplice of those who, fearing the Red Bolshevism of Moscow, capitulate before the Brown Bolshevism of Berlin."

"At the fire of the incendiary bombs the tranquility, the carefree mood in America was gone. The awakening is brisk and total. In a few days the United States has forded the distance that

Britain needed several years to pass," a French paper said.[18] "The invasion of Denmark and of Norway on April 8," another Frenchman commented, "raised the question of Iceland and Greenland: the Reich would obtain bases in the vicinity of America in these two Danish possessions. After the invasion of Holland, the United States began suddenly to worry about Japan's intentions with respect to the Netherland East Indies. It was at this point that American thinking changed. The public began to insist that America aid the Allies financially and economically much more than thus far, since this seemed to be the only way for them to win and also to prevent the war from extending onto the Western Hemisphere. The French ambassador, leaving the President's office on May 8th, stated that the United States could not let Germany win the war: this would be an immense danger to America." [19]

Again excitement rose to new heights when France surrendered. People began to realize that "even England might be invaded and lay America bare. Yet not even then did the public think of taking part in the war. But it was ready actively to prepare the defenses of the continent." [20]

"The sympathetic attitude towards the distress in Europe shown in the United States during the last few days," an Englishman thought, "may cause that country to adopt more constructive forms of assistance than have so far been forthcoming. But in all probability that assistance will come into effect only when the Allies have already fought the battle of life and death." [21]

France lost that battle before assistance could come. While her Premier sent desperate appeals to the President for "clouds" of airplanes, time ran out, and to the clamor for intervention the President was bound to disappoint the French. He knew that his inability to promise, however vaguely, American intervention, would constitute the collapse of the last barrier to surrender. But only Congress could declare war, Roosevelt reminded the French, who had already learned what to expect from Congress.

". . . the hand that held the dagger has struck it into the

back of its neighbor," Roosevelt commented when Mussolini attacked collapsing France on June 10, 1940, dismissing the President's repeated pleas to stay out of the war.

If the collapse of France awed the public in America, it drove the ruling circles into a panic. The Russians had calculated on a long war between the Axis and the West exhausting both, while the Soviet might would remain intact and growing. Hitler's quick victory had made him stronger than ever and might induce him to make Moscow the next target. The Soviets occupied the Baltic states in a hurry. Although *Pravda* still wrote on June 9: "The entry of the United States into the war is considered as possibly affording an opportunity for the governing sixty families to make a profitable war," and it still called those who refused to accept Hitler's peace warmongers and imperialists, Moscow resumed commercial discussions with Britain.

But Japan was overwhelmed with joy, after a period of embarrassment during which the German-Russian alliance had restrained them from making bold thrusts in the Pacific. "Now that France's fate has practically been sealed," Hochi commented on June 16, "Britain will have to meet with a similar fate soon. British influence on the seas, which has reigned supreme since Britain defeated the Spanish Armada, is now threatened with extinction." General Tanaka publicly scolded the "Japanese quarters" that dreaded American power to the extent of being "eager to avoid anything which may invite American displeasure. This is misreading the actual state of affairs," the General warned. "It would be playing into the hands of America, as a matter of fact. In the pursuit of her national policy, Japan should act courageously without regard to American sentiment. She must be prepared to come into conflict with America in the execution of her policy." [22]

The Japanese had to wait a few months until Hitler recognized his mistake in accepting Ribbentrop's assurance for the surrender of the British in the wake of the collapse of France. Then, in September, the German initiated the Tripartite pact, the alliance of the Axis with Japan, that was bound to extend the war over the entire globe. In the words of the Japanese military attaché in Berlin: "Japan has confirmed her resolution to march alongside Germany and Italy, whatever the difficulties. They are on the way to realize the new order in Europe so that, with common effort, a total new order may be instituted encompassing the whole world." [23]

Hitler's answer to American hostility was a sort of Nazi Doctrine that would keep Europe, united by and under Hitler, from political and commercial community with the United States. Darré, Hitler's Minister of Agriculture, declared in May, 1940: "The economic plan of the New Order will cause the United States to have from 30 to 40 million unemployed." [24] The Nazis explained the antagonism between the New Order and America as being a result of President Roosevelt's attitude toward the Reich. Yet an anti-American economic policy had been advocated as early as 1925 by F. Nonnenbrush. His book was made an official party textbook by Goering in 1940, shortly before he ordered total economic mobilization of Europe. "F. Nonnenbruch allayed an American attempt of economic invasion of Europe, and called for a German lead in the dual fight against European dependency upon America, and the fight against the threat of the domination of world economy by the United States." [25]

A German-dominated Europe was incomplete with a hostile Britain. She either had to be subdued by invasion or bombed into submission before Europe could be consolidated as the greatest power on earth, and through its colonies, economic, cultural, and political influence dominate the world. Britain and her fleet blocked those plans and protected America from direct danger. The most vital and immediate interest of America was to strengthen the British will and capacity to resist the Germans. "Hitler knows that he will have to break us in this island or lose the war," Britain's great war leader, Winston Churchill's call to arms rang out. "If we can stand up to him, all Europe may be free and the life of the world may move forward into broad, sunlit uplands. But if we fail, then the whole world, including the United States, including all that we have known and cared for, will sink into the abyss of a new Dark Age, made more sinister, and perhaps more protracted, by the lights of perverted science."

Yet there was pitifully little that the President could ship to Britain immediately. Even during those alarming moments when, in August, the Nazi Luftwaffe darkened the sky over Britain by day and inflamed her nights, important aid had to be sent by subterfuge, for isolationism still held sway in Congress and in the country.

In July, party conventions met to nominate candidates for the presidency. They knew the war would dominate the campaign and the public's choice for President. Developments in the war decisively influenced the tide and ebb of isolationist feeling and the election. The world understood that its fate was now at stake, but was bewildered by the importance of side issues to an America which still refused to take cognizance of the fact that her vital decision concerned no more herself alone, but the entire world.

". . . it is still true that the Americans are not adequately awake to the menace of Hitlerism. Despite the basic support they give national policies—which include the commitment to defeat Hitlerism—the people are far too apathetic and complacent. They are ready to be led. They are ready to be told what must be done. But if there is any leading into war, it will be the President who will lead Congress and the people, not the people who will lead the President. To date it has seemed as if Mr. Roosevelt were waiting for the people to make up their mind that the time for entry into the war had come . . . The longer he waits the more the obstructionists of national unity do their work. The President obviously does not want to go down in history as the man who manoeuvred and planned the American people into the great war. He fishes, rather, to be the man who sought and contrived for two years and more to defeat Hitlerism 'short of war,' and then only in response to public realization that war was inescapable, was willing to lead the nation into conflict," an English magazine commented.[26]

"Why does the United States not enter the war as a belligerent?" the same magazine asked. "The simplest answer is to say that to plunge a great nation into war, when it is not actually and physically under attack or under immediate threat, is a very terrible decision to make . . . To go to war, a democracy needs to be virtually unanimous. The task of coercing a substantial dissident minority is far too dangerous. Therefore the isolationist minority here has been given a tremendous advantage. It has only to retain the assumption of continuing minority existence to retain decisive authority." [27]

Another English magazine was more impatient with the American public. It reminded that the President "was bold enough to declare outright that the signal now for America was 'full steam ahead' in the provision of material help for the Allies," when Mussolini entered the war. "From the American as from the Allied point of view the danger was that help might come too late to be of any use to the Allies. [But] . . . the United States did not at once command enough internal unity to grant to the hard pressed Allies even the sort of 'non-belligerent' help that Italy had given Germany for nine months past." [28]

An embittered Frenchman was even more irritated with the ambiguous attitude of the American public. He saw Hitler's domination spreading first over Europe and threatening the world. America watched this drama as a spectator, "comfortably installed in an armchair, impassioned by the heroic struggle of G-men with a band of kidnappers, but not for a moment considering mounting the stage and helping her favorites." [29]

More pentrating observers were fascinated, however, with another drama of fateful suspense in which the President was making determined efforts to tear his nation from her complacency before the kidnappers overwhelmed the G-Men. This was the time of which the poet Lamartine had once portended that a century might be lost for the failing of a single man. Yet inside this single man a drama unfolded, too. Roosevelt wanted to keep the nation out of the war at the risk of even bigger catastrophe to her, when she might face alone the combined power of the totalitarian countries.

There were people in England, however, who remembered

how their own isolationism had helped Hitler grow to public danger. "When American visitors talk to British people nowadays," a writer warned, "their attitude resembles that of many Englishmen in 1938. Just as the British were dubious about running risks for the Sudeten areas, so Americans warn us that the United States will not entangle herself in a war fought, as they are apt to put it, to make Gibraltar and Malta safe for Mr. Chamberlain. We are now the 'distant country' struggling for existence, and America is the candid friend who lectures us in our hour of trial and warns us against trying to turn a conflict, localized in Europe, into what British Ministers used to call 'a world conflagration.' And now it is the Americans who are conscious of a moral dilemma. They want Hitler stopped, but they prefer someone else to do the job. . . . Cannot America remain, as President Roosevelt urged in his neutrality speech, aloof from Europe's horror and develop herself an unbattered haven for the future of civilization? . . . Heart and head can find arguments both for running risks and for isolationism." [30]

Others served notice that the character of the war would have to change before the Americans would feel obligated to join the fight. An Australian noted, "The British and French have not given sufficient weight to the obvious fact that for America to intervene in Europe with them would be a veritable Crusade, and one does not go crusading with people one suspects of having half their heart in the Crusade and the other half in the *lares* and *penates* of their own nation." [31]

The public abroad followed the conventions, the Presidential campaign, and the election from the single point of view of whether or not their result would promote peace or war with the totalitarian powers. It was taken for granted that Roosevelt's re-election would compel the dictators to make large-scale concessions or to extend the war. If anyone else were nominated and elected, even another Democrat, it was thought, a compromise, very favorable to the dictators, would result, and many believed that it would mean a new war soon after.

"The public in the Allied countries wish, of course, that [Roosevelt] be re-elected. His ideas are known. They are completely favorable to us," a French magazine commented, "and there is little risk that the President might in any way hamper seriously our actions. Yet one wonders what his relation will be, if re-elected, to Congress. . . . Many times he has manoeuvered with a caution bordering on timidity to get along with it. In the case of aid to Finland, for instance, he did not dare to ask Congress to allow him to sell arms directly to Finland despite universal sympathy for the fate of that country. It is thus an open question whether the President will not be blocked totally in his actions in case of his election for a third term." [32]

The Democratic Party convention nominated Roosevelt despite strong sentiment against breaking a precedent that excluded a third term for any President. In his broadcast accepting the nomination, Mr. Roosevelt said: "We face one of the great choices of history. It is not alone a choice of government by the people versus dictatorship. It is not alone the choice between moving forward or moving back. It is the continuance of civilization as we know it versus the ultimate destruction of all that we have held dear; religion against godlessness; the ideal of justice against the practice of force; moral decency versus the firing squad; the courage to speak out and to act versus the false lullaby of appeasement. . . . The fact which dominates our world is the fact of armed aggression."

Roosevelt's chances for re-election were considered to be good by Harold J. Laski. "Mr. Roosevelt has made government in these eight years genuinely interesting to the ordinary man," he wrote, "because he has related it to the ordinary man's interest. What do the Republicans offer instead. A desiccated version of the New Deal, suited to the palate of the Economic Royalists. That is why Mr. Roosevelt, despite the antagonism, due to personal pique, of John L. Lewis, will keep the full strength of the Labor vote, and, with the important backing of Mr. H. A. Wallace as his running mate, pretty nearly the full strength of the farmer's vote." [33]

Roosevelt ran against a strong opponent, Wendell Willkie, a colorful, fascinating personality who had become a popular figure in spite of the fact that as a corporation lawyer representing private utilities he had led an unsuccessful campaign against the expansion of TVA. He was practically forced on the Republican convention by the rank and file, and was no less internationalist than Roosevelt. But people in the democratic world feared the men behind Willkie, the old guard that he would have to appease or fight in his own party if elected. His internationalism notwithstanding, most people in Europe thought that Willkie's victory would mean less help to the Allies and eventual appeasement of the dictators.

Roosevelt made several moves just at that time. He sold fifty old but serviceable destroyers to Britain, in exchange for military bases in British possessions in the Western Hemisphere; he advocated conscription, a potentially explosive issue; and he appointed two known internationalist Republicans to cabinet posts. Such bold steps in the campaign constituted promises of determined action to help the Allies win once Roosevelt was elected.

For the world, this election was to decide whether freedom was to survive in the coming decade or whether might would rule over right, with the small and weak doomed to servitude.

The Economist followed the Presidential campaign and commented on its program. On July 6 it surveyed the two candidates: "Judged by the available evidence, Mr. Wilkie would make an able and distinguished President," the magazine stated. "But his historical importance lies less in his possible future virtues as a President than in his actual present character as a candidate. The strong probability is that the next President of the United States will be Franklin D. Roosevelt. Mr. Willkie's service to humanity—it is a very large one—will be to save the United States from its usual election-year predicament of having no foreign policy. Until very recently, it seemed almost certain that isolationism and intervention would be an issue, perhaps the main issue, of the Presidential campaign. If the President's foreign policy is criticized at all during the campaign, it will be for not moving far enough and fast enough in support of Britain."

Two weeks later, the same magazine set forth the issue in the election for the rest of the world: "The European war, and the President has the unique claim of having consistently used his office to teach the American people to see straight and to think realistically about the world tragedy. But in American eyes, there are constitutional issues at least as deep. There is revulsion against un-American strong government, against the 'personal' rule that Harding expressly repudiated when he succeeded Woodrow Wilson. . . . In sum, there is a wide belief that to take the unprecedented step of according to Franklin Roosevelt what was refused by George Washington, namely, a third term in office, might be to destroy the safeguards of 150 years of constitutional development. . . . In democracies no man is indispensable. Mr. Roosevelt is sincerely conscious of this, and his attitude towards a third term has been correct and scrupulous."

In further issues, the magazine warned the British public not to indulge in the attitude that there was no real difference between the candidates and that Roosevelt would win anyway. It elaborated on the difference in their views, purporting: "In the field of foreign affairs . . . Mr. Willkie's line of criticism lies not against the President's policies but against his manner of executing them. Mr. Willkie claims that he will be a more effective opponent of the Nazis than Mr. Roosevelt has been. All this, of course, makes the most excellent reading for the citizens of beleaguered Britain, though it is difficult to avoid a certain amount of suspicious doubt when Mr. Willkie attacks the President for the 'inflammatory statements' he has made on many occasions against the Dictators. It is not merely that this criticism ignores the great moral effects that Mr. Roosevelt's statements have had—an effect that should not be derided merely because it failed to prevent the outbreak of war; the real danger is that this line of argument might provide an entering wedge for those leanings towards appeasement of the Nazis which are present among the sectors of opinion who form Mr. Willkie's most devoted supporters, however absent they may be from his own mind."

The Economist made clear how deep the difference in outlook had grown between conservatives in a country fighting for its survival and those in another one, free from immediate danger. It called Willkie's arguments against the New Deal obsolete, saying: "No democracy can be successful unless it finds room for adventurous enterprise. These things are axiomatic. But it is the role of the statesman to emphasize them, or rather to reveal the other facet of the truth, that democracy will crash in ruins unless some means is found by which the State, without infringing the fundamental liberties of the citizen, can turn its attention to the problems which it alone can solve. That democracy and free enterprise are inseparable is true; but it is far more important at this stage of history to prove that democracy and communal enterprise are compatible. This, for all his mistakes, is the vision that Mr. Roosevelt has seen. This, for all his charm, his sincerity and his energy, is what makes Mr. Willkie sound like a voice from the past." [34]

Viewing the close of the campaign, the magazine found solace for the British in discovering that "after all the abuse that has been heaped by American writers on Great Britain for her blindness, her slowness, her effeteness, our brand of democracy is not so much inferior to the American, when it comes to the acid test. We both share the same weakness and the same strength. Indeed, it has become our historic mission to hold out in our fortress and give the Americans time to think things out. If we play our part, they will play theirs." [35]

Indeed, British fortitude in the Battle of Britain had a deep effect on the campaign. "News of the Battle of Britain and its various implications for American security, is almost swamping the Presidential campaign, with a corresponding advantage for Mr. Roosevelt, since Mr. Willkie must either parade his support for the President in every speech or else keep silent on the one supremely interesting topic." [36] In conclusion the magazine definitely gave up on the Republican candidate. It said: "We in England are rather more than mere spectators at this election; our fate is its main topic. Superficially, there is little to choose between the two candidates in the ardour of their desire to help Britain hold the fortress of liberty. If anything, Mr. Wilkie's protestations have been the stronger, and there is a good deal of substance in his argument that he, the successful businessman, would be better fitted than Mr. Roosevelt, the enemy of Big Business, to organize the great increase in munitions production out of which alone effective aid to Britain can come . . . [but] it is a little alarming to observe that Mr. Willkie conceives of the problem of munitions production so exclusively in terms of the sort of organization to which a successful businessman is accustomed. It needs more than that; it needs the establishment of priorities, the restriction of civilian demand, the mobilisation of labor, the rationing of plant capacity and raw materials. Is Mr. Willkie, whose campaign is based on the liberation of free enterprise from present controls, the relief of profits from the burden of taxation and the restriction of the sphere of government activity, a better man to accomplish this than Mr. Roosevelt, advised by men like Mr. Knudsen, of General Motors, and Mr. Stettinius, of United Steel? . . . Perhaps it is permissible, in an issue of *The Economist* which will not reach the United States until after the election, to endorse, from the British angle, the comment that the known vices of Mr. Roosevelt are to be preferred to the unknown virtues of Mr. Willkie." [37]

When Roosevelt was re-elected, it was "a more severe blow to the Nazis than many military victories," to an English magazine. ". . . a big and generous personality will lead America not only through the period of war but also in the momentous period of settlement." [38] Another paper called it "a very great personal triumph for Mr. Roosevelt." It said: "Everything was against him, including many papers that formerly supported him. Many of his personal followers—notably Mr. Farley, the organizer of his previous victories—were ostentatiously lukewarm. He had to fight against the prejudice raised by the third-term issue, and he was the target of an unparalleled volume of vicious and slandering personal abuse." [39]

"Mr. Roosevelt's re-election means to Europeans," in the view of a Swedish newspaper, "that America's foreign policy will be continued with the same force and consistency. This policy has been nearly unanimously approved by the American people because both Mr. Roosevelt and Mr. Willkie kept the same line." [40]

"The re-election of Mr. Roosevelt was just as vital for the destiny of the United States and of the world as was that of President Lincoln in 1864 for the second time during the secession war," Foreign Minister Aranha of Brazil stated.[41]

"The Americas never before have felt such a close sentiment of brotherhood as that which unites them today," *Dia,* in Montevideo, wrote the day after the election. "There never before has been an Americanist of Mr. Roosevelt's stature and it is doubtfully true that in the future all humanity will pronounce his name as a synonym of justice, law and democracy."

"I hail it as a most fortunate occurrence that at this awe-striking climax in world affairs," said Winston Churchill, expressing the relief of his countrymen at the result of the election, "there should stand at the head of the American Republic a famous statesman long versed and experienced in the work of government and administration, in whose heart there burns the fire of resistance to aggression and oppression, and whose sympathies and nature make him the sincere and undoubted champion of justice and freedom and of the victims of wrongdoing wherever they may dwell." [42]

He spoke for England, in the fall of 1940, where "Every morning the eyes show the lack of sleep more and more, and every evening the constant skyward glances and the hypersensitiveness to sound reveal the nervous tension and the dread of the night to come. The nights are indeed terrible with the malignant droning of the German bombers above, the glittering brilliance of the shell-bursts, the whining descent of the bombs, the earth-shaking roar of the explosions, the red glare of the fires that follow, the chattering rain of the jagged razor-edged shell-fragments, the reverberations (the one comfort on such nights) of the anti-aircraft guns, the houses, disembowelled and smashed and split into the deserted streets, the dead and the injured. No one who has lived through these nights, that have only just begun, will be the same when they are over. Awful as the horror and the tragedy are, and unendurable, almost, the apprehension of what is still to come, there is a pride and a glory in being a Londoner in London *now,* in London . . . last stronghold of freedom in Europe." [43]

In the view of a Japanese paper, the American people had missed a great opportunity by re-electing Roosevelt. "It is fair to conclude," the article ran, "that the Roosevelt Administration will adhere stoutly to its policy of positive aid for Britain and will take every possible measure to strengthen it. Since it holds that America's security and prosperity is inseparably bound up with Britain's, the future course of war events may eventually cause it to throw America into the turmoil of hostilities in breach of its pledge to the nation. . . . America's aid to Britain is understandable, in view of her traditional relationship with that country, but it is difficult to understand why America must continue her aid to Chiang Kai-Shek interminably. Mr. Willkie's election might have given America an opportunity to rectify her past mistaken policy, but Mr. Roosevelt's election has robbed her of this opportunity." [44]

Another Japanese paper concluded from the result of the election that Japan would "make redoubled efforts to establish an East Asian sphere of mutual prosperity and to promote the creation of a new world order in pursuance of the fundamental aim of the tripartite act concluded between Germany, Italy and herself, while closely watching the future development of American Far Eastern policy." [45]

The Germans argued that it was America who had forced England and France into war for American national interests and for Roosevelt's personal interest, because only in this way could he attain dictatorial powers. "America pressed for war against the newly won European consciousness, while following closely her own interests as she slowly changed her front from neutral to non-belligerent, eventually under various disguises to take actual part in the war . . . as frontier guards of a faraway unthreatened continent." [46]

People abroad, unfamiliar with the years of frustration the President had endured at the hands of his own rebellious party in Congress, and who did not know how powerless Roosevelt had been right after his first triumphal re-election, may have believed the rumor that he would become a sort of dictator. Some cultivated people in the Americas, who looked to the United States for democratic leadership in their dictator-ridden lands, despaired when Roosevelt ran for the third term. They echoed the arguments of Roosevelt's bitterest opponents. A social scientist from Haiti expounded: "It is impossible not to believe that Franklin Roosevelt's second re-election will completely upset the American democracy. It will enhance the personality of the President and lead to the growth of the central power which will have all the appearances of a dictatorship. Knowing the temperament of the Anglo-Saxon people, there will definitely be strong opposition in some of the forty-eight states to the increased power of the President, an opposition which might even give rise to a new movement for secession. . . . Such encouragement to dictatorship as a third term for the President might even sap the foundations of Christian civilization everywhere." [47]

But a French author exhorted those who feared a Roosevelt dictatorship to compare and distinguish between a dictator and a democratic statesman: "Did you happen to see shortly before the war a newsreel in which President Roosevelt appeared on the screen following Adolf Hitler? Do you remember the tense atmosphere of 'black magic' over the obscure room, pierced by the brutal burst of light from the projector, directed onto the Master who held the invisible and trembling masses by his frantic voice? Can you envision the inhuman glance in that implacable face from which the soul seemed absent? The strange power of Hitler's magnetism derived from his monstrous detachment. But then a familiar scene appeared on the screen, people crowding nonchalantly around a platform from which a man was making a speech. Do you remember that bright face reflecting intelligence and generosity, animated by a legendary smile, a living symbol of hope fighting against destiny? After an instinctive feeling of anguish and near panic that overcame every sensible person as he divined the satanic power in Hitler, Roosevelt by his mere presence made everyone feel relaxed, hopeful and safe." [48]

10

THE THIRD ELECTION

"After the election, President Roosevelt shot ahead with strikingly long quick strides. On November 6, 1940 . . . he announced that he had asked 'the most sympathetic consideration' for the British Purchasing Commission's request that the number of aeroplanes being built for Great Britain be increased by 12,000 to a grand total of 26,000. . . . On November 8 he announced that one-half of the United States war output . . . would now go to Britain, and one-half to the United States. On the threshold of his third term as President he seemed to be embarked on a policy of 'full steam ahead' in helping Great Britain, short of war. . . . Mr. Roosevelt on December 17 announced his plan. He prefaced it by the statement that American help was a matter of American policy and of American self interest, Britain's fight (he repeated) being America's defense against the common danger. He therefore indicated that the solution was to turn the British into American orders and to 'lease' the products or 'sell them under mortgage' to Great Britain. . . . There were other methods, he said, 'gifts among them' ('and we may come to it yet,' he added). . . . By December 17, therefore, Mr. Roosevelt had given warning to Germany that the United States was inflexibly disposed to supply Great Britain with all the armaments she might need, whether she could pay for them or not. It thereafter became the propagandist slogan in the United States that her role was that of the 'arsenal of democracy.'"[1]

"The tide has continued to run strongly, and the two symbols of its sweep have appeared. One is the general dropping of the last three words in the phrase 'all aid short of war'. . . . President Roosevelt has ceased to employ them. . . . The other symbol of the new American temper is the Lend-Lease Bill. It is one of the most drastic and momentous measures in all American history. It represents a sharp repudiation of the national platforms: a complete abandonment of the rules of international law regarding the status of a neutral. It also illustrates Mr. Roosevelt's remarkable ingenuity."[2] This ingenuity trapped Hitler; "[Mr. Roosevelt] played his cards with masterly skill. His own isolationists are disarmed by the force of his contention that the only hope of keeping America out of war is to enable Great Britain to win. . . . Hitler is left in hopeless hesitation whether deliberately to provoke America into war, thus courting hostilities with the most powerful State in the world or to watch that State methodically but with vast momentum mobilizing the whole of its gigantic productive force for the benefit of Germany's existing foes. It is a bitter choice for the Fuehrer, and whichever way he decides he loses. He has proclaimed his contempt for democracy. The greatest democracy in either hemisphere has taken up his challenge, and by so doing sealed his fate."[3]

One thing was sure, that Roosevelt's emergency actions between the elections and his inauguration had "solved the most formidable crisis with which Britain and the democratic nations had been faced." The British had no more money with which to buy war material, and unless they could obtain such material, the war was lost. And lost not only by the British Empire, but by the Americans as well, for, as Roosevelt said on December 29th, "if Great Britain goes down, the Axis will control Europe, Asia, Africa, Australasia and the high seas, and all of us in America will be living at the point of a gun."

The facile solution was that proposed by the international financiers and other "men of banal mind," as the President called them at a press conference on December 17. They suggested that the Johnson and Neutrality Acts should be amended to permit Britain to borrow from the United States, at low interest, the necessary billions. But Franklin Roosevelt, guardian at the gate of time, had no intention of repeating the worst mistake of the last war. Instead there was forming in his mind a solution which in grandeur of concept was greater than anyone dreamed. While the free world waited anxiously for his decision he went away on a long Caribbean cruise, during which, isolated from distracting influences, he formulated his plan.

On January 6, reporting to the Seventy-Seventh Congress on the State of the Union, he indicated something of its nature when he said of the Allies: "The time is near when they will not be able to pay for [munitions] in ready cash. We cannot, and will not, tell them they must surrender because of their present inability to pay for weapons which we know they must have. . . . For what we send abroad, we shall be repaid within a reasonable time after the close of hostilities in similar materials, or at our option, in other goods which they can produce and which we need . . ."

"Granted that this was a magnificent gesture of friendship and good will. Granted that it saved Britain from defeat. It is nevertheless true that the Act established a principle which may govern a new world order after the war is over. For in effect it lays down that no one nation can remain forever rich and prosperous if other nations lack the necessaries of existence. It was the first recognition of a 'have' nation that, for its own sake, it must share of its plenty with a 'have not.' The establishment of this principle has been awaited by the world for a thousand years."[4] Indeed, Roosevelt's Lend-Lease was the forerunner of the Marshall Plan, Point Four, and other postwar aid programs which ran on the same principle that the Lend-Lease program had established. "The happiness of future generations of Americans may well depend on how effective and how immediate we can make our aid felt," the President warned in his State of the Union message.

The Nazi press branded Lend-Lease "an eccentric idea" which one need not even discuss seriously. "It is but a provocation that reveals the President's warmongering. He acts as if he were pushed by public opinion, by the voice of the people. Actually he is a warmonger. He himself feels this strongly. Otherwise he would not need always to excuse his policy with the statement that it is to serve to keep America out of the war."[5] But Hitler did not miss the meaning of Lend-Lease, as a Swiss paper pointed out when it remembered that the Fuehrer had on January 30 called the year 1941 the year of decision.[6] His statement acknowledged the need for a decision in the war before Lend-Lease aid actually reached Britain. The Swiss paper reported that it was supposed in Berlin that the aid could not come forth before 1942.

The Italian press attributed the new concept of aid for England as part of "a plan by Roosevelt and an alien Jewish group behind him for economic and financial conquest which, at the same time, would serve the revenge of the Jewish minority on 'the great Aryan nations of Europe.'"[7] Mussolini himself debunked the pretense that the aid was to serve the defense of democracy, in his reply to Roosevelt's State of the Union speech, following at a respectful distance the speech of the Fuehrer. "What is now happening in the United States," he thundered, "is one of the biggest hoaxes in world history. The American interventionalism is based on a lie. It is a lie that America is still a democracy, since it is an oligarchy ruled by an economic ally, financed by Jewry and practiced through a highly personal form of dictatorship."[8]

Europe, accepting Pax Germanica, denounced the Anglo-Saxons who were disturbing its peaceful development. This was the Nazi slogan for use among its satellites and collaborationists, as against democracy, which would require victory in a new world war before it might establish peace and prosperity in Europe. A French collaborationist took exception to the part of Roosevelt's speech in which he had predicted that the oppressed people would rise against their tyrants. "Thus despite our defeat," he wrote, "they still count on us. We remain continental soldiers, this time not in a foreign war but in a sort of European civil war which they want to inflame with our help."[9] A Swiss magazine also faithfully echoed Nazi propaganda. "No European power, except England during the American War of Independence, ever has taken a menacing attitude nor committed the tiniest hostile act toward the great American Republic. As Mussolini said in his latest speech: 'It is more probable that the inhabitants of Mars might invade America than the soldiers of the Axis.'"[10]

America's aim was obvious to the Nazi press. "It is Roosevelt's plan," they repeated, "to block the path of Europe toward peace and to exploit the continuation of European crisis for the advantage of a giant continent, which, in any case, is about to smother itself in the riches of its gold and resources." [11]

Nazi propaganda in Britain stressed that Roosevelt and America were bent on acquiring all profitable British positions in the world while they helped Britain ruin herself. In America the fifth column denounced Roosevelt for wanting the Americans to fight Britain's war. One and the same German author alternated between both lines. First he tried to find a reason why Roosevelt was so keen on sacrificing Americans for British interests. "Franklin Roosevelt, in contrast to most of his compatriots," he said, "has never broken inwardly with Europe. He admires the old European traditions and the life and attitudes of the British aristocracy. He has an unmistakable weakness for European rulers. He was also the first American President who invited an English king to Washington." But the author admitted also the opposite point of view. "The question was often asked," he wrote, "whether Roosevelt and his government did actually play sheer American power politics, England being but the means to that end. This supposition is being confirmed in the columns of the American newspapers, by speeches of American politicians, even by Roosevelt's own words." [12]

However, when it appeared that it was in vain that the Battle of Britain had been won, since the Germans were about to win the Battle of the Atlantic by sinking ships carrying war materials and food to Britain, even some English papers, in their bitterness, repeated Nazi propaganda slogans against America. ". . . President Roosevelt made a certain statement," a respectable magazine wrote, "of which the effect was to warn Hitler that the war would continue until victory for democracy was won. Yet the United States was not at that time taking any part in the fighting. Her hands were free and her forces intact. No man can tell how those forces will be used, before we see the end of this war; but the present fact—and it is facts we need for our sustenance—is that Washington is already helping to call the tunes, but is hardly helping to pay the piper. While Germany and Britain are reducing each other's cities and industries and their citizens' health to ruin, there are three Great Powers, the United States, Russia, and Japan, who are thereby being placed impregnably in the position where they, and not either Germany or Britain, may decide what is to be built upon the ruins. What President Roosevelt said on June 6 was, it is true, on the face of it merely designed to squash the suggestion, at that time being freely made, that his talks with Mr. Winant (the U.S. Ambassador to Britain who had lately flown home to consult with the President) had had to do with the possibility of peace. 'Absolutely nothing like it,' he said. 'Not even the tenth cousin of a peace offer (from Hitler) or anything like that.'"[13]

While the writer was baffled by the revelation that the head of a foreign country appeared to decide on Britain's life and death, he resented that the British people accepted it as a fact of life.

"The interesting thing was that he [Roosevelt] spoke with such decisive effect about a European affair, and that the men and women of Great Britain hung upon his words. Would it be going too far to say that we have reached the pass when British opinion looks to Washington as much as, even more, than to London for guidance about the prospects in an affair that is being financed, so to speak, by British lives and British welfare?"

The article was written while Rudolf Hess was parachuting into Scotland. Rumor had it that he was carrying a peace offer by Hitler. The British public was not informed on the details of the interview with the Fuehrer's favorite, but the American Ambassador received and forwarded complete information to the President.

Those people in England who believed the fate of democracy in the world hinged on the outcome of the war were rather irritated with America's reluctance to enter the fight. But those who remembered how long they had hesitated to go to war admired America's generosity and the broad concept of her foreign policy with respect to the war in Europe.

"If the American people," a magazine stated, "are not themselves deeply interested in the struggle, then they have given 'aid to Britain' on a scale more lavish and generous than any people in history have ever given in war to any belligerent. If, as their Government constantly reiterates, their own vital interests are concerned, then they have not nearly done enough, not for us but themselves." [14]

Others refused to look upon America's attitude toward the war as determined by her consciousness of her own interests and freely admired American idealism. "It would be doing the great American democracy a grievous wrong to attribute her constantly increasing help solely to practical considerations. The moral factor weighs heavily in her determination to assist Britain and her allies in their fight against gangsterism. Signs are not lacking that under the wise and inspiring guidance of President Roosevelt the Americans are rapidly moving towards a decision to take a hand in the fight themselves if circumstances make this imperative. They realize the futility of goods, food and equipment, which they are generously providing under the Lend-Lease Bill, being sunk in mid-Atlantic instead of reaching safe destination. Whatever they choose to call it, there is little doubt that before long they will be convoying or protecting their shipments." [15]

In fact, this logic did not escape Hitler. He had seen the handwriting on the wall when the cash and carry provision had been added to the Neutrality Act. When Britain ran out of cash it was to be expected that American credit in one form or another would enable them to continue getting war material. When Nazi U-boats endangered delivery of the goods bought in America, what was more logical for America than to help Britain fight off the U-boats by extending the United States defense zone, occupying Iceland and Greenland, and convoying the shipments in the extended zone of the Western hemisphere, until it became necessary to shoot Nazi submarines at sight. America was bound to enter the shooting war.

Foreseeing such developments, Hitler's plan was to finish off Britain before America was strong enough to launch a massive attack on Germany. This plan suffered a setback when Britain leased military bases to America. The Nazis became afraid that Britain might transfer military bases in the Eastern Atlantic and the Mediterranean and force them to risk a war with America lest they lose the Battle of the Atlantic. Prompted by their fear of total American intervention before Britain could be defeated, the Nazis concluded the Tripartite Pact with Japan in the Fall of 1940. Commenting on the Pact, *Pravda* in Moscow wrote: "The front against Britain is being extended and the war may take on huge proportions. Undoubtedly the extension of military help to England by the United States was an important stimulus to the Pact; also, the transfer of bases to the United States in the Western Hemisphere and British consent to transfer her bases in the Far East and Australia also." [16]

Nothing so drastic followed. Sober British opinion did not expect America to rush into the war, although the Battle of the Atlantic remained critical for the British in the year 1941. "I can imagine," a writer commented, "that after accepting some form of naval action, the Americans might soon come to tolerate a gradually extending use of their Air Force by an offensive arm. . . . But I cannot imagine Americans consenting to the despatch of an expeditionary force to Europe. . . . The President is very properly bent on preserving the nation's unity, and my own decided impression is that if ever he crosses the line into war—if ever, in plain words, he orders shooting—it will be under clear provocation in defense of undisputable American interests." [17]

Another writer even wondered whether an immediate American armed intervention would not do more harm than good in the battle. "The Battle of the Atlantic is now severely straining our resources," the article ran, "in ships and maritime personnel. The air attack upon our ports is also formidable; it will test to the full our powers of organization and civilian morale. But we are making better head against the attack on commerce than we made in 1917, and there is no indication to suggest any weakening of civilian spirit and staying powers. . . . It is doubtless true that actual American entry into the war would make a great moral difference, it is certainly open to question whether the immediate physical effects would be of value to the British cause. There is no telling how American opinion might react. . . .

You cannot declare war in a democracy when as many people are against it as now take this stand in the United States." [18]

Under such conditions, German optimism was understandable. One of their more serious political magazines stated: "The British people more and more are becoming convinced that Hitler's Germany has seized leadership of Europe not only with respect to military successes but also to her production, which surpasses hers by far, even considering American aid to Britain . . ." [19]

The British and their allies did not underestimate the strength of American isolationism, although it was slowly losing ground. A French analyst noted that, unexpectedly, heavy industry in America was resisting the country's involvement in war. "They thought that the extension of war production would increase government powers on a large sector of industry," he asserted, and they were even afraid that the President would make use of this opportunity to institute nationalization. Nor did they forget the effects of the war of 1914-1918 on production. An excessive industrialization might again generate over-production, leading to social upheaval as soon as war needs were over." [20]

The strength of isolationism fluctuated. It appeared to be on the wane in the spring of 1941. A Swiss newspaper reported. "In the fall of 1940, the surprising resistance of the British made a deep impression on the American public, which then began to listen to arguments other than isolationist. Tremendous propaganda in the press, movies and radio hammered into the public mind that the British position in Europe was the 'first defense wall' for the Western Hemisphere. From that moment on a policy of intervention, which the President could not take seriously before, became probable to the highest degree. The change in public opinion could be observed from week to week. The conviction spread that America ought to give England all, literally all, aid that she could. The qualification 'short of war' that had played such an important role in the Presidential election campaign faded into oblivion. The power the President received from Congress to handle Lend-Lease aid eliminated the constitutional obstacles of a policy of intervention. The law conveys the power of a dictator on the President in the sense this word once had in Ancient Rome." [21]

"Thus, step by step, the United States became engaged, in the course of 1941, on a world-wide policy," a French observer noted.[22] "It extended over the two oceans that tied her to the Old World. The idealistic and political factors as well as the economic impelled her to intervene in the war under all but the military form to prepare the 'American peace' for the future."

However, when a situation arose in which the dire need for American military intervention appeared to have vanished, the public fell back into isolationism. This was the case when, to the surprise of much of the world public and to many governments, among them that of the Soviet Union, Hitler on June 22, 1941 hurled his full military might in an attack on Russia.

Although it was the generally accepted opinion that the Soviet armies would not be able to put up serious resistance to the Nazi onslaught, the attack caused immense relief in Britain. Even a beaten Russia would bog down huge Nazi forces and deter them from Britain. Ultimately, the British thought, a big continental army could be recruited from the huge Russian manpower. This in cooperation with British sea and air power and with American aid, would inflict the decisive blow to the Nazis. People the world over wondered why Hitler had attacked Russia, since Stalin was apparently ready to make great concessions in order to deter him from that fateful course. A Swiss magazine pointed to the historical analogy with Napoleon: "The most stupefying fact is the similarity of the political and military situation, and consequently the reactions. At that time Britain and France had almost equal empires, the first on the seas and throughout the world, the second on the continent, in Europe. Today Germany has taken the place of France. At that time the entire Continent was afraid of France because of the revolution of 1789 and its consequences, as it fears today Germany because of the Hitlerian revolution. Hitler's attempt [to invade Britain] corresponds exactly to that of Napoleon." [23] Indeed, both dictators gave up the invasion of Britain and attacked Russia instead, in order to avoid war on two fronts.

In London, according to a Swiss newspaper report,[24] it was believed that "Hitler hoped to gain fresh sympathy in the whole western world by his attack on the Bolshevik Soviet Union. This was to be the case first of all in America and Vichy France, in the countries already occupied by the Germans, and perhaps even in England when the moment would be propitious for a new peace offensive. In London it was firmly believed on the next day following the attack that Hitler's reasoning was clever, but that it had not the slightest chance of success in the really important circles in America and Britain." But the same paper printed a United Press report from Washington to the effect that "President Roosevelt might be reluctant to alienate the Catholics in the United States by measures friendly to Russia. . . . It was expected there that Roosevelt would follow a cautious course towards Russia and concentrate on his aid to Britain." [24]

Churchill left no time for a display of bewilderment or hesitation. He immediately declared Soviet Russia to be an ally in arms. Roosevelt, on June 24, promised American aid to Russia.

The British, relieved of German bombing and grateful to the Russians, were enthusiastic for helping the new ally. "It was, perhaps, inevitable," a magazine stated, "that the entry of Russia into the war and the gallant and determined resistance of her people should have been received with a sense of relief, almost of relaxation, in the British Commonwealth and even more in the United States. When air bombardment dwindles to a negligible formality, and the unknown perils of invasion recede into the haze of the future, the optimist comes into his own again. . . . It is with feelings of disappointment, almost frustration, that the British people and their friends in the world have come to realize the narrow bounds set at this moment to our power of giving effective military help to Russia. By day and night, in all weather, the Royal Air Force has maintained attacks of increasing weight on enemy shipping and on targets in Germany and the occupied territories. . . . But this offensive, powerful and successful in itself, has not deflected the German command from its objectives in Russia, and has fallen far short of the assault with all arms which the German adventure invited." [25]

"In September, 1939, when Germany flung all her armed might against Poland," an article recalled, "leaving some nine divisions at the Siegfried line, the Allies missed the great chance of attacking Germany from the West. Today we are confronted with a similar, if not identical situation: the whole armed might of Germany is battling Russia and some twenty German divisions are holding the front from Petsamo down to Biarritz. The golden chance of erecting a second and most inconvenient front for Germany, is there." [26]

An official British communiqué announced the conclusion of a twenty year Treaty of Friendship with the Soviet Union and that "full understanding was reached between the two parties with regard to the urgent tasks of creating a second front in Europe in 1942."

Official policy in America was heavily influenced by the almost unanimous opinion of military experts that the Germans would overcome organized resistance in Russia within six weeks. Any effective aid to Russia would require more time than the experts gave to the Russians. Many already were worrying about what was going to happen when Hitler defeated Russia and again turned with full fury against England. Others were more concerned with what the future might bring if the Russians should succeed in stopping the Nazi offensive and become one of the main powers dictating the peace.

"The massive reluctance of the American people to enter the 'shooting war' was powerfully reinforced by the attack on Russia," an English magazine purported.[27] "When the nearly incredible news came over the cables, I watched that nation lying back into its easy chair with an audible sigh of relief. Ex-President Hoover drew the moral on the very first day, when he declared that such case as there was for American belligerency had now been destroyed. . . . The Russians would do all the necessary fighting on land; it would suffice that Americans should make the munitions. I heard this said even by experts who predicted that the Russians would collapse in a few weeks. . . .

"My reading of the public pulse is that America as a whole would acquiesce in any moral and aerial action which events rendered necessary. But I can imagine no set of circumstances, even in the distant future, that would exhort its assent to a European expedition. Before that happens its mood must radically change. Is the President trying to change it? I cannot answer that question with confidence, but I will venture to say this: the nearer I got to the White House during my stay in Washington, the less confident were those I met."

At this point the writer asked the agonizing question that was unspoken on so many lips in Britain.

"Here, then, is the problem that we have to face in our dealings with America. Can we hope to win this war, save by an expedition in the West? And if that be necessary, as it surely is, are we strong enough or can we soon be strong enough, to undertake it without American participation? . . . If, as I believe, we need American military aid, we must begin without delay to state the case for it, plainly and frankly. . . . The Americans without our prompting will not 'spontaneously' come in. In that event it is with the Russians that we must come to terms over the eventual European campaign in two fronts. Are we doing that? . . . I do not know the answer to that question."

Another English weekly analyzed the recurrent American isolationism. "There was a definite slump lately in participationist sentiment in the United States," it reported, "and a proportionate gain in isolationism. Why was this so? . . . It is certainly significant that the recession of American opinion was that a readiness to envisage going to war coincided fairly closely with the Nazi invasion of Russia. People in America, very rationally, said to themselves: Hitler has turned east instead of west, and so the threat to us is no longer imminent." [28]

With the relative passivity of the British, the war took on a new meaning—a gigantic struggle between Slav and Teuton. If this momentary turn could be accepted at face value, outsiders were free to wish for or help attain the victory of the race that stood closer to their ethnic origin or preference. But in the moment one of the two defeated the other, the rest of the world would be threatened by either Nazi or Bolshevik domination.

If the President wanted to make clear what the war was about and what kind of a world should emerge from the struggle, he had to do so without delay. The newspapers in the lands of the Tripartite Pact dwelt stubbornly on the anomaly of the situation. "As the upholder of Democracy, President Roosevelt has declared that the current international conflagration is a struggle for the supremacy between Democracy and Autocracy," a Japanese newspaper jibed, "but he is assisting the Soviet Union which is the upholder of Communism and the most autocratic of all autocracies." [29]

The President dispelled the confusion at his momentous first meeting, in August, 1941, with Winston Churchill. The President laid down the principles of the peace that were to follow the struggle, the same principles that, in his view, were at issue in the armed conflict. The result of the meeting was the Atlantic Charter, to which all the nations opposing Nazism were expected to adhere.

"Roosevelt and Churchill have worked out a Magna Charta of freedom," wrote a Swiss paper.[30] "It will affect not only the course of the war but also the future history of mankind. . . . It means that America takes on herself the moral responsibility not only to do what is possible to eliminate the Nazi regime in Germany, but also to take part in the peace conference and help to create a better world. . . . As a propaganda instrument," the Swiss paper further remarked, "it prepares the American public for a direct community of action with Britain."

The Charter reasserted the "Four Freedoms," containing those "principles of morality" which the President had stated in his message to Congress of January 6, 1941. He also declared that only a peace based on the following freedoms would be acceptable to America:

(1) Freedom of speech and expression—everywhere in the world.

(2) Freedom of religious worship—everywhere in the world.
(3) Freedom from want everywhere in the world.
(4) Freedom from fear, through world-wide reduction of armaments—everywhere in the world.

Thus the President declared an ideological war. He accepted Hitler's challenge, admitting of no compromise. "The President wants to assure the freedom of the individual but he also wants to free humanity from misery and from the fear of misery," a Swiss paper commented.[31] "The task he set to himself is immense when one realizes that even in England, indeed even in the United States, one-third of the population lives below the level that has been officially noted as existential minimum. Roosevelt undoubtedly wanted to take the wind from the sails of totalitarian propaganda. While they declare social freedom to be the right of master races alone, Roosevelt will help the masses without regard to geographical borders or racial differences. . . . This is a realistic peace program and liberal in its means, definitely the best that can be planned under the present circumstances. The American President recommends a 'New Deal' among all peoples of the world."

The Charter elaborated on the Four Freedoms and declared the right of all nations to trade on equal terms and promised the establishment of a permanent system of security that would prevent the use of force by any nation. "The picture of Franklin [Roosevelt] and Churchill meeting to confer, surrounded by their experts, on battleships on a foggy northern bay, was certainly confirmation that it was intended to back to the limit those who were fighting the aggressors," a biographer of Roosevelt avowed.[32] "It was more than that—it was a public acknowledgement that the United States had gone all the way over to a foreign policy based on collective security."

The Charter actually established American leadership of the anti-Nazi allies and the incorporation of American principles of democracy into future institutions.

"The concrete fact, as most of us and the Americans saw it," an English weekly expounded, "was that a fully armed British

Empire and American Republic would together for several years wield a quasi-monopoly world-power, as we hope for disinterested ends, over a disarmed enemy and an exhausted Europe. This vision of benevolent hegemony of the English-speaking powers culminated in the Atlantic Charter. Its actual wording may not explicitly bear this interpretation, but the fact remains that it was drafted at a meeting at which no representative of Russia was present and that the political and ethical outlook it reflected was unmistakably Anglo-American. Mackenzie King's recent broadcast is only one of several proofs that neither half of this English-speaking partnership has yet begun to make the necessary adjustment . . . we can only guess at the reactions of the Russians. 'What!' they might well say, 'these Americans, who had not yet declared war, nor spilled a drop of American blood, are to dictate the world's future?' " [33]

Although the Charter was the result of a compromise, some British circles disliked its anti-colonial flavor. Others recognized American interests behind the pretty façade of principles. Yet, there were warnings in the British press not to see only egotism behind the winged words. "We may assume that genuine proposals for the betterment of the world will be made. . . . They will involve some immediate sacrifice probably in most of the countries which accept them. There may also be proposals not so genuinely altruistic. The danger is that we should be so suspicious of the Americans—*et dona ferentes*—so ready to see a selfish policy camouflaged as idealism that we shall not be able to distinguish the evil from the good." [34]

Stalin was not in a position to raise objections to the Charter, and he knew that its wording left room for manifold interpretations. Moreover, he wondered whether the Russian masses, having suffered heavy losses in life and property, would not demand real representation in the government after the war was over. The country's need for American help after the war in rehabilitating the Soviet Union also might impel a democratization of the Soviet society. With these possibilities in mind, Stalin was ready to adhere to the Charter, the more so because he must have recognized the immediate advantage of implicitly becoming one of the democratic powers sponsoring the Charter. This tacit recognition of the Soviet system as a sort of democracy was to play a fateful role in the implementation of war-time agreements.

The Nazi press was aroused. Its anger and indignation made it clear to the world that in Nazi circles there was fear of the effect of the Anglo-American declaration on the oppressed peoples.

"The Two War Criminals In The Role Of World Benefactors," ran the headline of the report of the *Völkischer Beobachter*.[35] "The great world betrayal another American President committed against us is still too deeply and painfully engraved in the memory of all Germans not to hear with wrath that the initiators of this war have resorted to such criminal methods of fraud again."

"It is not only a bluff and swindle but also an unmeasurable stupidity," another Nazi paper raged.[36] "The world is witness to a gigantic liquidation of Bolshevism that should bring about a new order everywhere, not only in Europe. It will free all peoples of the world of its dangers and these peoples will listen no more to the voices of Churchill and Roosevelt that entertained the silly hope of outroaring the speech of the guns which make way to the world of the future."

Count Ciano noted in his memoirs a discussion between the Duce and the Fuehrer on the effects of the Charter. The Duce asserted that it had, rather, harmed Roosevelt in the eyes of public opinion at home. "The Fuehrer gave a detailed account of the Jewish clique which surrounds Roosevelt and exploits the American people," Ciano added. Hitler thus gave the Axis newspapers the lead to explain why capitalist America had accepted Communist Russia as an ally. The Jews were trying to split the non-Jewish nations with the instruments of capitalism and communism, both being their invention.

It was easy to misread the President's intentions since, as many observers pointed out, he spoke to the world in lofty terms, but at the same time insisted on addressing his own people that the help he requested for Britain served the outright self-interest of the American people. As a Frenchman put it: "President Roosevelt and his supporters were constantly obliged to deny that the support of England was motivated by any other reason than the most selfish American national interest. Although the American people condemn 'power politics' as immoral and destructive of international order, they would not accept cooperation with England or other nations in the mutual defense against the Nazi peril unless it could be proved to them that they were not aiding anybody but themselves . . . Only the most incorrigible idealists have dared to assert that the essence of this world conflict was moral and spiritual and that its other aspects—the political and economic—were in fact subsidiary and absolutely insoluble as such." [37]

The Atlantic meeting and the resultant agreement on war and peace aims between the English-speaking nations put an end to this duplicity. A British writer stressed what American participation meant for the organization of the peace. He wrote: "This is not 1917, 1918, 1919. America will not come to a Versailles as a recent partner, with half a dozen boasting European states who have 'rigged' matters beforehand behind her back. As I see the end, the world will by then be completely ruined—all save the United States and India. Inflation was not invented in 1918. Not only will the United States be the predominant partner, but all these dreams of reconstruction will be entirely dependent on the continuing good will of that country. Nor is Franklin D. Roosevelt Woodrow Wilson. With all his virtues, Mr. Wilson came to Europe almost with an inferiority complex, anxious to please men of great name but less merit. The same European diplomacy is now a little fly-blown (or as Mr. Churchill would say, 'dusty'), and one trusts that the next Peace Conference will be held at Washington." [38]

As when the Declaration of Independence rang out, America again has become "the hope of the human race," an English weekly asserted, and added, referring to the Lend-Lease Act, "If the time needed for developing its tremendous implications can be gained by the fighting efforts of Britain . . . during the next six months the eventual results of America's decision will save the world." [39]

American leadership was embodied, however, in President Roosevelt's personal world leadership. The same weekly emphasized this by saying: "without [Roosevelt's] personal genius for national leadership the thing now accomplished [Lend-Lease] never could have been done. With flexible patience of method and iron steadfastness of aim, he has combined in a marvelous way the gifts of practical management and moral inspiration. As executive head of the Republic, the Act equips him with potent authority to mobilize for war-production the entire industrial resources of the United States. The President is astonishing his own people again by acting with what they call electrifying speed. . . . As in our Prime Minister's case, Mr. Roosevelt's words are battles like his acts. On these two extraordinary men destiny depends. That the world's crisis has produced them both, and raised them to the head of their respective nations, is the supreme good fortune of freedom."

Some sources still were impatient with the Presirent's slowness in moving toward inevitable participation in the "shooting" war. An English magazine echoed these old misgivings in the month following the Atlantic meeting: ". . . it is still true that Americans are not adequately awake to the menace of Hitlerism. Despite the basic support they give national policies—which include a commitment to defeat Hitlerism in the world—the people are far too apathetic and complacent. They are ready to be led. They are ready to be told what must be done. To date, it has seemed as if Mr. Roosevelt were waiting for the people to make up their mind that the time for entry into the war had come. And . . . the longer he waits the more the obstructionists of national unity do their work. The President obviously does not want to go down in history as the man who manoeuvered and planned the American people into the great war. He wishes, rather, to be the man who sought and contrived for two years and more to defeat Hitlerism 'short of war,' and then only in response to public realization that war was inescapable was willing to lead the nation into conflict." [40]

But even in the worst days of the Battle of the Atlantic the British press understood and appreciated the President's position.

"It will be a calamity," a magazine warned, "if President Roosevelt steers his country, which he handles as a master navigator, into a European war without making it clear on what terms and for what purposes America wages war." The same paper surmised that Roosevelt did not want to embroil his country in war, stating that "Mr. Roosevelt is genuinely desirous of taking his place in history as the President who kept his country out of physical participation in the conflict. . . ." [41]

It appeared that America could go very far in provoking Hitler without having to fear that the Germans would decide to go to war against her. "Hitler swallowed the repeal of the embargoes, the release of the destroyers, and the passage of the Lend-Lease Act; he will, it is suspected, swallow United States convoys, the new scheme of training RAF pilots at American airfields, or any other expansion of American aid which involves a smaller risk to Nazi prospects than would an American declaration of war." Indeed, not even the President's "shoot at sight" order in September, 1941 in response to the sinking of an American ship provoke war. Thus the President's reluctance appeared justified, in the view of the magazine, under one condition: ". . . if with American material, economic and diplomatic aid Great Britain can destroy Hitlerism. . . . But the chance grows ever slimmer, and this country has ceased to expect miracles from its Chief Executive, or to regard war as a game of marbles, from which one can withdraw at any given stage. And the average American has a dark suspicion that those sweeping powers for which the President asks are going to be needed before our world is much older." [44]

"Until that moment of decision comes," another English magazine reported from Washington, "the national morale is poor and the debate and disunity will inevitably continue. Once the die is cast, we shall see a real closing of the ranks, with many who now oppose participation in the war joining loyally and enthusiastically in the war effort. The present situation is a vicious circle. Until the public shakes off its apathy and recognizes that this war is 'one' war, the decision to participate will not be taken; until the decision is taken, the apathy will not cease to be. President

Roosevelt is now a tight-rope walker, alternating between a forthright statement of policy or striking act and a cautious word or deed of recession. . . . The major tenet, as enunciated by the President and accepted by the people, is the defeat of Hitlerism in the world. Tacitly most Americans realize this probably means eventual entry into the war. But they are not anxious to enter. Responsible officials, even including President Roosevelt and Secretary Knox, still publicly express the hope that the United States will be able to avoid 'shooting war.' But their hope is strictly pious. . . . People know that from the Lend-Lease Law onwards the United States has bound itself to give safe delivery and all-out aid to Britain and its allies. With such an obligation, the eventual need of American participation seems certain to arise.

"Perhaps the President expected an incident that would arouse the people sufficiently to accept a program of action." [45] The reporter thought that this seemed to be the course being pursued, and he continued: "But it leaves the initiative to Hitler, and there is a large question whether any sufficiently startling incident will be forthcoming, or whether, in the present case-hardened state of public thinking everywhere, it could suffice to arouse America . . ."

An Australian magazine paid tribute to the President for the instructive handling of his opposition. "I have heard people over here," the report from Washington noted, "criticizing the length of time it took to get the bill [Lend-Lease] through Congress without understanding the reason why that time was taken. Lindbergh and the isolationists were allowed to hang themselves by being given so much rope. The Bill was allowed to go on and on and everyone in America who was opposed to it was allowed to come and state his case. Everything was brought out into the daylight." [46] This was the democratic way of handling a controversial issue, according to the report, until the public was informed of all arguments and could approve of the President's initiative.

Roosevelt had adhered to his Third Inaugural Address in which he purported that "there were men who believed that democracy, as a form of government and as a frame of life, was limited or measured by a kind of mystical and artificial fate—that for some unexplained reason, tyranny and slavery have become the surging wave of the future, and that freedom is an ebbing tide. . . . We know [that democracy] cannot die because it is built on the unhampered initiative of individual men and women joined together in a common enterprise—an enterprise undertaken and carried through by the free expression of a free majority. . . . We know it because democracy alone has constructed an unlimited civilization capable of infinite progress in the improvement of human life. We know it because, if we look below the surface, we sense it still spreading in every continent; for it is the most humane, the most advanced, and, in the end, the most unconquerable of all forms of human society."[47]

Because his words inspired the democracies, the British looked on Roosevelt as second only to Prime Minister Winston Churchill as a producer of striking phrases. According to a report from London to the *New York Times,* "Mr. Roosevelt is better than Mr. Churchill in that he speaks for a country that—this is the view of best informed Britons—will win or lose the war. But, the British ask, when are these inspiring and cheering words going to be translated into guns and planes actually fighting the Germans and the Italians?"[48]

The eagerness with which the British public listened to the President's words on the radio caused the British Broadcasting Corporation's magazine to sigh deeply, regretting that there had been no radio to transmit the speeches of American leaders in the past. "If the voices of Alexander Hamilton and Abraham Lincoln had been as familiar to us as the vigorous tones of President Roosevelt, many misunderstandings might have been avoided," the paper reflected, with the usual British understatement.[49]

Even the Nazis appreciated the President's fortunate phrasing of unprecedented actions, or actions whose connotations made it dangerous to call by their accustomed names. One of them wrote: "As a Harvard man, Roosevelt speaks free of accent, but in public he uses a genuine American way of speaking. He cracks a slogan that immediately spreads about, uses a picturesque turn that sheds light into difficult problems, a quick flash of idea that steers around trouble spots, disarming those who harbor doubts, even in a mass meeting. When he noted in 1940 that the war was still unpopular, he coined the phrase 'short of war,' that was to hide all measures bordering actual warfare, although by that the neutrality of the country was undermined. In his struggle with a Congress that did not favor the idea of convoying aid to Britain, Roosevelt discovered in the beginning of 1941 the slippery expression of 'sea patrol.' This all distinguishes him from his predecessors. He is entirely indifferent to the means he makes use of in his extraordinary ambition that strives to be satisfied and that will grow with the years." [50]

But there are times when even the most telling phrases are no substitute for action, stated a newspaper of a strictly neutral country. "Roosevelt said as late as May 27 that he still believed that military intervention by the United States in the war could be avoided. On the 4th of July, however, he said only that he hoped for such a development. Roosevelt's statesmanlike talents and art will be on trial in the moment he will hit on the right measures, as he did so far, at the right time, which in the case of the constitutional impediments existing in America meant usually the last moment." [51]

Was the President fit to bear the strain which was to be his lot in the years ahead? A Swiss journalist measured him up physically and mentally to the tasks waiting for him in the mist of the future.

"Roosevelt is now 59 years old," he wrote,[52] "and, according to his physician, Admiral McIntyre, he is now in better shape than he was ten years before. Anyway, he comes from a particularly strong and healthy family and is himself of robust constitution. He has developed his upper body and his arms since his sickness through consistent gymnastics, and as a result his muscles have become those of an athlete. Those who see the President for the first time are impressed with his dynamism and with his kindly nature. They cannot miss the elasticity of the President's moods, his almost actorlike ability to shift from hearty laughter to deep earnestness, and his ability to make contact without any difficulty with the most divergent persons. After a long series of conferences lasting to about 5:30 P.M., without having a moment's rest, the President either returns to his apartment for his cup of tea or he is taken, three times a week, to the swimming pool which was built for him in the White House. Alone or in the company of a domestic, he performs there strong and methodic exercises for about twenty-five minutes. He gets a massage afterwards and goes to bed for a nap before dinner. The White House is usually full of dinner guests. Members of the family and high functionaries mingle with strange types, social workers, students and leaders of youth organizations invited by Mrs. Roosevelt. Dinner is served in the large dining room, but at times the President eats his dinner alone. After dinner a film is shown, but lately the President has rarely had time to watch it. He likes the documentary films and enjoys Mickey Mouse; recently he saw Chaplin's dictator film. Thereupon the President withdraws into his office. He spends his week-ends on his estate at Hyde Park, or else embarks on a cruise on the Potomac or Chesapeake Bay on his yacht."

A correspondent of the Japanese paper *Yomiuri* reported his impressions of Roosevelt. "On leaving the White House after a press conference," he wrote,[53] "a reporter asked me what impressions I had formed of the President. I replied that he seemed to be full of both physical and mental energy and much more alive than the newsreels would lead me to expect. The American reporter then said that he also was impressed by the vitality of President Roosevelt. The public cannot be blamed for noticing the signs of age and weariness on the features of the President on seeing him in the newsreels. His position and responsibility are far greater than those of any former President of the United States, because of the importance of any national or foreign policy he may decide on in the face of the current delicate international situation. . . . Although the President's press conferences are held in a most easy-going and cordial atmosphere, it is easy to see that he weighs every word he utters. . . . Since American capital is aiming to gain control over the world it is evident that President Roosevelt favors an imperialistic policy.

This is why Washington has extended its defense line from the Western Hemisphere to Britain, Africa, the Balkans, Australia, and even to Asia . . . In order to control the world, Washington will have to gain possession of Britain . . . The same country that bought Louisiana from France and purchased Alaska from Russia, is now buying Britain. The materials being sent to Britain are the 'down payments' on purchases. This is why Britain is certain to become a subsidiary economic organ of the United States whether it defeats Germany or not . . . Despite his continued anti-Axis policy, President Roosevelt is preventing an open clash with these powers, for such an event would tend to antagonize the Soviet Union. Before either Britain or the Axis Powers become worn out, President Roosevelt is amassing the wealth of the world in the United States and strengthening the position of America. If he is to remedy the internal friction caused by clashes between capital and labor, he will have to take drastic measures against labor and resort to totalitarian measures. The United States will take active measures against its enemies when it has created the powerful weapon of economic power and super-production. . . . We wonder whether the President will be able to bring about national unity and so realize his objective."

The British public was delighted to hear of the President, his personality, his public and private life. Above all, the press conferences fascinated them. This is how a correspondent described such a conference over the radio: [51]

"The President talked without any notes . . . reporters may question any Presidential statement, and may in fact say anything that comes into their heads, for it is impossible to embarrass the President, who knows a hundred ways of not answering a question with great charm. There is no such thing as indiscretion: you ask him not only why such a policy was decided on, but what he had at the back of his mind in committing the country to it. A fortnight ago, for instance, after he had explained how he proposed to send out American armaments to Britain, somebody asked him to explain the psychology of this idea. He leaned back and waved with his cigarette-holder. He said: 'Figure this way. The President has a neighbor whose house is catching fire.

The President also has a length of garden hose. He doesn't ask the neighbor to pay fifteen dollars for the hose; he goes and attaches it to the hydrant. When the fire's out the neighbor returns the hose with thanks and agrees to replace the damaged section of it.' If as an Englishman you shut your eyes and listen to the flow of explanation, jokes, exposition of old laws, you realize this: the active head of a great State is telling the secrets of his policy to a hundred newspapermen and then sitting back to defend himself against their criticism. If there was even the slightest possibility of its happening at Berlin or Berchtesgaden, there would be no further need to make armaments, no more call for black-outs, no more need to fight."

The popularity of Roosevelt with the British people was intense and general. "They felt in their bones that Mr. Roosevelt was their lifelong friend," a British diplomat reminisced, "that he hated the Nazis as deeply as they did, that he wanted democracy and civilization, in the sense in which they believed in it, to prevail, that he knew what he wanted, and that his goal resembled their own ideals more than it did those of all his opponents. They felt that his heart was in the right place. . . . They knew that he would, to the extent of his enormous energy and ability, see them through. . . . There is probably no such thing as long-lived mass hypnotism; the masses know what it is that they like, what genuinely appeals to them. What most Germans thought Hitler to be, Hitler, in fact, largely was; and what free men in Europe and in America and in Asia and in Africa and in Australia, and wherever else the rudiments of free political thought stirred at all—what all these felt Roosevelt to be, he, in fact, was. He was the greatest leader of democracy, the greatest champion of social progress, in the twentieth century." [55]

11

AMERICA IN WAR

On December 7, 1941, Japan struck, not at Indo-China or Malaya, as had been expected, but at Pearl Harbor, the main base of the American Pacific Fleet. Japan attacked without a declaration of war, as she had done in her war against Russia in 1904. It was a quiet Sunday when the Japanese bombers and midget submarines attacked. The first report registered the loss of three destroyers, one target ship, a minelayer, and a second battleship capsized and there were almost 3000 dead. The President called it a day of infamy, since negotiations with two representatives of Japan were going on while the Japanese fleet plowed toward Hawaii for the deadly blow.

The next day the President asked Congress to declare war on Japan. The President knew the implications of the American losses; they would allow the Japanese fleet to fan out through the huge area of the South Pacific and occupy the Netherland East Indies and Malaya abounding in the raw materials Japan needed for the successful waging of war. Three days after Pearl Harbor, Japanese planes sank, off Malaya, the two most modern warships that had been dispatched to the Far East to assure British-American naval superiority in the Pacific.

With a single stroke, the "Greater Asia co-prosperity sphere," the dream of the Japanese militarists, was within reach.

How did the Japanese attack catch the Navy unprepared? Negotiations with the Japanese had been practically at a deadlock. Moreover, the President as well as the Secretaries of State and the Navy knew that the Japanese fleet had been sailing out to the high seas, and they must have been aware of Japan's history of striking first and declaring war afterwards.

In answer, an English quarterly noted, "For America, it is doubly plain that the first and greatest problem is within themselves. Pearl Harbor might have been turned into a disastrous defeat for the Japanese if the American forces had been adequately vigilant and active, just as air protection would have prevented some of Britain's naval losses. Likewise, the great loss of aircraft in the Philippines on December 8, which has been just revealed, was preventable. The 'enemy from within'—not especially the Fifth Column, but the enemies who consist of disorganization, over-confidence, lethargy, and sheer stupidity are the main source of disaster." [1]

The Japanese official report on December 9 rather understated the success. "With this blow the successful operations of the American navy in the Western Pacific have been jeopardized. It is, to say the least, impossible now to speak of them as equal in power to Japan." [2]

The sweeping success of the Japanese attack took the world by surprise. "What is really surprising," a magazine wrote, "is that the attack did so much damage." The magazine recalled that the President had sent a direct appeal to the Japanese emperor to break the deadlock in the negotiations. "Such a grave step should have alerted the military at the far outposts. If the growing strain was not sufficient to keep the United States on the alert it is not easy to understand what warning was required. Indeed, the whole of this extraordinary episode bristles with the inexplicable. It may be admitted that it is not easy for peaceful, orderly nations to provide against an outbreak of gangsterism, and yet the whole of this war that is now girdling the earth depends upon our finding some solution for the problem. Almost every nation takes some precautions, and even though it was only this year that the United States decided to fortify Guam, this at least suggested that some sensing of the growing strain in the Pacific had reached Washington. But, as Mr. Roosevelt pointed out in his Message to Congress, the distance to Hawaii implies that the Japanese attack was planned some days or weeks ago, and it is difficult to understand how the aeroplane carriers failed to escape the ordinary work of reconnaisance." [3]

However, friendly as well as neutral and even enemy voices warned that the Japanese military success might backfire morally and psychologically.

"The tactical surprise achieved by Japanese treachery at Pearl Harbor was admittedly complete and disastrous," an English magazine asserted. ". . . the disasters in the Pacific, the fall of Singapore and the consequent threats to the Burma road, to Australia and to the ocean communications of the Empire and the United States, force us to recognize how formidable is the enemy's bid to win the war before the power of the United Nations can be deployed. The issue may turn on the question of time . . . and the problem of mobilizing the reserves of military and industrial power. . . . To create the organization for waging a new world war, into which are henceforth merged the Chinese war in Asia, the British war in Western Europe and Africa, and the Russian war in Eastern Europe, was the object of Mr. Churchill's mission to Washington, supplemented by the simultaneous visit of Mr. Eden to Moscow. . . . Fundamental to the whole scheme is the common declaration of the twenty-six United Nations made on January 3. By this act the Allied States have pledged themselves to a unity of purpose, expressed in their subscription to the Atlantic Charter." [4]

"Psychologically," wrote a German in retrospect, "the Japanese attack on the United States was certainly a mistake that was to backfire. Public opinion in the United States was divided until December, 1941, about whether or not the country should go to war. Roosevelt was not sure whether he could get from Congress a declaration of war without an enemy attack. Now all obstacles have been wiped out. . . ." The Japanese attack was expected, according to the author, but it was a complete surprise that it had been directed against the United States. "The Americans broke the Japanese code and deciphered some highly informative telegrams. But the attack on Pearl Harbor was not anticipated. Through its brutality it whipped up public anger." [5]

Its moral effect far outweighed the strategic setback. "It galvanized the American public and fused them into a national unity that proved indestructible and immediate," a French author commented.[6] "Had Japan attacked Thailand instead of Hawaii it is probable that the electric current of popular outrage would not have swept the country," an English newspaper thought. "The United States might have decided that Thailand constituted her Poland, but certainly not without debate. . . . Popular support for Mr. Roosevelt's foreign policy, which had previously been extraordinarily high, has become virtually unanimous." [7]

"Anger flamed from coast to coast. And though people were bewildered by the attack on Pearl Harbor . . . they did not let into their minds the possibility that the Japanese had already won the first battle of the war. . . . That fanatical nation, with its sacrificial mysticism and its super-Hitlerite ambitions, possesses in the immediate circumstances one of the strongest strategical positions ever known. The Japanese dream of empire over all East Asia, the South Seas, and a thousand million of mankind—half the human race—is on the way to materializing," an English weekly related.[8]

Another English weekly showed concern over the public anger, fearing that it might compel Roosevelt to make the Pacific the main theater of war. "The problem will be," it asserted, "to preserve a sense of proportion in a people which has made savagely angry by as treacherous a piece of infamy as even the Axis has so far organized. . . . Japan and her allies . . . have killed the credit of all who have had any truck with isolationism by vindicating each phase of the President's approach to the war. Even Mr. Westbrook Pegler, who has written an almost daily hymn of hate against him for years, now sighs his relief that Mr. Roosevelt was given a third term." [9]

But the public resented also the criminal negligence of the military authorities that had made the Japanese gamble a triumph. "The American public has been justly stirred to anger by the disastrous negligence of the commanding officers in Hawaii revealed by the report of the board of inquiry," an English magazine reported. "It shows that the officers failed to confer and cooperate, and neglected to take the precautions actually ordered, which, had they been taken, would have found the defenses in a high state of readiness. . . . The commanding officers are found 'guilty of dereliction' and are to be tried by court-martial. No wonder the American nation is shocked at the revelation of incompetence productive of a disaster so grave that it has dislocated the whole Allied strategy for the Pacific in its earlier stages. . . . But Great Britain, too, had its naval disaster in the Pacific, due to defects which have not been so fully analysed in public." [10]

A spokesman of the Japanese Navy denied that the attack on Pearl Harbor was a sneak attack. He said to the reporters: "Roosevelt cannot state in truth that America was not warned of an attack on Hawaii from the air. During the discussions between Tokyo and Washington, the Japanese delegates repeatedly declared that their government hoped that the negotiations would lead to a peaceful settlement, but that there was a time limit. After that limit expired Japan would be compelled in self-defense to give up diplomacy and take up arms. Unfortunately, Roosevelt and his government took the warnings of Tokyo for a bluff. Now it is too late for the Roosevelt clique to recognize that Japan meant it in earnest." [11]

In truth, the Japanese government, as late as December 5, 1941, in an official release, had this to say on Japanese-American relations: "Official circles let it be known that negotiations in Washington would continue. . . . The official spokesman related that there are still some differences of opinion with respect to some points of issue, but some progress has already been noted. . . . Therefore, Japan will continue the discussions in the hope of eventually finding a formula for the solution of the crisis in the Pacific." [12] But the same Swiss newspaper which printed this report from Tokyo revealed the next day: "The conflict between America and the Japanese island empire, which extends far back into the past, appears to be headed towards a dramatic turn."

An Indian was not impressed by the extent of the Japanese initial successes. He wrote: "I feel profound sympathy for the Japanese government in its present predicament. If Germany defeats Russia, the Big Bully of Berlin will be too near to be comfortable. May he not have his own designs on the rubber and oil and tin of the South Pacific Islands? And has not Hitler written something in his Bible about the Yellow Peril? On the other hand, if Russia holds out, it means the ultimate and complete defeat of Germany. What then becomes of the Axis and of all the ambitions which Japan has hugged to its bosom all these years?" [13]

A year after the attack on Pearl Harbor, an English newspaper analyzing the military, moral, and political impact of the event, stated: ". . . the Navy Department in Washington issued a report on . . . the treacherous and deadly attack at Pearl Harbor. . . . It was announced, quite correctly, that two battleships, and two only had been sunk—Arizona and Oklahoma—but rumor was busy with tales of other losses; and it is now reported that, in fact, three other battleships were completely disabled, and three others damaged to an extent that put them temporarily out of action. Three of the seven cruisers present were also temporarily out of action. Thus, at one blow before the immediacy of war was fully realized, the American Pacific fleet suffered crippling losses in capital ships which for the moment gave the Japanese that superiority at sea without which their lightning successes could not have been gained. But the very magnitude of the losses . . . was not without a compensation, in that it brought home to the Americans the full meaning of the war, and started them in the resolve to throw the whole of their energy into providing the means for victory. What is scarcely less surprising than Pearl Harbor itself is the rapidity with which the United States has repaired the situation. Three of the damaged battleships and three damaged cruisers returned to service months ago and, in addition, new ships under construction have been completed." [14]

Another magazine attributed far more significance to Pearl Harbor: ". . . it marked the decisive opening of North American power in the Pacific, and for the American people it meant much more than that. During this first year of war there has been established in the United States a power and range of federal authority such as few American citizens could have imagined twelve months ago. By one stroke of legislation after another a political democracy of 130 millions is being enrolled for total war . . . the most energetic and unrestrained, the most unregulated and competitive of all great nations has confronted the need, and accepted the logic, of complete central authority for a single overmastering purpose. In the United States a startling new epoch has been opened."[15]

The road that led Japan to Pearl Harbor was traced by a quarterly magazine: "It was believed at first that the Army's ideas on foreign policy had been finally discredited by the Russo-German pact, and that there would be no further prospect of a military alliance between Germany and Japan, but that was far from being the case. Every other turning that Japan tried to take was found to be a blind alley leading nowhere. Her attempt to destroy Chiang Kai-Shek was defeated, her attempts to make peace were pathetic failures, and her half-hearted overtures to the democracies were accompanied by the condition that they should recognize the new order. Hitler's treachery lay on one side, concession of failure on the other. . . . The invasion [of Western Europe] opened up the problem of the Far Eastern colonies of the European powers. If Japan was to take full advantage of this opportunity, she must clearly condone the treachery and betrayal of the previous August [1939] and join the winning side. It was also necessary to enlarge the conception of the New Order, so as to include within its limits the South Sea region. . . . Thanks to the abject policy of Vichy, Japan had a great measure of success, but Japan has made no progress at all with the Dutch in the Netherland East Indies. . . . Foreign Minister Matsuoka paid a visit to Berlin and Rome and on his way back signed a non-aggression pact with Soviet Russia. . . . It was a reasonable inference that Japan might withdraw a large number of her troops that she kept in Manchukuo . . . and embark upon aggression in the south."[16]

A Berlin correspondent of a newspaper in a neutral country related, the day after the attack on Pearl Harbor: "In political circles it is pointed out here that Roosevelt has desired and prepared the war on the Axis powers. Concerning Japan, he tried to avoid war and hoped that by the interplay of threats and concessions he might convince Japan to refrain from entering the conflict between the Anglo-Saxons and the Axis. The fact that Japan was able to destroy this plan is considered as a major political defeat for America. But this was to be foreseen, since the tripartite pact of Berlin, signed last November, was a clear warning to America. In Berlin they take note with great satisfaction that the Americans were completely overwhelmed and that, according to the first Japanese announcements, the American navy suffered a catastrophic blow on the first day of the war." [17]

"As Theodore Roosevelt once imposed naval imperialism so now does Franklin Roosevelt force on America an Atlantic expansionist policy," a German magazine commented in comparing the two Roosevelts.[18] "Theodore Roosevelt issued the order for the conquest of the Philippines. The war policy of Franklin is known. Both were influenced by Admiral Mahan, whom Theodore called his friend and teacher and whose ideas Franklin, as Under-Secretary of the Navy, adopted." [18]

The Japanese attack introduced a new, widely expanded plan in the councils of the Axis, but Hitler had failed to force the war to a decision in 1941. The battle of Britain ended without the capitulation of Britain and the Russian winter arrived before Hitler was able to defeat the Soviet army. He did not seize the two highly symbolic objectives: Moscow and Leningrad, though in the south his troops penetrated deeply into the territory of the Soviet Union and reached the Caucasus.

Hitler had not broken Soviet power nor had he thrown the Russian armies behind the Urals out of Europe. In 1941, he could not claim victory in Europe. He had to give up plans for ruling over the greater part of the world by maintaining puppet governments in Britain, France, Belgium and Holland and by holding part of Russia and leaving the rest in a state of anarchy. Instead, he resolved to expand the war to embrace the whole globe. By this resolution Hitler accepted the Japanese thesis and signed a pact with Japan that aimed at conquering the British Empire and America.

According to the plan, the Japanese attack on America was to open the decisive phase of the new world war. In 1942 the Germans were to penetrate the Caucasus and march to the

Persian Gulf; they were to occupy the oil fields there as well as those of Baku. By establishing their power in the Middle East oil centers, the Germans would inflict a devastating blow on the British Empire. At the same time, however, a German desert army was to replace the Italians in North Africa whom the British had completely routed, and with their tanks sweep through the desert to Alexandria. By taking Alexandria and Suez, they would break the backbone of the British Empire. Simultaneously, an inexorable U-boat blockade of the Atlantic would frustrate American aid to Britain, starve her, and prevent America from transporting large scale troops and equipment over the ocean to open a front in Europe or Africa. Meanwhile, Japan would reach India, incite the Indians to revolt against the British, and set up an "independent" government. Marching through India, the Japanese would meet the Nazi armies in the Middle East and the gigantic pincer would be closed.

The prestige and power thus acquired by the Nazi-Japanese alliance with the active help of German and Italian fifth columns, could not fail to influence the countries of South and Central America and help raise to power dictators friendly to the victorious Axis. The British Empire would be definitely dissolved and the United States completely isolated.

This fantastic plan was about to turn into reality in October 1942. The coalition was a hairbreadth away from ruling the earth. But Hitler, who, true to his pact with Japan, declared war on the United States, ascribed the responsibility for it to President Roosevelt's imperialist policy. "Hatred of the authoritarian powers in Europe and of rising Japan in East Asia is a component of the Rooseveltian world policy. So is his utopian dream of turning this century into an American century as the last was a British one," a German magaine editorialized.[19]

To justify the declaration of war on America, the German press accused Roosevelt and Churchill of "making Bolshevism an instrument in the fight against Germany. They kept the will to fight burning in England for a long time by assuring people that Stalin would take care of Hitler. This promise became a weighty factor in sustaining British morale."[20] Hitler himself shrieked, in his New Year's message: "The Jewish-capitalistic forces have allied openly with bolshevism so that now only the tripartite powers stand against the Jewish-capitalistic-bolshevik conspiracy. Churchill and Roosevelt have delivered Europe to the Kremlin." [21]

Mussolini had to resort to bigger lies to brush off his responsibility in declaring war on America: "Neither the Axis nor Japan wanted an extension of the conflict," he stated from the balcony of the Palazzo Venezia. "One man only, an authentic and democratic despot, through a series of infinite provocations, deceiving with supreme fraud the very people of his own country, has desired the war and has prepared for it day by day with diabolical tenacity." [22]

Roosevelt said, in his annual message to Congress, "We cannot wage this war in a defensive spirit. As our power and our resources are fully mobilized, we shall carry the attack against the enemy—we shall hit him and hit him again whenever and wherever we can reach him. We must keep him far from our shores, for we intend to bring the battle to him on his own home ground."

An English weekly compared this message with those of the dictators. "Those who listen to the voices of the Axis leaders in Germany, Italy and Japan," the article ran, "will search in vain for a message which still stirs enthusiasm in any country but the speaker's own. . . . Mr. Roosevelt, broadcasting on Monday, called on the listeners to have a map of the world before them; and men in every allied or neutral country were made to feel that the United States had made the world cause its own cause, and was prepared to fight on every sea-lane and every battlefield both in the interest of America and for 'liberty and justice everywhere.' . . . America is totally in the world war and will be in the world peace." [23]

In his annual message the President compared the faith of the democratic front with that of the totalitarians that propelled the fight. "We are fighting," he said, "to cleanse the world of ancient evils, ancient ills. Our enemies are guided by brutal cynicism, by unholy contempt of the human race. We are inspired by a faith which goes back through all the years to the first chapter of the Book of Genesis: God created man in His own image."

As if to confirm that the Nazis represented the denial of the principle of the creation of man as set forth in the Bible, Goebbels stated, "The bourgeois era of false and deceiving humanistic principles is over. It will not be mastered by ruse but by manliness and force. The world has split into those who love and those who hate. Only he stands on firm ground who knows perfectly well where he has to love and where to hate." [24]

Reacting to developments within the democratic front, Axis propaganda simultaneously warned listeners and readers that the Anglo-Americans were playing with Bolshevik fire or that America was bent on liquidating the British Empire and acquiring its assets.

At the signing of the pact of the twenty-six United Nations, an Italian journalist asserted that the alliance of communist Russia with the capitalist powers was against nature. "One of the two plays sharp," he wrote.[25]

Expecting a Japanese attack on India, Britain tried to organize Indian cooperation in the defense of the country. Gandhi rejected any cooperation with belligerents. His Congress Party, however, saw their opportunity to gain independence for India in exchange for cooperating with the Allies in fending off a Japanese invasion. The Party broke with Gandhi and accepted as their leader Nehru, who agreed to cooperate under the condition that the British allow a responsible Indian government to be formed. Churchill was not willing to go beyond a vague promise of independence after the war, refusing to set any date. But Roosevelt made unmistakable gestures to the effect that he favored Nehru's point of view, and the American press gave more and more outspoken expression to the nation's unwillingness to fight for the integrity of the British Empire. Since Churchill had stated that he was not the King's Prime Minister to preside over the dissolution of the Empire, the result was an awkward conflict between the two principal allies while the war was raging.

The Nazis, of course, made use of this opportunity in their propaganda. When the United States and Australia signed a military pact, the Berlin press wrote that the collapse of the British Empire was imminent. It was said to be being absorbed by the stronger partner, the United States, whose government was exploiting the current situation mercilessly. "President Roosevelt," they purported, "wants to build an American empire out of the ruins of the British, and increasingly he has his way. First the British had to deliver to him their dollar assets, then bases in their possessions in the Caribbean seas; then Canada fell into the North American economic zone, and now finally America takes over Australia, the latter practically leaving the Commonwealth." [26]

When MacArthur took over the command of the allied forces on land, sea, and in the air in the Southwest Pacific, the Nazi press commented: "The impression is general that Roosevelt made the appointment over the head of both London and Camberra. But in their terribly grave situation they could not oppose Roosevelt's decision. It appears that both England and Australia see clearly that their only hope consists in letting America 'take things in hand.'" [27]

An English magazine analyzed the development of public opinion in America: "It was not long ago," the survey ran,[28] "that public opinion was overwhelmingly opposed to sending a single soldier outside the Western Hemisphere and the Administration had to approach every move with the utmost wariness. Now it can be sure of support for any enterprise, provided it is sufficiently vigorous and daring. The only danger is that if public expectations are raised too high the American people may become impatient of the inevitable weary months of waiting, disappointments, and reverses while the training, the shipping and the supplies necessary to a successful offensive are built up. . . . So far America's war has been if not 'phony,' at least remote and undramatic with little fighting, and equally little opportunity for direct sacrifice at home. . . . The immediate effect of the outbreak of the war was, of course, very greatly to enhance the prestige of the President, partly because of that recourse to the executive arm which always accompanies a war, but mainly because events have proved Mr. Roosevelt to have been so completely right in his foreign policies. But criticism, and even opposition, are creeping back . . . there is a rising volume of criticism of the Administration. . . . The hatred of Mr. Roosevelt, when it is combined with hatred of Britain and reinforced by hatred of 'entangling alliances,' can lead to the most astonishing doctrines. . . . The persistent and growing clamor is that American forces should be kept at home, that the Navy should do nothing more than patrol the coast, that Japan is the only enemy, that America is being cheated by her allies."

Real opposition to Roosevelt appeared in both houses of Congress when he submitted a bill against inflation, which had begun spiraling. The bill called for a program of price and wage stabilization that would hurt labor and especially the farmers, who hated the idea of missing their long absent opportunity to raise prices while demand for their produce was expanding. In 1942 the House of Representatives and one-third of the Senate seats came up for election. At such a time members of Congress were reluctant to antagonize strong blocs of voters, but the national interest demanded action.

"The situation, if unchecked, can lead to disastrous inflation," was the view of an English weekly.[29] "But the President, with or without the help of Congress, is determined to stop it. In his special Message to Congress . . . he asked for the passage of legislation . . . authorizing him to stabilize the cost of living, including the price of farm commodities. His plan is to put a stop to the process in which prices and wages chase one another upwards in inevitable sequence. . . . President Roosevelt, in his determination to increase taxation and spread it over the whole community, has not had the support from Congress which our Government has from Parliament. He appears determined, if necessary, to act without that, and there is every indication that the country, apart from the farmers, will be with him." But, the same weekly commented later,[30] "Members of Congress have been behaving like a body of perfect politicians. President Roosevelt sees where that road must end—in inflation; and as supreme executive officer of the nation he is concerned to stop it. Hence the growing divergence between him and Congress, which has come to a head over the question of statutory farm prices. Ever since he took office Mr. Roosevelt has been known as the farmers' friend, and no American statesman had treated them more generously. It is the more significant that he should now be resisting these claims to a raising of farm prices, which would, he says, constitute 'an immediate threat to the whole price structure.' . . . Unless a compromise is reached it will fall to the President to take the matter into his own hands."

A Swiss newspaper wondered whether the President would be able to find a formula of compromise between national and powerful bloc interests. "Can the government, in their struggle against inflation, afford to antagonize all parties as well as the powerful leaders of organized labor?" the paper asked and answered its question: [31] "Roosevelt's administration will be at any rate reluctant to risk losing the unprecedented support of the masses. They need the support of the workers in the life-struggle of the land. . . . It appears that the present condition of total war will soon lead to a far-reaching socialization of the world economy. It has begun with state control of agricultural produce and with the shift of industrial production to wartime demands, so that, by the end of 1942, the civilian population will be able to buy only bare necessities. It remains to be seen in what spirit this revolutionary change will be accomplished in America."

On the strength of the powers voted him for the duration of the war, the President was entitled to take the necessary measures without the assent of Congress, but Berlin rejoiced at the prospect that "the American President is about to set up an economic dictatorship in order to find a way out of his towering difficulties." [32]

The President played no politics and stood squarely for the national interest. In the coming years, America produced an economic miracle. She not only supplied her own military forces and her allies with equipment, ammunition, and food, but in the meantime produced enough for her civilians to live better than ever before in the past.

However, as the year 1942 continued, the situation on the various fronts became dangerously unfavorable to the Allies. The only good news was that the Russians were standing fast heroically in the face of a formidable new offensive of the Germans. But they insisted more and more on effective help from the Allies that would compel the Nazis to remove some of their armies from the Russian front. There had been an agreement between the President and Churchill on the latter's visit to Washington at the end of 1941 to open a front in the Balkans or the West in 1943, but the decision was vague, and the Russians needed a second front immediately lest they collapse under the sustained drive of the enemy. The Russian clamor for a second front struck an echo in the British people, who were deeply grateful to the Russians for saving them from the horrors of the steady bombardments of the previous year. Molotov, the Minister of Foreign Affairs of the Soviet Union, eventually came to visit first England and then the United States, to get down in writing a promise that the Allies would open up a second front without delay.

An English magazine described the unrest of the British public in the spring of 1942 over the lack of a second front: ". . . the government has been subjected to the steady pressure of public opinion, expressed both in and out of Parliament, to make our promise good. The possibility of a western offensive by Britain has been debated in Parliament, in the press, in the homes, in the parks, at the street corners and even on the screen, but in military matters the government has always the answer that it alone knows the facts, and that public discussion of the strategy must in such circumstances be largely irresponsible and may even do harm. . . . The comparative peace which Britain is enjoying, owing to relative immunity from air raids, has stirred in the people a feeling that they ought to be doing something more to help the Russians who now carry the full brunt of the German attack."[33]

Commenting on the agreement reached with Molotov on the second front, an English weekly noted: ". . . That there must be a second front everyone is agreed. The intention has been put on official record in the identical statements issued by the British and American Governments after Mr. Molotov's visit to London and Washington in June. The actual wording of that declaration deserves notice: 'A full understanding,' it was affirmed, 'was reached with regard to the urgent task of creating a second front in Europe in 1942.' Ambiguity could no doubt be discovered here. . . . But the conviction the plain man could derive from the words is that there will be a second front in Europe before 1942 ends. . . . But that he is not satisfied is intelligible enough. None of us is satisfied. With the spectacle of the irresistible impact of the German force in Russian gallantry, with the relentless progress of the German armies towards Russia's richest cornland and oil-fields, all our impulses both of self-interest and of sympathy for a heroic ally impel us to desire above all things the opening of a second front tomorrow. . . . The state of mind of the average Russian can well be imagined. His country is facing the very crisis of its existence. . . . What, in the face of that, are British and Americans doing to help? . . . The question is inevitable, and if it is left unanswered the consequences may be dangerous." [34]

The President in a fireside chat in early September confirmed that a second front would be opened. His speech was recorded and played several times a day on the British radio to calm the public. In the meantime Stalingrad, now an immense heap of ruins, held out, true to Stalin's order that there was to be no more retreat. For this reason, also because Hitler had announced its capture only to concede later that a chunk of it actually was not in German hands, and since the town carried Stalin's name, it became a symbol. Ribbentrop's words on Stalingrad, written in his diary on September 27, 1942, are ambiguous when read now: "Perhaps this battle will be elevated to a symbol of Europe's fight for freedom. By capturing this city, the great connecting center of North- and South-Russia, which also controls the Volga, the main communications artery of the land, we shall inflict a blow on the enemy from which it will never recover." [35]

During September and October, Washington had to consider

the possibility of imminent Axis victory on a world-wide scale. However, the Axis tide had reached its high point, and began to ebb during those same months. Rommel's African army was stopped before Alexandria. The Nazi groundswell was blocked on the river Don and at Stalingrad. The poet, Boris Pasternak, commented in a Moscow broadcast: "The Germans thought they could win the war on the basis that two and two make four—by adding up the planes and tanks; they had more than anybody else at the beginning. But you don't necessarily win the war in such a crude way as that. True they did have some idea of psychology when they invaded France. But here they knew much less about us and were groping in the dark." The Americans launched an offensive on the Solomons and Aleutians as a result of a naval victory in the Pacific at the Battle of Midway.

The big change took place in the first days of November, with General Montgomery's offensive at El Alamein, followed soon after by the landing of American and British troops in North Africa. Was it the second front the Russians had insisted upon? It was generally believed that the Americans were arguing for an offensive in Western Europe while Churchill advised an attack on the 'soft underbelly' of the Nazis—Italy or the Balkans—and that North Africa was the result of a compromise. In October of 1942, a Swiss paper blamed the Americans for the absence of a second front: "Till a short time ago one was inclined to believe that the British government or the British military were holding back the establishment of a second front, and that the Americans were far more willing to take the risks involved in that enterprise. However, the *Times* and other papers, urging better coordination of allied strategy, have let it be known that the Americans have resisted British efforts to transform the military leadership into a 'United Nations' command and general staff. These hints may give Stalin a clue where to find those responsible for Allied reluctance to open up a second front. The same papers remind one how much more distant relations between the United States and Soviet Russia have remained than between Russia and Great Britain. It will not be surprising if Stalin comes to the conclusion that certain American circles dislike the perspective of a Soviet state emerging too powerful from the war." [36]

Stalin aired his own views at a meeting of the Moscow Soviets on November 7. He said: "How can we explain why the Germans were able to seize the initiative and reach such results? In answering this question I would point out the absence of a second front that made it possible for Hitler to throw all his reserves into the battle and thus hold the numerical superiority. Should the Germans have been compelled to withdraw sixty of their own divisions and twenty of their allies, they would now stand on the brink of the abyss. As it is, 240 German and allied divisions are fighting on the Russian front while only four German and eleven Italian divisions are taking part in the African campaign." [37]

In this atmosphere, on November 3, a few days before the Allied landing in North Africa and Montgomery's break-through could influence the voters, the American public went to the polls to elect members to the House of Representatives and one-third of the Senate. It was after nine months of harassing experiments in meeting wartime demands, and in an atmosphere largely made up of bewilderment and frustration, that the voters went to the polls, if they did not stay home, as an unprecedented number of them did. An English magazine commented: "There were no recognizable political issues to fight over. Absolute victory, and as early as possible, is the single present aim of the American people. The bitter and unrelenting antagonism to the Roosevelt regime, in which certain sections of the public have been absorbed, was of necessity submerged, for the President is also Commander-in-Chief, unchallengable Head of the Republic, to whom, as the newly elected Governor of New York declared, unwavering support must be accorded. There could be no party or organization standing for an anti-war program; nor could the isolationists—powerful still, and unrepentent as regards America-First and no European entanglements—do other than uphold the national course. . . ." [38]

Roosevelt the politician faded, and the statesman, leader of all peoples fighting for their freedom, rose to the august and tremendous task that became his lot to carry to accomplishment.

"The news of Rommel's defeat in Libya pushed the election results off the front page. The announcement of the American expeditionary force's landing in French Africa was made on the following Sunday. If these sensational events had occurred one week earlier, the Republican party gains might have been reduced by half," the same article pointed out: "As it was, the President was called upon to proclaim the American invasion of Africa, and deliver his historic appeal to the French people, four days only after bracing himself to meet the shock of an election reverse which at that moment cannot have appeared to him as anything other than a grim irony of the democratic process. . . . It is now being asked: To what extent do the November results affect the power and standing of the President, and what line of action in Congress is to be expected from a greatly strengthened opposition? The reply as to the first question can hardly be in doubt."

At this juncture the German Fuehrer reiterated his unshakable conviction in final victory. He saw its guarantee in the fact that the National Socialist Party wielded all power in the State and that the Army was becoming more and more permeated with National Socialism. But it was just as strong a guarantee of victory that he, Hitler, was the leader of the country. He drew a comparison between himself and Emperor William II and said, "The Kaiser of that time was a man who lost the capacity to fight the enemy. In me you have a man who never thinks of capitulation. Even as a child I always had the last word." [39]

Hitler had drawn another historical comparison before, in his declaration of war on America on December 11, 1941, when he said: "It is a fact that the two historical conflicts between Germany and the United States were instigated by two men in the United States, namely by President Woodrow Wilson and President Franklin D. Roosevelt. History has spoken out its judgment on President Wilson. His name will forever be connected with the basest breach of faith. . . ." As to Roosevelt, the Fuehrer, comparing him with himself, said: "I understood all too well that there was a world-wide gap between Roosevelt's outlook on life and mine. When World War I came, Roosevelt took part in it under Wilson. I tried as a private in the German army to do my duty for two years in the face of the enemy and returned as poor as I had been in the spring of 1914 when I joined the army. And when Roosevelt took up the career of politician, financially well-equipped, well-protected, possessing influential connections, I was struggling as a nameless unknown man for the resurrection of my people to which the greatest injustice in history had been done. The power that carried Roosevelt forward was the power which I fought from inner conviction in the strength of the fate of my nation." [40]

Mussolini stated to Ciano, on the occasion of a Roosevelt speech that the Duce had particularly disliked, "Never in the course of history has a nation been guided by a paralytic. There have been bald kings, fat kings, handsome and even stupid kings, but never kings who, in order to go to the bathroom and the dinner table, had to be supported by other men." [41]

When Churchill addressed both Houses of Congress, an English magazine had this to say about him and Roosevelt: "The power of words is one of the weighty factors in this war; the eloquence of these two men has given form and coherence to the previously undefined aspirations of the Allied peoples, and has established for them personally a joint leadership of their two nations, which is different in kind from the collaboration of, for instance, President Wilson and Mr. Lloyd George." [42]

An Englishman described the daily routine of the wartime President: "The Roosevelt day begins when he is awakened at 8:30 A.M. Admiral McIntyre is his first visitor. After the routine physical check-up, the President eats a hearty breakfast, during which he begins his first conference—usually with his secretary; sometimes with his wife. From then on until midnight or after he is hard at work—receiving interviewers, conferring with his chief subordinates, drafting legislation and speeches, telephoning Mr. Churchill in London, etc." [43]

Dr. Hans Thomsen, ex-German Ambassador to Washington, told the foreign correspondents in Stockholm that President

Roosevelt was a super-intelligent man with great energy and Mrs. Roosevelt was undeserving of the caricatures and ridicule aimed at her by the German Press. "She may not be a beauty queen," said Dr. Thomsen, "but she has great charm and purpose of mind and is, therefore, a great asset to her country." When a neutral correspondent asked him what prompted his remarks, deviating so radically from the propaganda line, he replied that in his opinion the first requisite in engaging in successful warfare was to size up one's enemy correctly. Underestimation was fatal, he added.[44]

Mrs. Roosevelt as a personality, her influence on the President, and her role in his attitudes and decisions were amply commented on abroad. "How any one could have held the official position as First Lady for ten years and still no bit of her shirt front stuffed I can scarcely explain," a London magazine wrote.[45] "She is informal, interested and interesting. And yet she is one of the most dignified of human beings. You feel, as she pours out tea from a large silver teapot, that you are in the presence of royalty. She has always maintained her own individuality and runs her separate public existence. She talks with great freedom and admirable common sense. She cannot possibly write in public what she says in private, and her column 'My Day,' which many people in this country have now seen, is a model of banality, but it is also an extraordinary sign of an independent and vigorous personality. There is not a word in it that is not commonplace, but as it is quite simple and sincere and written from the White House, most people want to read it."

An English writer found her development rather unexpected. "Anna Eleanor Roosevelt was brought up," he noted, "by a dowager aunt to believe that politics was something no 'nice' woman should go near, lest she spoil her skirts. There is something ironic in the memory now, for Mrs. Roosevelt's whole married life has been that of a politician's wife, and of late years she had become expert in the art herself, having been forced not only to share her husband's interests, but to bring to practical realization some of her cherished ideals. For many years now Eleanor Roosevelt has been the foremost champion of democracy.

She talks, and writes and—what is more to the point—lives democracy."[46]

"Mrs. Roosevelt is a great many things," another author asserted, "but among others she is a political force. A political force, not a politician. . . . It may pain professional feminists to have to face the fact, but the woman who in American history has played the greatest role in public affairs, has never run for office, never won the votes of others, and got her chance by becoming the wife of a master politician. There is a woman in the Federal Cabinet; there are women in both Houses of Congress; there are women judges; . . . but the woman who best justifies female emancipation is, above all, a mother and a grandmother. . . . It took the politicians some time to realize that ordinary political rules didn't apply to the Roosevelts, less even to Eleanor than to F.D.R. They began to think that, however distressing it might be to admit it, she was an asset. . . . Indeed, more than once, it was apparent that the President's wife, far from being a parasite on her husband's popularity and prestige, was able to lend him, at low moments, some of the political capital she had accumulated . . ."[47]

"In the kaleidoscope of Washington and the United States, Mrs. Roosevelt stood still. Not politically, of course—few people have ever travelled as much—but morally and intellectually. For her, the New Deal was not just an experiment, a rag-bag of expedients; it was a chance to get into the American system some of the social conquests of less fortunate countries. In the expressive American term, Mrs. Roosevelt had a concern for the 'underprivileged' and she did not conceal her preoccupation. She talked and wrote. . . . And as she moved all over the country, winning friends and influencing people by her candor, her courage, her competence, she became a serious political force, an embodied League of Woman Voters. Of all her assets, courage was the most striking. Mrs. Roosevelt was forever disdaining the human prudence of the politician to which her husband as President and head of the Democratic Party had to pay some deference. Mrs. Roosevelt paid none. . . ."

"If Mrs. Roosevelt had one political speciality, it was youth.

And from a politician's point of view, youth is important, because it is going to have votes and is going to vote a long time, while many of the soundest party voters are old, or indeed, dead. But although it is necessary to cultivate youth, it is hard to do so; for the young are especially good at seeing through the personal ambitions of politicians. They did not see through Mrs. Roosevelt, since there was nothing to see through; no hidden ambitions, no desire to pull a fast one on some rival—just sympathy, just a desire to help, just, perhaps, a memory of a not very happy youth, for there are more ways than one of being 'under-privileged.'"

Julian Huxley, returning from a visit to America, quoted Quentin Reynolds who, at a public dinner, told of his impressions of America after his stay in Russia. He had expected to find America engaged in an all-out struggle to lick the Japanese and Hitler, but so far as he could see that war seemed to be chiefly against Britain and Roosevelt. "This rhetorical exaggeration," Huxley wrote, "contains a considerable kernel of truth. The United States is still very far from being united. The sudden emotional flame of national unity which swept the nation after Pearl Harbor died down after a few weeks. The real unity, international as well as national, has to be forged through effort, suffering and disaster. It is steadily, if slowly, taking shape; but meanwhile its emergence is being veiled and delayed by the old disunity which is still very much there, though often manifested in new ways." [48]

Then Huxley explained what Reynolds called the war against Roosevelt and wrote: "It is as difficult for many Englishmen to realize the bitterness against President Roosevelt which exists in many quarters in America, as it is for most Americans to realize that there is serious criticism of Mr. Churchill, let alone hostility towards him, in Britain. But it is a fact. Mr. Churchill came in as a new broom; Mr. Roosevelt has ten years of New Deal behind him. Thus to that large minority of Americans who hate the New Deal, Roosevelt, in spite of their acceptance of his foreign policy, is still 'that man,' he and all the works of the New Deal an un-American anathema. He is accused in the press and on public platforms of using the war to further his New Deal domestic policy, of being a good politician but a bad administrator, of allowing old grudges to stand in the way of war appointments, of taking too much on his own shoulders until he becomes, in Walter Lippmann's words, the 'bottleneck of bottlenecks,' of not tolerating first-class men in his vicinity, of favoring labor at the expense of business and the nation. When it is impolite to attack him directly, the attack is made on one of his pet schemes, or on Mrs. Roosevelt. . . .

"It is true that he has not offered satisfactory positions to opponents of high calibre like Willkie, that he has no Inner War Cabinet and no Ministers Without Portfolio or their equivalents whose main job would be to help him to think and to make decisions on general policy; it is also true that he has tried to ensure that labor's hard-won gains (won a generation later than in Britain) shall not be lost as a result of war fever. But many of his opponents go far beyond constructive criticism in their attacks. They use any policies of his which happen to be unpopular as means of discrediting the Administration."

A magazine sized up Roosevelt before the elections of 1942 and when the war had reached its lowest ebb. "This President is a very different man from Mr. Wilson. He has the tact, geniality, humanity which the other lacked, and when interested groups in Congress are petty and obstructive, he usually knows how to rally the common man and average elector to his side. Few rulers of his stature have been so little disposed to play the dictator. But events may be driving him to assert himself in a way which he would be the first to regret, and it is unlucky that this should happen on the eve of the midterm elections." [49]

A Swiss newspaper, reporting on how the American public was informed on the world situation, wrote: "The most significant comments are undoubtedly made by President Roosevelt himself whose speeches, messages and fireside chats impress the American public with their unusual brightness and exemplary clarity."

The reporter elaborated on Roosevelt's popularity: "Before Pearl Harbor only about half of the population was satisfied with the policies of the President. Right after the Japanese attack, the figure of those who approved of his policies rose to 84 and since that time it stands with little deviation at 78 per cent. The public demonstrations and meetings also show that his war policy is by and large popular. In New York there was a mass demonstration on June 14, called 'New York at War' in which about two and one-half million people took part. The press did not exaggerate when it noted that it was the most powerful demonstration of its kind in the entire history of mankind. No less significant is, however, the attitude of the political professionals, the circles which have followed Roosevelt policies in the last years with outspoken displeasure, even those belonging to the Democratic Party. The yearly convention of the State Governors, for instance, issued a resolution on July 2 that expressed its full approval of Roosevelt's policies 'which had warned the nation of the dangers that had threatened it.' On July 23 one experienced the entirely unusual spectacle of the National Association of Manufacturers and two Unions fighting one another, accepting a common resolution supporting the President. The great majority of the population unquestionably is ready for even greater sacrifices in the interest of warfare as an inquiry of Fortune Magazine made clear." [50]

"Indeed, Roosevelt is a most uncommon man," R. G. Menzies told his fellow Australians, who knew little of America and her President. "He is singularly endowed with the graces of life. He is a man of great personal charm and magnetism. He has that quiet and smiling humour which we so readily understand. His selective command of language is remarkable. He is perhaps the most effective living politician: his knowledgeable finger is always on the pulse of public opinion. Each of these things is a useful attribute for a great man to have, but not one of them of itself will make a man great. Roosevelt's greatness proceeds from a combination of two things: First, his indomitable courage. No man stricken down by infantile paralysis in his adult years, who literally rises from his bed to become three times President of the United States, is to be denied that superb attribute. No man whose political programme puts him at odds with almost everybody in his own circle, and who pushes on with it, can be denied admiration. And second, his far-reaching and sensitive understanding of the real problems of common humanity. . . . In

1935, when I was passing through the United States, every newspaper was attacking Roosevelt; all the people of a conservative or comfortable turn of mind were belaboring him; he appeared to have no 'big' friends. Yet he has passed from triumph to triumph. Contemporary valuations are all too frequently astray, because superficial and flashy weigh too heavily in the scales of contemporary judgment. But, allowing for all this, we may surely name Franklin Delano Roosevelt among the greatest of the Presidents of the United States." [51]

"It is undeniable that in the succession of great rulers Franklin D. Roosevelt will be accounted among the greatest," an English review of his Public Papers averred. "These pages present the portrait of a man of high courage, of wide vision, of great tenacity of purpose; above all of unquenchable faith. Critics of his administration there must needs be; but even critics will agree that in the gravest moment of its history America has found a leader endowed with rare beauty of character, disarming in its humanity and simplicity, and endowed also with a capacity, never excelled among its long succession of great rulers, for prudent planning and vigorous action." [52]

"Roosevelt is a Jeffersonian democrat, projected into the industrial age," wrote Harold J. Laski. "Deeply religious, profoundly American, an aristocrat with that magnanimity of spirit which loathes cruelty and special privileges, he is less concerned with inferences from a system than with adaptation of intuitions. He is quick, vivid, agile, incisive, rather than profound. He is a born political strategist, feeling the moves of his enemy months ahead, always prepared for the tactical withdrawal, never losing hold of the supreme end of the campaign. He thinks in the terms in which his public naturally thinks, with the result that he has a unique power to put his issues before it in the language it understands; and he has the capacity to put them in that historical background which makes them relevant to permanent principles of American history. He understands how much of popular thinking is done in concrete terms, and it is rare for him to define an issue without searching for the phrases which will grip the mind of the radio listener. There is not an atom of evidence which would justify the ascription to the President of either the Socialist outlook or the dictatorial habits of which his opponents have accused him. His political measures make him, if any label is sought for, a Liberal of the experimental school of Mr. Lloyd George; while his political habits show, as in his press conferences, a passionate faith in the urgency of educated public opinion."[53]

12

A WORLD LEADER

The Soviet army followed up its great victory at Stalingrad with a powerful offensive on a sector over sixty miles long on the Don front. The Anglo-American armies landed in North Africa to meet Rommel's tanks fleeing from El Alamein. Victory was on the march, though the way still appeared long and tortuous. Yet, postwar problems already were cropping up, especially due to the relocation of power. Military strategy, even tactics, became heavily tinged with postwar fears and ambitions, eating away at the cohesive force of the alliance.

Dissension broke into the open and kept alive Nazi hopes for a final victory, even though their situation on the battlefield had deteriorated. The Nazis even expected to place themselves in a position to choose between allying with the West or with the Russians. In such a hypothetical case they would have unquestionably preferred joining with the West in an anti-Bolshevik front, since leaders and led alike dreaded the Russians, whose land they had scorched and whose people they had killed or enslaved.

Nazi hopes thrived on suspicion among the Allies and vanished only with the destruction of Germany in blood and fire.

During this period President Roosevelt began planning to set up an international organization to arbitrate conflicts between the principal powers. He also took care that Congress, this time, would pledge itself to join the new world organization before the approaching end of the war encouraged dissensions that would allow the alliance to crack.

The organization would rest on agreement among the three great powers emerging from victory—America, Soviet Russia, and Britain. They, in Roosevelt's view, were to assume the heritage of the dissolving empires, Japanese, German, French, Dutch, even British, and see to it that the peoples liberated from colonial status would establish self-government in the spirit of the four freedoms. Such policies would demand great power agreements on principles and policies, and on their manner of execution. Roosevelt believed that agreement might not prove so difficult if the powers saw clearly the alternative of chaos and a new world war.

Roosevelt deemed decolonization the most formidable postwar problem. Far from trying to slow its progress, he was resolved to expedite and support it. His policy was bound to clash with the policy of the British, but Roosevelt doubted that peoples once liberated from Axis overlordship would submit again to colonial rule. Their expected movements for independence were to be channelled into a peaceful process lest they lead to upheavals and wars.

When Japanese troops reached the Indian border, the cooperation of the Indians with the Allies became indispensable to effective defense of the subcontinent. Indian leaders wanted a definite British promise of independence upon the conclusion of the war. Churchill was reluctant to give anything but vague promises, but the President made no bones about his support for the Indian claim, even though the British authorities in India considered his envoy there *persona non grata.*

Roosevelt counted on the Russians to join him in ending colonialism. He related this idea to Molotov in 1942 when the Soviet Foreign Minister visited Washington, but Molotov had come to exact a definite date for a second front, and he put first things first. For his country, still largely occupied by the enemy, the first aim was to defeat the Nazis.

By 1943, however, as Russian might began to be felt, the second front took on a new political meaning. The colonial question moved into the foreground as the result of the liberation of North Africa, where a decision had to be made whom to commission with the administration of the liberated French colonies. In view of Roosevelt's intentions with respect to colonies, he could not be sympathetic to a man like General de Gaulle who was dead set to restore the integrity of the French empire and its great power status. But in opposing De Gaulle, Roosevelt for the first time ran into adverse liberal public opinion at home and abroad.

General Dwight D. Eisenhower, in his *Crusade in Europe,* related the President's point of view on the future of the French colonies. "He speculated at length," Eisenhower wrote, "on the possibility of France's regaining her ancient position of prestige and power in Europe and on this point he was very pessimistic. As a consequence, his mind was wrestling with the questions of methods for controlling certain strategic points in the French empire which he felt that the country might no longer be able to hold."

An Englishman recalled Roosevelt's preoccupation with the colonial question as far back as in 1940, after the collapse of the French army. Early, the President's private secretary, had said to the press "that the United States considered that every continent should have a Monroe Doctrine of its own. For instance, in the case of Indo-China, we think the disposition should be decided among the Asiatic countries." [1] To General Stillwell the President revealed an instance of decolonization he expected to take place: "I have a plan to make Hong Kong a free port: free to commerce of all nations—of the whole world. But let's raise the Chinese flag there first, and then Chiang can the next day make a grand gesture and make it a free port. That's the way to handle that! I am sure that Chiang would be willing to make that a free port, and goods could come through Siberia—in bond—without customs examinations." [2]

His viewpoint was in line with traditional American policy, as an English magazine reminded its readers.[3] "[A policy] . . . which has been accentuated by American participation in the Second World War, and particularly by her association with China in the struggle against Japan . . . is a revived policy against what is called colonialism. The British government in India and the colonies, as well as Japanese aggression, is seen as the present form of the spirit against which the American colonists rose in revolt in the eighteenth century. Present-day Americans are concerned to help in a Declaration of Independence for all subject peoples. Where independence is not immediately practicable, they want some international control of the backward areas. The abolition of imperialism and the colonial system, though not mentioned in the Atlantic Charter, is likely to take a prominent place in the peace programmes of World War II as the abolition of militarism and vindication of the right of national self-determination took in the American peace programmes of World War I."

At the conference of Casablanca in January, 1943, Roosevelt's main concern was colonialism, "a problem upon which, in his feelings, future peace depended. The colonial system, Roosevelt thought, implied wars. If it survives, all organisation of the peace is futile," a French author stressed.[4] Such deep conviction involved increasing difficulties with America's traditional ally, France, and with America's closest associate in latter-day world conflicts, Britain, both colonial empires. It seemed far more difficult to deprive Britain of her colonies, since her people had shouldered the greatest burden of the war in the West, than to refuse to help restore the colonial empire of France, whose administrators and armies had received the Americans as enemies. Such French publicists as Pertinax would refuse to believe the rumors according to which "American diplomacy has strange views in regard to the French empire after the war. In its plans France would not resume her historic place as a great power,"[5] but, in fact, when at the Teheran conference in December, 1943, Stalin spoke against restoring France's colonies to her, he met with Roosevelt's full approval.

In the face of these formidable opponents, General de Gaulle stood fast, representing the phantom of French grandeur that threatened to dissolve in a cold wind of realities. A Frenchman in Egypt asserted: "We have to follow him, the Chief, who spontaneously, on the very day of the defeat of our armies, upheld against everything and everybody the position of France. His instinct was so sure, corresponding so fully to the then yet unexpressed sentiment of the community, that the people of France are now lining up behind the man, who yesterday was unknown to them."[6]

The divergence of American policy on France from that of the British became clear when America kept diplomatic ties with the Vichy regime, and again when Roosevelt refused to entrust de Gaulle with the administration of the liberated French territories in North Africa. *The Economist* analyzed the American attitude: "The United States was not in the fight at the time of the French collapse, and Americans did not come to think of Vichy as a personal betrayal. Hence a much greater tenderness for 'men of Vichy' and a greater readiness to distinguish between '*attentists*' and traitors. President Roosevelt has stated his full support for the North African arrangements . . . as a matter of immediate military necessity, and Mr. Eden has confirmed Britain's concurrence, presumably on this temporary basis. But the problem is not solved because it can be shelved for the moment. It will remain a serious problem in North Africa itself; and the same question will arise, whatever point is chosen for the re-invasion of Europe . . ."

By June 1944, the problem of whom to entrust the administration of the liberated territories of France made it imperative for Roosevelt to revise his attitude toward General de Gaulle. Roosevelt had always been irritated by the French leader's faith in his calling to embody the spirit of France. Since the time was close when the Allied forces would advance in France, the President relented in his distrust. The invasion required an undisturbed civilian administration behind the lines.

General de Gaulle was finally invited to Washington where he was received with all the formalities due to a visiting head of state.

"During my five days' stay in the Federal capital," General de Gaulle related in the last volume of his 'Memoires de Guerre' (Paris, Librairie Plon, 1956), "I see with admiration a torrent of confidence carry the American *élite* and I note that optimism becomes those who have the means. President Roosevelt has it without doubt. In the course of our discussions he . . . gives me an idea of political objectives he intends to attain thanks to victory. They appear to me grandiose but at the same time disquieting for Europe and for France . . . it is a system of permanent intervention instituted through international law. In his view a Directory of four, America, the Soviet Union, China and Great Britain will take care of the problems of the universe. A parliament of the United Nations will lend a democratic aspect to this power of the 'Big Four' . . . his words imply that American forces will be stationed on bases located in all regions of the Globe, some on the territory of France.

"Roosevelt counts on attracting the Soviets into a unit that will satisfy their ambitions. In this unit China will need his assistance and Britain will be compelled to play ball lest she lose her dominions. The middle and small powers will be influenced through assistance. Eventually, the right of the peoples to self-determination, the support tendered by Washington, and the American military bases will cause in Africa, Asia and Australia new sovereignties to rise, increasing the number of those obliged to America. In such perspective, questions like the fate of Germany, that of the Vistula, the Danube, the Balkans, the future of Italy appear secondary. Surely he will not go, in order to find a happy solution for these problems, as far as to sacrifice the monumental concept he dreams to realize.

"I listen to Roosevelt as he describes his projects . . . the words of the American President definitely convince me that logic and sentiment do not weigh heavily in matters between countries in comparison with the realities of power; that, what is important is to take what one is able to keep; that France to find her former place should rely on herself alone. I tell this to Roosevelt. He smiles and concludes: 'We shall do what we can. But it is true that in the service of France nobody can replace the French people.'"

An episode reveals how widely known it was that Roosevelt had been resolved not to return her colonies to France, particularly those in Asia. On August 22, 1945, three months after the President's death, "on his way to Saigon, General Leclerc was informed by Lord Mountbatten of the Potsdam decision that Indo-China be cut into two zones, one north, the other south of the 16th parallel; in the North the Japanese were to be disarmed by the Chinese, in the South, by the British. Mountbatten is reported to have said: 'If Roosevelt were still alive, you wouldn't stand a chance of getting back to Indo-China—but maybe it can be fixed now.' "[8]

The Economist noted that liberal opinion in America was so much disgusted with the political wrangling in Africa that it was turning away from Europe, and especially from 'imperialistic Britain' towards Russia and China, "which hold pride of place as partners in world order. . . . The paradox is that their indignation is meat for the isolationists." (February 6, 1943) The *Washington Star* went on record this way: "Recent developments have shown that we can deal with Russians in a friendly manner even more successfully than we can with others of our close friends and associates. One thing appears certain; we shall have no major disputes with Moscow over economic zones of influence of the air routes of the world."

Fortunately, not all postwar political questions divided the Allies. The first conference of the "United Nations" at Hot Springs, Virginia, in September, 1943, was a most promising prelude to their cooperation in and for peace. "It was in the President's view the first of the conversations between nations of like mind which were contemplated in the Mutual Aid Agreements to give, as the President said in his speech to the delegates, practical expression to the principles of the Atlantic Charter," a magazine commented.[9] "If Mr. Roosevelt succeeds in his design there will be built up a series of agreements . . . between the nations in the economic sphere sufficiently concrete to bear the strain which peace will impose upon the whole structure." The subject of the conference was furnishing relief, first of all food, to victims of war in the liberated countries. To those who considered the program rather modest, the magazine offered the reminder that "those who built the great cathedrals of Europe, which were designed to serve and have served successive generations, did not lay the foundations and build the whole framework at once, but started with modest beginnings and built on them, so that one part of the structure was in use while building was in progress in another.

"Our generation will have deserved well of posterity if it succeeds in doing no more than driving a few supports here and there into the morass which will confront us when the flood of the barbarian invasion has receded and been dammed at its source. . . . It may be that President Roosevelt had some such notion in mind of the limitation of the theoretical when he chose his subject for the first United Nations conference. He was looking for a topic of universal interest and appeal which would strike the imagination both of his own people and of the people of other countries."

Only a year after the disastrous start of the war the President's yearly message to Congress reflected the nation's satisfaction over the decisive turn in the European war. Congress, though its new majority was hostile to Roosevelt, was transformed into a friendly audience by his unusually mild appraisal of the general situation. "Not since the black days of early 1933," a magazine commented,[10] "has any address of the President been so overwhelmingly applauded. Even his most bitter critics were condemned to silence or grudging admiration. Congress was palpably impressed both by the production figures and his accounts of the war; and the 'hurt feelings' of legislators, industrialists and farmers alike have for the moment ceased to be headline news."

War production took, indeed, huge strides, and the program for 1943 accounted for about two-thirds of the national income. Even the Germans had to admit, though in a left-handed way, that America had more than lived up to expectations. "The power of the American economy is a fact; the unlimited power of the American economy, however, belongs to the realm of fables," a German magazine cautioned.[11] "It was unable under Roosevelt's presidency to solve its peace-time problems; it will even less be able to cope with the more difficult war problems. Stagnant and mainly consumer industries can neither structurally nor organizationally be turned into war production. America lacks manpower, and no importation of labor can help fill up the gap as in our country. Its finances already show the symptoms of inflation. All these factors affect production, as Mr. Nelson made manifest when he stated that the figures of production in August fell behind the figures provided in the plans. Anyway, this war is not going to be won or lost in the factories as our enemies in their overestimation of the economic factor believe, but in the battlefields."

The President, in his message to Congress in September, 1943, gave these production figures: ". . . during the two months of the recess of the Congress our factories produced approximately fifteen thousand planes. There was an especially important increase in the production of heavy bombers in August . . . During those same two months American shipyards put into commission 3,200,000 tons of large merchant ships—a total of 281 ships, almost five ships a day."

In that year, however, John L. Lewis threatened a walkout of the half million miners of his union, disregarding the national emergency. Many considered it as a challenge to the President's authority. However when an anti-strike Act was passed by Congress under the impact of national censure of Lewis Roosevelt vetoed it. Lewis had been a supporter of the President originally. An English weekly explained the labor leader's attitude: ". . . About mid-way of the President's second term a change became evident in his temper. It was clear that he expected more concessions than he received. . . . By 1939 it was obvious that he was in opposition; and in 1940 there was no more zealous opponent of the third term. When the CIO refused to follow him in his support of Mr. Willkie, he not only resigned from its leadership, but took with him the United Mine Workers, whose strength had been the foundation of CIO. When Roosevelt was re-elected, he had worked himself into a fury with the President. . . . His recent action in bringing out the miners on strike for an extra two dollars a day . . . was rather an effect than a cause of his inexhaustible willpower. . . . He has done a remarkable job for millions of American workers. . . . They rewarded him with a salary of $25,000 as well as their loyalty. But his vanity traps him. It has transformed a man who once looked as though he might be among the most creative Americans of his time into a man to whom hardly any political cause is wrong if its service enables him to hit back at those who have wounded his vanity." [12]

A reporter visited the mining areas, whose workers had blindly followed John L. Lewis even to the extent of damaging the nation's war effort.

"I should like to picture for you, not so much the country the miners live in but the sort of way these miners live and have lived," he related. "I will mention only one man, and he can stand, without knowing it, as a fair symbol of the miners' problems. . . . This man happens to be a Roosevelt man. He voted for him three times, and two years ago he felt badly about the way we shipped steel to the Japs. When the strikes were called last spring, he never hesitated. He isn't mad at anybody, and he will point out with some pride that when the strike was called, there was no need for a picket line anywhere along the valley. This is what he says: 'Well, if John L. says we walk out, that's all there is to it . . . I feel sorry for President Roosevelt. It must be an awful headache to him; but in all that time there's been only one man who promised things to us and got them. He said he'd get us decent wages: he got it. He said he'd get a mine inspector law: he got it.' I need hardly tell you that the name of the man is John L. Lewis." [13]

Meanwhile, the President and Prime Minister Churchill at Casablanca were agreeing upon the invasion of Sicily in order to insure command over the Mediterranean for the Allies, to permit them to unload huge amounts of supplies and add to the safety of the convoys in the Atlantic. The Conference adopted Roosevelt's principle of unconditional surrender, which while it might lengthen the war against the Germans, would not again give them a pretext to accuse the Allies of having lured them into surrender by fraudulent promises. However, Stalin did not accept this principle as guiding his war policy toward the Nazis. On the contrary, he allowed a German group in Russia to set up a Committee which reverted to the Bismarckian policy of friendship with Russia, and he stressed in his speeches that he had no intention of wiping out Germany.

Stalin would not consider the North African or Italian invasions as the second front that had been promised by the Western allies. While the Soviet armies were maintaining their rate of advance on the immense eastern front, Stalin warned that the offensive was bound to lose momentum in the spring if a second front in Western Europe did not force the Nazis to withdraw large contingents of their army and air force from the east.

Roosevelt and General Marshall were unable to overcome Churchill's stubborn resistance to opening up a second front in France and the Low Countries until more supplies and ports were available, and supremacy on the water and in the air assured.

The invasion of Sicily sealed the fate of Mussolini's empire and of his ambition to turn the Mediterranean into an Italian lake. He resigned in July, 1943, a prelude to the downfall of other fascist regimes.

Successes notwithstanding, victory for the Allies was not yet in sight, and while Americans and British repeatedly held conferences among themselves, there was a grave danger that the Soviet armies would reach Poland before an understanding among Stalin, Roosevelt, and Churchill could be worked out with respect to military rule over the liberated territories. Without a western front on the Continent, such an understanding, moreover, might be reached on terms excessively favorable to the Russians. Roosevelt and the American military leaders resolutely opposed Churchill's tenacious advocacy of a Balkan front which might have put the western armies in possession of eastern Central Europe before the Russians reached it. However, the price of this advantage might have been immediate Russian hostility.

Secretary of State Cordell Hull visited Moscow in October, 1943, to prepare a conference of the Chiefs of State. His mission proved to be a resounding success. In the last days of November the first conference between Roosevelt and Stalin took place in the Persian capital, Teheran, with Churchill, who had met the Soviet dictator before. They adopted a statement of common military objectives that foreshadowed measures to be applied in the liberated countries.

But final liberation was not yet in sight. The Allies met resolute resistance in Italy as soon as the Germans took up positions there and no one could guess when the Nazis would be ready to recognize the game was up, or whether the end of the war in Europe would affect the Japanese enough to save the Allies from a long and arduous campaign at the very source of the inflated Japanese empire.

A commentator compared the general situation in September, 1943, with that of a year before. ". . . It is legitimate to believe for the first time," he wrote, "that this is the beginning of the end for all our enemies. Little more than a year ago Mussolini was in Benghazi, waiting to enter Alexandria in triumph. Now nobody except Marshal Badoglio and a few Italian policemen know where he is. A year ago the Germans were in full cry for the Caucasus and the Volga. Now they are retreating from a desperate defense of Orel. A year ago the Axis bestrode the world like a Colossus. Today it is doubtful whether there is any Axis at all. A year ago the U-boats were eating out the heart of the Allied mercantile marine. Now they are eating their hearts out in harbor. A year ago Germany was only sporadically scarred. Today general ruin is spreading from her western provinces, as spilled ink spreads on blotting paper. . . . The contrast is no longer between bad and less bad, but between bad and good. Nothing is ever certain in war; but it is long odds that the next contrast will be between good and better. . . . In the Far East the Japanese have been driven out of three big bases . . . they have lost all the central Solomons. The Allies have been able to deploy real air strength, and in the middle fortnight of October alone destroyed 900 Japanese aircraft." [14]

The same magazine cheerfully surveyed the diplomatic field from the vantage point of its reporter in Washington. ". . . the nation welcomed the tripartite conference in Moscow," it asserted. "The rank and file of Americans want an understanding with Russia. The nation's attitude towards the Soviet Union is a mixture of admiration, astonishment and apprehension. Certainly Russia puzzles us. Our diplomacy has been reconciled to the need of putting relations with the Soviet Union on the basis of the right of each nation to a feeling of security. It is prepared to go far in recognizing 'strategic frontiers' for Russia."

British magazines were no less optimistic in the first months of 1943.[15] "By the time Hitler speaks on Saturday the last vestiges of the German army encircled at Stalingrad will have ceased to exist—a fact that can hardly fail in Berlin to recall the assurance given by Hitler the last time he addressed his people that 'Stalingrad will be taken, you can be certain of that.' This was on September 30. On November 8 he added the information that 'we have got it except for some very small parts.' There was some truth in that. The Germans had come within an ace of taking Stalingrad."

A month later an English weekly commented on the tenth anniversary of Hitler's accession to power: [16] ". . . It was an occasion on which the leaders of the Nazi party did not conceal their gloom . . . The crushing defeats of the German armies in Russia, and their lack of success elsewhere, has compelled the Nazis to change the technique of their propaganda. Hitherto Hitler has been represented as infallible organizer of victories, confronted by enemies powerless to stand up against his irresistible strength. But now his appeal is not the success motive, but fear. . . . Hitler sees the menace of the Central Asiatic flood let loose to surge 'upon the oldest civilized continent.' "

But the Germans tried to turn a terrible defeat into a moral victory as the British had done at Dunkirk in 1940, when they rescued their armies stripped of weapons and equipment. "The capacity of the German people for sentimental twaddle about themselves," an English magazine registered,[17] "is greater than that of any other people. . . . Anything that happens, good or bad, can be turned to the Nazi purpose provided it be treated in the right sentimental manner. The fall of Stalingrad, for instance, was announced in an elaborate technique of melodrama with music and funeral dirges designed to extrude gloom and tragedy. . . . it is clearly dangerous, even with so malleable a material as the German character, to argue that black is the same thing as white, that defeat in the field is actually the same thing as invincibility in the field. Yet in his address to the armed forces on January 30, Goering resorted to a bold tour de force of putting Stalingrad in the same light as the British had put Dunkirk, although the British had saved their men while General Paulus surrendered his army. Goering declared: 'of all the terrific battles, the battle for Stalingrad stood out like a gigantic monument . . . ; every German would come to pronounce the word Stalingrad with holy awe and remember that it was there that Germany stamped the seal of final victory, because people who could fight like that must win.' "

A Swedish writer warned the Allies that a political collapse inside Germany might rob them of the fruits of their victory:[18] "If the German military front," the article ran, "proves stronger than the home front . . . it may happen that a German capitulation will confront the Allies not with a beaten opponent capable of negotiating, but with a smashed-up state and a gigantic rioting army. More than one Finnish writer has been speculating on the nature of Russia's plans in a way that suggests a possibly mischievous motive . . . Russia, they say, is trying through the German National Committee set up in Moscow, to alleviate the good will of the German masses in order both to defeat Hitlerism the more quickly and to lay the foundation of a preponderant Russian influence in postwar Germany. They add that Russia's present offensive . . . is dictated by the political strategy of forcing a decision with Germany before the Allies can land in western Europe so that the victory and the settlement will be alike Russian; a rather piquant variant on the more common theme of a Russian insistence on a second front."

However, an English magazine found the Nazi position far from being hopeless. "The weapon on which they rely," it explained, "to wear down the Allied strength so that the plans concerted at Casablanca will be still-born, is the U-boat. It has been stated that the excess of U-boat building over sinkings is ten per month. If we are to take this figure seriously, it reflects a very grave state of affairs indeed. It has been pointed out that the Allied shipbuilding also shows a positive balance over the enemy sinkings; but we cannot consider the position relieved. It is still possible that the enemy can weaken, if not forestall, the Allied offensives by this means. . . . There is little value in the immense number of trained troops and manufactured material in Britain and in the United States if they cannot be transported to the points were they are needed." [19]

A Swiss monthly had authentic information about Nazi aspirations, which it wholeheartedly supported. "There are three parties and not two with regard to Europe: Germany, the western Allies, and Russia. Each is fighting to make his point of view prevail. From this basic aspect one should not be misled by appearances. . . . The fact is that Russia avoids any compromise with the capitalistic powers. Each wages war for its own aims. They go so far as to create on their territories temporary governments like those established in London. In case of Soviet victory these 'governments' will become sheer instruments of Moscow in its plans of intervening in Europe at a later date. Would the British and the Americans abandon our continent to Bolshevism? No matter what happens, Germany believes that sooner or later events will take place to her advantage. A century ago, under Louis Philippe, Stendhal said: 'In a hundred years Europe will be either republican or cossack.' The first alternative hasn't come true. Will the second materialize?" [20]

A weekly thought it saw a more immediate chance for the Germans to redress the balance. "For the next six months," it asserted, "it will be the main Axis object to prevent the United Nations from concentrating shipping which will enable the building up of a great Allied striking force for the assault of Europe. Hitler's urgent need is to create a second front against our shipping. . . . His one great hope is Japan. It is evident that the Allies have given priority—rightly—to the European theatre of war. Such forces as are in the Pacific are maintained on the basis of strict economy of force. Only a major Japanese attack either on India or Australia would lead to an alteration in the present distribution of Allied shipping and armed forces . . . It is sometimes suggested that the Japanese do not care overmuch about the fate of their partners in Europe. That is a false conclusion drawn from correct premises. Japan's policy will be not to do anything which might go against her own interests. . . . But Japanese interests dictate very definitely that the two naval powers and the one land power which can challenge her hegemony in Asia shall not be triumphant in Europe. To that extent therefore she is vitally interested in German victory and will go to great length to prevent a German defeat at the hands of the United Nations." [21]

A Swiss newspaper mused over the changing times on the occasion of a Hitler-Mussolini meeting in April, 1943. It commented: "The world is paying little attention to the latest meeting of the dictators. How different it was when they met in 1940 on the Brenner! People held their breaths, feeling they were witnessing the encounter of Gods. . . . At one time Hitler staged legendary weekends to baffle the world, now they have lost much of their frightening effect. . . . They have become if not banalities, at least events of which the world simply takes note." [22]

Yet what Hitler was perpetrating ought to have alarmed the world. It could not be called falling back into barbarism because the extent of his inhumanity had no parallel in history. "The Nazis are making good Hitler's promise," *The Economist* reported, "to exterminate the Jews. Since July last the ghettoes of Poland have been emptied, and Jews have been deported from enemy-occupied countries to the east. The journey of these unhappy men, women and children is designed to guarantee that few of them will survive. They are packed in cattle-trucks so closely that the dead have no room to fall to the stinking lime-strewn floor. At their destination the slaughter camps await, where all—young and old, mothers and children, the sick, the infirm—all, in a word, whose strength cannot be exploited for the German war effort, are massacred by mass-methods of destruction. Of the six million Jews of Europe, over two million are gone already. Thousands more are being herded across Europe to their death. The mind falters before such horrors." [23]

Shortage of shipping space prevented the Allied governments from saving more than a fraction of those Jews who had fled to places accessible to the Allies. The moral indignation of the world had long ceased to mean anything to Hitler and his henchmen.

Shortage of shipping space also compelled firm priorities to be established in regard to the assignment of manpower and equipment. Differences of opinion inevitably arose about the standards by which priorities were determined, reflecting not so much the temperament and individual judgment of the leaders as their nations' attitude to the war, their concept of its meaning and aims, and their interests in waging it in a particular way.

The personal conviction of a political or military leader as to the interests of his nation led also to dissension within commanding national units. MacArthur resented the island-hopping strategy dictated to him as commander of the Pacific theatre of war, but the decision remained firmly with President Roosevelt, even though in military matters the President normally relied on his trusted generals and admirals. Roosevelt yielded to Churchill over the question of a second front in the west, but he resisted Churchill's stubborn insistence on a Balkan campaign. As American power unfolded in producing for and supplying all Allied armies, the American point of view increasingly prevailed. The President, in also being Commander-in-Chief, stood for America. The two were identified in the eyes of the world to an extent unprecedented in the past, except for the short period when Woodrow Wilson's messages appeared to be remaking the world. Roosevelt's long tenure in office and the expectation that he would hold the Presidency at least until the end of the war, furthered this image. The dictators also increased his prestige by their inclination to call Roosevelt the arch-enemy, who had somehow succeeded in mesmerizing the "real" America. By making Roosevelt Enemy No. 1 the dictators raised him to Hope No. 1 in the eyes of their victims, the oppressed and persecuted of their realms.

As world leadership accrued to America Roosevelt became the leader of the world. ". . . The very excellence of America's war performance has thrust that country so prominently into the world arena," an Australian magazine stated, "and is so clearly fastening on her a responsibility for the war's global outcome commensurate with her war-time prestige, that she cannot help realizing that destiny in postwar matters is inevitable. Whichever way America may decide to go, whatever decision she may make, these will affect not her alone, but all the world."[24] In the writer's view, the perspective of a post-war community of free nations was opening. . . . [There is] a conflict in American minds as to the content of their most cherished ideal—Liberty. Is it to be confined to freedom of business for the business man, or freedom from outside competition for farmer and worker, or even freedom as an American national prerogative to act independently in the world as an unconditional unit? Or is it an ideal which, starting in the thirteen States, eventually covered the present Union and is now destined to link with other islands of Liberty to cover the whole earth?"

Nothing illustrated so eloquently the difference between American and Nazi world leadership as the way each affected other peoples. A Frenchman noted: "The United States, in supplying the United Nations with goods useful for waging war, reserve the right to request later a compensation in kind. She gives cash value and is supposed to receive values when peace will be restored. The Reich does not give away but receives cash value from all countries associated with her, in goods she needs, and it is she, the powerful protector, who makes the dubious promise to pay for them by deliveries of industrial articles after the war."[25]

MacArthur's dissatisfaction with the secondary role of the Pacific war stirred not only the isolationists but also other Americans who considered the war against the Japanese to be the genuine American war, free from the complications of political wrangling between the Allies in North Africa and Italy. The priority of the European war rested, however, on sound judgment. "Between two evils one had to choose the lesser one," explained a French writer. "The United States was incapable in 1942 of stopping the Japanese except near the confines of Australia, having lost mastery of the sea and air and needing time to build ships and planes to reconquer it. It is true that

Australia and China were in danger in 1942 but so were Russia and England. Should the latter have been defeated it might have made ultimate restoration impossible." [26]

In the meantime the Japanese acquired territories so vast and so rich that it appeared a most formidable undertaking to dislodge them. When General Tojo, the Japanese Prime Minister, reviewed the situation in the Diet, an English magazine commented: "Some of the claims made by General Tojo . . . are true and cannot be ignored by the Allies. It is a fact that important natural resources of what he called 'the world's greatest treasure house' are now in Japan's hands, though she may lack the technical means and the shipping to exploit them fully or sufficiently transport them. She has access to rich supplies of rubber, tin and cinchona which have been lost to us. She is in possession of numerous and advantageously situated air bases for the control of the Western Pacific. In view of the fact that the longer she has to make use of these gains the stronger she will be, it cannot be said that time is on our side in the Pacific war." [27]

Later, in the face of officially-inspired American urging that the British grant independence to India after the war, the same English paper took up a rather considerate position: "It is entirely salutary for us," it conceded, "to be faced with temperate American criticism of our Indian policy or our colonial administration, and equally salutary for America to have the facts of the situation temporarily put before her and be given an opportunity of considering which of her criticisms is just. . . . At the moment it is British colonial policy which most needs elucidation, for the impression exists in large circles in the United States, fostered by left-wing critics both there and here, that exploitation and maladministration figure largely in British colonial administration not only of yesterday but of today, and that in consequence some kind of internationalization of colonies is to be desired."

The anti-British mood of the American public was, in the view of an English weekly, a reflection of the opposition to the President for a fourth term. "Against this background," the paper asserted, "all discussion in America on war issues is conditioned by the prevalent anti-Administration feeling; this fosters isolationist, anti-British and anti-Russian attitudes. All are closely related. Much criticism of the war effort is opposition to Roosevelt and the New Deal; much of the anti-British feeling is fostered because Roosevelt is identified with friendship with Britain, and to attack her is to attack him; isolationism is political opposition to Roosevelt. . . . Despite Pearl Harbor, which many Americans will tell you occurred because America was already aiding Britain, the war is not yet America's war in the sense that she is under attack and in danger." [28]

Relations with Russia also caused concern within the Administration. "In the course of the year 1943," a French author wrote, "clouds appeared to gather between America and Russia. The fate of Poland, Finland, and the Baltic States became points of friction on the one hand and the absence of a veritable second front on the other. The Americans resented that the Russians had kept silent about the contribution they had made to the Russian war effort through American supplies. The United States Ambassador to Moscow, Admiral Standley, publicly complained about it when he arrived in Moscow in March, 1943.

"President Roosevelt, at his press conference on March 13, expressed his hope that all the United Nations would give up territorial ambitions, which was undoubtedly an allusion to Russia's attitude toward Poland. Stalingrad gave her such self-confidence and such power that her partners are afraid that she might abuse it. In the same month, Ambassador Bullitt declared that if the United States should not win the war this would mean a Russian victory with all its consequences. The Russians certainly noted that the same Ambassador stated in Montreal, right after Hitler's attack on Russia in 1941: '. . . Stalin now reduces Hitler's means of destruction, doing against his will a service to civilization. We shall hope that he should continue to sap the forces of Hitler and be happy that the fight was on between Satan and Lucifer. For that reason, however, sentimentality should not blind us to believe that Satan would ever aid the establishment of a peace of Christian liberty.' [29]

"The anti-Russian wave began to disquiet President Roosevelt," the French author continued, "who authorized Vice-President

Wallace to make a speech in which he emphasized the need for a better understanding between the Anglo-Americans and the Russians. A third world war might be the result, Wallace said, if the Allies put obstacles to the claims of the Soviet Union."

It was to coordinate war and peace aims as well as means whereby they intended to realize them that the Allied heads of state met in a series of conferences. However, at first only Roosevelt and Churchill conferred, in order to create a common front before they faced Stalin's requests. This aroused Stalin's distrust, although he had declined an invitation, stating that military duties did not permit his leaving the country.

"The importance of [the meeting at Casablanca]," as an English weekly assessed, "is better measured by the mere fact that it took place at all, inviting as it did journeys from Washington by President Roosevelt and from London by Mr. Churchill, than by the necessarily colorless communiqué in which the result of the discussions is presented to the world . . . and yet there is sufficient color at any rate in the closing paragraph, in its sober but inspiringly suggestive intimation that 'the President and the Prime Minister and the Combined Staffs having completed their plans for the offiensive campaign of 1943, have now separated to put them into active and concerted execution.' The only commentary needed on that is the reminder that the last time President and Prime Minister met in conferences the result was the landing in North Africa and the occupation of the very territory in which this month's conference has been held. The former synchronized with the capture of Tobruk by Rommel, the latter with the capture of Tripoli by Montgomery." [30]

The Casablanca conference was followed in August, 1943, by the meeting in Quebec, again attended only by the heads of state of the western Allies. A neutral opinion had this to say on the occasion: "Our surmise that among the subjects to be discussed at the Quebec conference between Roosevelt and Churchill will be the revision of the formula of 'unconditional surrender' set at Casablanca in the beginning of the year; it has proved to be a political mistake. The Casablanca declaration was supposed to assure the Soviet Union that the Western Allies would not conclude a separate peace. Instead, Moscow intends to exploit for its own purposes the disadvantages which the Casablanca declaration created for the Anglo-Saxons. Important German circles dreaded Bolshevism and thought in the critical last hours they could always make a compromise with the comparatively harmless Anglo-Saxons. After Casablanca the West lost sympathy, a fact that was noted in Moscow and turned to their advantage. They put on a show of magnanimity in the hope of gaining popularity, by setting up a committee 'Free Germany,' which in its preamble painted in dark colors the evil threatening the Germans by the Western demand for unconditional surrender. At the same time the manifesto opened an easy way out in the form of a negotiated peace which would allow the German army to march home, keeping their arms and luggage." [31]

Following the Quebec conference, Stalin recalled his ambassadors from Washington and London, creating a situation that required immediate remedy. It was decided that Roosevelt and Churchill would meet Stalin at a place not too distant from Russia, and Stalin accepted a conference of the Foreign Ministers in Moscow to prepare the meeting. Foreign Secretary Cordell Hull went to Moscow, where he found and contributed to a favorable atmosphere for a successful meeting of the heads of state. His report relieved Congress and stirred great hopes of Russian participation in the war against Japan and postwar international policies. The Senate passed a resolution that approved in advance what it had refused to President Wilson. Hull's Moscow propositions were approved by the emphatic vote of 85 to 5. "The Senate is thereby on record as favoring American participation with other free and sovereign nations, in the establishment of international authority with power to prevent aggression," a British magazine noted.[32] Roosevelt's hand was thus strengthened for negotiations with Stalin and Churchill.

The conference at Teheran in December, 1943 gave Stalin and Roosevelt the first opportunity to size each other up. As a result of the conference an agreement was reached on the date of a second front in the west, to be synchronized with a Russian offensive action and a second Allied landing in the South of France. Stalin made a definite promise to join the war against Japan after victory in Europe. There was agreement over the main lines of a future United Nations organization and about the political administration of the territories liberated by the Soviet Armies. In many instances Roosevelt sided with the Soviet dictator against Churchill, and hopes ran high that the two countries that were to emerge from the war more powerful than when they had entered it would keep their forces joined in making peace.

In September the Axis was broken when Italy surrendered unconditionally.

Churchill, on behalf of his King, presented Stalin with a splendid sword dedicated to the glory of Stalingrad. "Mr. Roosevelt, inspecting the sword," an English weekly wrote, "is said to have looked towards Stalin and remarked, "Truly a heart of steel." The Teheran agreements and the proximity of victory recalled the mortal dangers of yesterday.

"On thinks of this time a year ago when the German armies were almost at the gates of Moscow; one thinks of the next Nazi drive towards the oil wells of the Caucasus; one thinks above all of Stalingrad, city of imperishable fame . . . we dare prophesy, Stalin will be remembered—the man whose skill and steadfastness, supported by the courage of his people and by the help his Allies gave him, turned a retreat into a glorious advance and freed his native soil." [33]

"We may assume that the present century will be near its close before the surviving nations can begin to estimate what the vast conflict of the fifth decade involved for Europe and Asia," wrote another English magazine. "But as to one thing in that terrific accounting there will be no dispute. Historians will agree that this Presidency of Franklin Roosevelt, and his national leadership from the Fall of France onwards, marked one Great Divide of the modern age. . . ." [34]

A Swiss paper, comparing Roosevelt with the two other great leaders of the Allies, wrote: "Roosevelt has neither the monumental calm and inexorableness of Stalin nor the robust go-getter spirit of Churchill. But without yielding to his great colleagues in genuine stature, Roosevelt is the more skillful politician, the man who learned in his many years of experience leading a democracy that the surest road is not always the shortest one. . . . Such judgments concern, of course, but a single feature of Roosevelt, and they do not mean that he and his policies are not consistent in their broad lines. His policy triumphed again and again until it came to pass in America what Roosevelt had wanted to happen.

"But it cannot be denied that Roosevelt's willingness to compromise made him many enemies. This explains why Roosevelt, although powerfully popular with the great majority of the people, has more opponents, even personal enemies among prominent Americans, than usually is the case with statesmen. Interestingly, many, perhaps the majority of his enemies, are recruited from former friends and collaborators of the President. . . . It is said of Roosevelt that he once stated that he would not be a dictator for anything in the world since dictatorship would make it so easy to govern as to deprive it of all its attractions.

"Roosevelt learned what it meant to lead the fate of a nation in war without dictatorship when the miners of John L. Lewis walked out. But he showed so often in the course of his not easy career that he was able to handle the gravest difficulty not only with the help of tact, cleverness, manoeuvering, but in the long run, with inexorable resolution, that he prevailed over a labor leader's power also." [35]

"When I walked into the President's room," Alan Brooke, the British Chief of Staff told, "I felt very ill at ease, being in such slovenly clothes. He was sitting at his desk and, after Winston had introduced me, I apologized for being so badly dressed and gave him the reasons. He replied, 'What's wrong with you? Why not take your coat off like I have, you will feel far more comfortable.' It was so nicely said that it at once made me feel at ease and broke down all my discomfort. On all occasions that I met him he was perfectly charming to me. . . . General Marshall's relations with the President were quite different from my relations with Winston. The President had no great military knowledge and was aware of this fact and consequently relied on Marshall and listened to Marshall's advice. Marshall never seemed to have any difficulties in countering any wild plans which the President might put forward.

"The President's writing table interested me owing to the congestion on it. I tried to memorize the queer collection: blue vase lamp, two frames, bronze bust of Mrs. Roosevelt, bronze ship's steering wheel clock, four cloth toy donkeys, one tin toy motorcar, one small monkey made of two hazlenuts, jug of ice water, pile of books, large circular match-stand and ink-pot, plus many other articles that I cannot remember." [36]

A visitor told Alfred North Whitehead: "I understand that you have compared President Roosevelt with Augustus Caesar. I am a Republican. I can't bear the man." Whitehead turned to the speaker with a look of glistening hesitancy, then replied in his urbane tones: "I know of only twice in history when there was a gentleman on the throne." Comparing Roosevelt to Churchill, the philosopher asserted: "Churchill thinks in terms of the eighteenth century. . . . He has two sides to his nature; on one side he is a British statesman of the type one knows, and, in many aspects, admires. But I knew his mother—a lightheaded young thing . . . and on that side he is a back-slapping Rotarian, singing jovial songs with 'the boys.' You are more fortunate in your man. Mr. Roosevelt does, I believe, think largely in terms of a new epoch. It was shown before this war began, in his domestic policies which so infuriated some of our wealthy friends. Let us hope he lives to have a large hand in the shaping of the peace." [37]

The Cuban government invited all Latin American governments and Canada "to express their approval of the manner in which President Roosevelt has been promoting the harmony and community of interest of the nations of the Western Hemisphere." The Argentine government dissociated itself from the sister republics when they declared war on the Axis. Referring to President Roosevelt's visit to his country in 1936 when he had praised

Buenos Aires and called it "the capital of peace," the foreign minister hinted that Argentina would remain true to her "tradition of peace" but he added: "There is no weakening of the effective collaboration that Argentina gives to her brother peoples who fight the battle of the ideals of peace." [38]

Madame Chiang Kai-shek had this to say of the President: "Neither we nor posterity can withhold unerring tribute to the foresight and statesmanship of President Roosevelt when he envisaged to the full the implications and consequences of the struggle of right against might and took decisive measures to make America the arsenal of the democracies. History and posterity will panegyrize your President's unswerving convictions and his moral courage to implement them." (New York *Times,* April 5, 1943).

The President's chronic difficulties with a hostile Congress did not escape the attention of foreign observers, however, despite his overwhelming accomplishments as a war leader.

Looking back on the year of 1943, which had seen the Allied armies on the march toward victory, an English survey related: "The year has been filled with multiple difficulties for Mr. Roosevelt. With the assembly in January of the new Congress the President was made to realize the full effect of the opposition gains in the mid-term elections. Untried Republican members felt themselves to be the advance guard of a victorious army pledged to attack the New Deal but determined to vote against any proposed measures that bore the President's signature. They were aware that the anti-Roosevelt Democrats, and particularly the Southern reactionaries, were ready to join in assaults upon the Administration. He had entered the second half of his third term amid conditions that would have been dismaying to a Chief Executive without the dauntless Roosevelt temper." [39]

"American politics have been bitter for a decade past," another magazine commented, "and they are no less bitter today. The Administration is on the defensive; it has almost, if not quite, lost control of Congress. . . . Eyes are fixed on next year's elections, Mr. Roosevelt's no less than anyone else's. His very proper object is to avoid a change in the Commander-in-Chief in the middle of the war—or at least such a change as would risk a reversal of policies and an administrative overturn. Unfortunately, it seems to be the case that the only candidate who both stands a chance of winning and also would follow Roosevelt's policies is Mr. Roosevelt himself. He is thus forced by inexorable pressures into a position where he is the defenseless object of charges of personal ambition. A fourth-term candidature would unleash a catalogue of abuse beside which the performance of 1940 would be insignificant. This might not hinder Mr. Roosevelt's chances with the electorate. But it would immeasurably embitter the atmosphere in Washington and turn his opponents in Congress, of both parties, even more severely against him." [40]

Speculating on Mr. Roosevelt's chances at the elections, still more than a year ahead, a magazine ventured: "Two overwhelming questions present themselves: President Roosevelt's future as it relates to America's role in the post-war world, and American action on the race problem in relation to the world race question. . . . President Roosevelt has been willing to remain a strictly party leader in the eyes of many American people. He has not sought by large measures to conciliate his opposition. He has won many political victories in the past by riding out the storm, and that is what he appears to have determined to do now. That means that, if the war is still on in 1944, he is presumably intent upon running for a fourth term. If the war situation is then sufficiently grave, and its gravity cannot be blamed to maladministration through President Roosevelt, his chance for re-election would be thoroughly strong. Even politics-torn America may hesitate . . . to dismantle the war administration that has been erected." [41]

Another appraisal of the President and his situation pointed out: ". . . We must face the fact that the Republican party is almost equal to the Democratic party in the lower house, is very strong in the upper house, and is in control of the governments in all of the important States outside the solid South. And the Republican party since 1939 has opposed, by large majorities, all the measures taken by the President to thwart the designs of

Hitler. Had it had its way, the United States would not be at war yet; there might, indeed, be no war for the United States to be in, only a world dominated by the Axis in which the American people would be hurriedly and remorsefully preparing to withstand pressure and attack from all sides of the globe. To forget this is to be unjust to Mr. Roosevelt, and to prepare to be full of irrelevant moral indignation at the consistency of the leaders of the party which has almost won the elections of 1942, and has good prospects of winning the elections of 1944. . . . If Mr. Roosevelt were an autocrat, we should be able to count on intelligent, courageous and flexible world leadership. We should have been able to count on it in the past. We should not, in all probability, have been at war at all if the lead given by Mr. Roosevelt in his 'quarantine' speech of 1937 had not been firmly repudiated by the American people. If Mr. Roosevelt had been able to give any indication of his determination not to permit a Hitler triumph in his reply to the despairing last-minute appeal of Paul Reynaud, we should not, in all probability, have had to endure the long, disastrous and still unfinished farce of Vichy. If Mr. Roosevelt had been able to act more freely in the summer of 1940, we should not have had to close the Burma road and America would not have had Pearl Harbor to avenge. Nobody who comes to the study of American foreign policy with any knowledge of its limiting conditions can do less than wonder at the skill with which Mr. Roosevelt, compelled by American tradition and constitutional practices to bid only minor suits, has managed to give the impression that he had only to choose to bid in any suit he liked. Only if we realize the superb timing, the masterly rhetoric with which this weakness has been concealed, can we appreciate what we owe to Mr. Roosevelt." [42]

Another observer cast a very dark view on the situation: "In 1943, the relation of the President to Congress is ominously similar to that of President Wilson to Congress in 1919," he claimed. "In 1943 a liberal President again faces a Congress in which the majority is unstable and his opponents are bitter enemies who hate his whole social and international policy. . . ." [43]

Similarly, a pastor is said to have remarked: "God has led the President by the hand for a long while, but even God gets tired sometimes." [44]

A conservative English weekly was entirely pessimistic as to the re-election of Roosevelt if he chose to run. It commented just a year before the election: "Most of the political pundits in the capital regard Mr. Wendell Willkie's selection as Republican candidate for the Presidency as a certainty. There is not the same confidence in respect of the Democratic nomination. . . . Mr. Roosevelt will, of course, be the party's choice if he wants a fourth term, but the President, it is said, may remove all speculation by taking up some office higher even than the American Presidency in connection with world organization after the war. . . . It is felt even by Mr. Willkie that Mr. Roosevelt is in a class alone. If he decides to run, then the battle will be fierce. . . . Mr. Willkie will start out with the solid anti-Roosevelt front of the Republican party. He has angled successfully for the Negro vote having made more than one speech against discrimination. No longer are labor and agriculture, on which Roosevelt's strength depends, unanimously pro-Roosevelt. The farmers are as much incensed over the truckling to John L. Lewis and other union leaders. Even the union workers are not solidly with the President. Certainly, his bitterest enemy is Lewis, to whom the President just bowed in ending the fourth coal strike. No man has done more for organized labor than President Roosevelt. Yet labor seems in a state of uncertainty. . . . Philip Murray, President of the Confederation, declared he was 'in no mood to deliver the Confederation lock, stock and barrel' to any man or party in the world." [45]

13

SHAPING THE POSTWAR WORLD

Roosevelt gave the reporters some good copy when he told them a spy story in explanation of his move to the Russian embassy in Teheran. Marshal Stalin had asserted that German spies had been roaming about town who might have made an attempt on the life of a leader of the Allies while he was driving through the streets. The Russian and the British embassies were located close to one another outside Teheran; thus his acceptance of Stalin's hospitality eliminated all risk. The Germans angrily denied any plot, stating, "The idea of three world criminals meeting in an occupied and enslaved country and living in the Soviet embassy guarded by the OGPU while hundreds of German spies are supposed to be roaming the streets is ludicrous in the extreme. Having nothing concrete to tell journalists about the actual Teheran conference, he told them this instead, knowing very well how the Americans love such tales." [1]

In his Christmas address over the radio, Roosevelt had softened the meaning of the unconditional surrender without altering it. "The United Nations have no intention to enslave the German people," he stated. "We wish them to have a normal chance to develop, in peace, as useful and respectable members of the European family. But we most certainly emphasize that word 'respectable'—for we intend to rid them once and for all of Nazism and Prussian militarism and the fantastic and disastrous notion that they constitute the 'Master Race.'"

"President Roosevelt opened the year (1944) with a series of messages to Congress," an English magazine [2] commented that "They were bold in conception, and in form as positive as they could be. . . . Mr. Roosevelt was addressing a Congress which during many months had displayed both hostility and bitter feeling. He had returned from Teheran and Cairo in a mood of the highest confidence. By the end of February he was involved in a conflict with the Senate which revealed harder antagonism between President and Congress than America has known for three-quarters of a century. . . . Very rarely does a President approach the end of his term with a majority upon which he can rely, and Mr. Roosevelt has been in power for eleven years. His supporters are now outnumbered in both Houses. It was taken for granted that Mr. Roosevelt would consider most seriously the task of conciliating Congress in order to ensure the passage of certain measures which had been perilously delayed. He did not agree with this view.

"The course he adopted in the new year broke all the rules of the regular pre-election game. In the message devoted to general policy he delivered a five-point programme of far-reaching importance. The first place was given to a plea for full compulsory national service. The other proposals were concerned with adequate war taxation, the soldiers' vote, the combating of inflation by means of price control and stabilization, and the revision of war-contracts with the aim of effecting large economies and establishing a fair scale of profits. Each one of these is controversial in the extreme. . . . None could be piloted through Congress without the backing of organized public opinion, and the President has against him a formidable array of newspapers and organizations of national scope. . . .

"The storm in Congress, inevitably, gave a fresh and violent turn to the continuous debate upon Mr. Roosevelt's plans for, and chances to, the election. . . . There is . . . a high probability that before the decision of midsummer the news from all battle-fronts may be of a character so tremendous that domestic disputes and Washington politics will have shrunk to the dimensions of the trivial. . . . It would not be a matter for surprise if the American people were to become entirely absorbed in the world struggle, in its overwhelming drama. If this should be so, we cannot doubt that the President will stand out, more sharply than he stands to-day, alongside the two European leaders to whom has been entrusted a power and responsibility never before approached in the modern age. He is the first member of the trio to come up for judgment before a great assize of his own people.

"They see in America an elected leader, three times endorsed by large popular majorities. He is directing a great nation which, in a war of unlimited scope, has carried out a task of unified will and power beyond the range of words or imagination. They compare this spectacle with that of their own land, governed by a statesman of kindred vitality and command, yet markedly dissimilar in gifts and temperament and habit; and they marvel at the contrast between the positions and experiences of the two men. Mr. Churchill toils from day to day in the deep assurance of a united nation. He knows that, so long as the awful emergency remains, there will be no need for him to worry about political and other disputes, to anticipate any challenge of his leadership or any assault upon himself. Mr. Roosevelt lives and moves in an atmosphere of conflict: of political bitterness, industrial and racial tension, and of an enmity against himself so intense and persistent that for a parallel in Britain we should have to go far back. . . . It is all the more amazing because the fierce political and sectional conflicts and the variegated personal animosity do not, and will not, make any difference to the national purpose or in the result of the global struggle."

In that struggle, however, Roosevelt could proceed only through compromises so as to preserve Allied unity. The British, preoccupied with India, wanted offensive military action in Burma. Roosevelt prevailed over them, but as a compensation he had to accept a campaign in Italy instead of a second front in the west. He knew perfectly well and was prepared to compensate Stalin for the further delaying of the invasion of the Continent from the west. "This is how one compromise entails another one as a compensation. . . . But to believe the testimony of his son, Roosevelt was worried that it would be even more difficult to preserve unity at the making of the peace. That is why he was anxious to avail himself of any opportunity offered to him by the war to work for the unity in peace. This is the sense of the conferences in Cairo and Teheran."[3]

However, in the view of an English magazine the conferences either did not produce results or they could not be disclosed, with the consequence that the general political and diplomatic situation remained deplorable. "The diplomatic setbacks of the first half of 1944 are," the paper stated,[4] "the measure of the Teheran failure to issue a communiqué calculated to impress . . . Turkey, Sweden, Spain and Portugal. . . . [They] continued to supply vital war material to Germany, and have had to be coerced by the Allies into other conduct; Poland, though an Ally, openly and with some show of reason accused Russia of the very 'tyranny and slavery,' oppression and intolerance that the Teheran declaration promised to eliminate; Finland, Rumania, Hungary and even Bulgaria refused a virtual Russian invitation to put their trust in Russia rather than in Germany. Quite apart from Japan, and within the restricted scope of the European theatre, the effect of Russia's magnificent military victories was in some measure offset by the effect of Russia's political purpose, or what was assumed to be her political purpose. The Red Army, as it were, struck Hitler down, and the Kremlin set him up again: by galvanizing a reluctant European support for him."

Russia disappointed many people by her resolution to keep the territories obtained on the strength of the agreement with Hitler in 1939. It is true that Poland had acquired the same territory in a war against Russia twenty years before in defiance of the Peace Conference. Also it appeared that Russia was intent on using the small countries liberated by them as buffers against Germany by insisting that they have governments friendly to her. A Swiss newspaper looked at the situation with less pessimism. "Whether Roosevelt gained the conviction in Teheran that Stalin really wanted to cooperate may not be so sure, but there are facts pointing to such intention. Statements are being made lately in Moscow, repeatedly admitting that the Soviets would for years be compelled to rely on the supply of goods from America and England and also that they would need considerable long-range credits which might convince America that it would be possible to set limits to the Russian claims." [5]

But the pessimism of the English writer issued from a more general consideration. "Political philosophers will note in passing," he averred,[6] "that war, being the negation of all moral principles and a recourse to brute force as the arbiter in affairs, always defeats its object. It is not merely that force settles no problem. It creates more problems. What is worse, it creates the 'chaos and confusion' to which both Mr. Churchill and Mr. Roosevelt referred as a pressing danger, on November 9 last. Force being the arbiter, whether measured in man-power, military skill, economic and financial resources, it follows that decisions are impressed by those most able by force at any given moment to impose them. Russia, as General Smuts observed on November 25, is the new master of Europe. Russia therefore decides the fate of Poland and of the other border states."

General Smuts caused great stir in the public of the European neutral countries when he declared "with unsparing clarity" that the history of the West after the war would be administered and guided by the three great powers. "The residence of the Fuehrer will simply be transferred from Berlin to Moscow. . . . Where the armies will meet will be the border of the east and west. . . . Europe will be returned to the old misery of spheres of influence." [7]

"There is no reason to doubt that Marshal Stalin sincerely wants a free and independent Poland," an English weekly cautioned those who feared that the grand alliance might crack at the first act of liberation.[8] "The Russians have had plenty of experience of trying to rule an unwilling Poland, and it is hard to believe that they want to repeat the experiment. But for perfectly intelligible and legitimate reasons they want Poland to form part of the Russian security system, in much the same way as the Czechs will. The fact that the past history of Russian-Polish relations makes the Poles wary of such an arrangement puts the Russians, as well as the Poles, in a dilemma. . . . are they to sacrifice their own security to Polish independence, or Polish independence to their own security? It is not an easy situation for any Great Power to handle, for twenty years, and they have not been very patient or clever in dealing with it—any more than we were in dealing with a somewhat similar situation in Ireland. And the Russians welcome our advice about Poland about as much as we should have welcomed theirs about Ireland."

If the West was disturbed by the consequences of the invasion of eastern central Europe by the Soviet armies, the Russians found the rising anti-Russian agitation in the west equally disturbing, especially in the "numerous Catholic communities in various countries, and by an idea which seems to exist in some quarters that it is the Catholic mission to give an anti-Russian slant to western European politics," according to a Moscow correspondent broadcasting on BBC.[9] "The appointment of Robert Murphy as political adviser to General Eisenhower in Germany has been met here with as little enthusiasm as in British liberal quarters. And when an article appears in an American journal with an enormous circulation, like former Ambassador Bullitt's article in which he anticipates war against Russia in fifteen years, Russians begin to wonder. As one Russian said, 'Are we to take this article with us to the peace conference for reference? In the Red Army people ask: Is that the thanks we are getting from some Americans for our contribution to Allied victory?"

A French author found words of approval for President Roosevelt, a Protestant who appeared to have been in close touch with political guides at the Vatican. "Mr. Roosevelt is not a New England Puritan," he explained.[10] "He is no descendant from those dissenters whose robust but narrow mind in its rigor was inseparable from anti-papism. Born in the median and cosmopolite zone of the old colonies, he has preserved its more open and supple intelligence sustained by frequent travels in Europe. This undoubtedly helps to explain his haste to establish contact with the Vatican and also that the cleverness of his diplomacy proved equal to the largeness of his views. . . . Msgr. Spellman, Archbishop of New York, went several times to Rome during the war, was received by the Holy Father, and again returned. . . . One is struck by the new spirit of the great American statesman

. . . [who] understood that the influence of the Vatican was not to belittle. . . ."

In the countries liberated by the West, a Catholic political revival took place. One reason was the lower clergy's participation in the resistance, another was that the Christian Democratic parties appeared most to conform to the pattern of rule which American governing circles envisaged for the Europe of the future. Catholic-led government in inveterate anti-clerical countries, such as France and Italy, or in the formerly Protestant-ruled (West) Germany, was a most remarkable development.

The problem of what principle to follow in support of the provisional governments emerging upon the appearance of liberating armies was not an easy one. Whether they wished or not, the Allies faced ideological problems on the forming of local governments from the resistance groups, a situation which created distrust and suspicion between the Anglo-Americans and the Russians.

When Western leaders showed a preference for conservative elements in governments invested with the temporary administration of the liberated countries—some of whom in the past had been in sympathy with former autocratic regimes—they aroused a storm of protest by liberal public opinion at home. Not even obvious military expedience—as in the use of Admiral Darlan in North Africa—the benefits of which events soon showed, succeeded in calming the liberal uproar that reproached the breach of the Atlantic Charter. Moscow, however, greatly helped the West by advising the groups under its discipline against revolutionary actions or subversion of the social order, although it observed with uneasiness the principles underlying the Western political manipulations. In vain the Allies emphasized their common anti-Fascist, democratic platform, for they represented ideologies attractive to one, repulsive to other popular groups. Such identification could become dangerous to Allied unity when one or the other side, involved in civil discords or war, would be rumored to be supported by the Russians or the Anglo-Americans.

Stalin's difficulty in Poland was that, due to her traditional fear of Russia and her more recent fear of Soviet communism, no representative Polish government could be formed friendly to Russia. Countries like Greece, on the other hand, if left to spontaneous popular action, would empower Communist-led governments while the British army liberated and fed them.

Either a policy administered in common by East and West, or an agreement delineating the spheres of influence of each, was in order. Churchill rushed to Moscow and reached an agreement with Stalin regarding southeastern Europe in October, 1944. Roosevelt, however, was not party to the agreement.

The *London Times* told the story of the Greek guerilla movement, considering it as most instructive, "for it illustrates the peril of the acute political discussions which menace almost every occupied country in Europe. When the Allies began to take in hand the organization of the movement of resistance in Greece about sixteen months ago," *The Times* related, "they found there a secret political organization called EAM, Greek initials for National Liberation Movement, with ramifications in most parts of Greece. . . . It was an extreme left-wing organization under strong Communist influence. With Allied support this organization formed bands of partisans eager to fight against the invaders. . . . In the meantime other patriotic organizations had sprung up and also obtained Allied support. . . . For some time those various organizations worked smoothly, with the result that the Germans and Italians were practically driven out of the countryside which was and still is under the complete control of the patriots. This continued until the recent outbreak of hostilities between them. . . . [The non-leftist organization] is accusing EAM of trying to monopolize the movement of resistance with the ulterior motive of establishing Communism in Greece. EAM, in its turn, charges the other group with being a Fascist organization encouraged by the Germans and working for the continuation of privileges of the ruling classes." [11]

The disregard for the Atlantic Charter by both East and West when it did not suit their plans for the liberated countries, greatly depressed the public in the west. Was the Charter no more than a pious wish? "There has been a great deal of disillusioned talk from American Liberals," a magazine reported,[12] "to the effect that the Atlantic Charter seems to be pining away from neglect. Old-time isolationists have been quick to mourn the Charter they once never even recognized; they say that it only goes to show that you can't trust Roosevelt. This is dangerous talk, whether it comes from a crusading Liberal or a calculating isolationist. And so a reporter at the press conference asked if Mr. Churchill had signed that document. The President replied that nobody had ever signed it and added that no formal signed document exists. By this single sentence the President hurled a bombshell onto every front page of the nation's press. A most ardent pro-Roosevelt columnist, Marquis Childs, lamented yesterday that the President's performance on Tuesday was, in fact, completely mystifying."

After the Russians turned the tide and kept advancing they began to lose their popularity with the American public. In the summer of 1944, a Gallup poll showed that 70 per cent of the people thought Communist more dangerous than Nazi propaganda. An English magazine commented,[13] "It is perfectly clear that for over a century America has entertained an aversion and distrust for Russian domestic policy. When America needs the Russian alliance in an international crisis, the United States has condescended to overlook these differences or even deny their existence. It is, therefore, extremely unlikely that the fond hope so many seem to hold for Britain's future as an honest mediator between the two landmasses will be realized."

Not only the public but even the government in America was said to be much less friendly to Russia than their British counterpart. Yet, to the surprise of an English magazine, the Russians preferred the Americans to the British.[14] "Americans in government circles are firm and intransigent in their intercourse with Russian government officials and have little inclination to honor them. In spite of this there is more understanding in Russia for the United States than there has been for Britain, and on the whole more sympathy. The ambitious young Russian compares himself to the early pioneer in America a century ago; he foresees the development of his country somewhat on similar lines; he is enthusiastic for the efficiency of American methods in industry and in organization generally and wishes to emulate them. The personal intercourse recently established between Russian and American technicians and men in the services has led to good understanding and is cordial. They are like two people of different education and ways who find each other in spite of the different level on which they have been brought up, and to their surprise can speak the same language. The difficulties they will have to overcome in the future are less than those between England and Russia."

But in England public enthusiasm for the Russians lasted. "The views about Russia," the same magazine commented,[15] "now expressed by our most responsible—and occasionally conservative—public men would have been considered dangerously pro-Bolshevik two or three years ago. Thus it is that the basis for post-war confidence and cooperation is being laid."

Also in the military field British and Russian soldiers got along nicely, as this report from Belgrade emphasized. "Yugoslavia is really the only country in Europe which has seen British and Red Army cooperation on any scale; and many liberated towns have now watched British and Soviet officers riding with the Yugoslav Commanders at the head of the triumphal procession. A British officer told me how, in one place, the Red Army representative was invited to enter a town and insisted on waiting for his British colleagues to come up and join him. When I left Belgrade, driving down in pitch darkness to the airport, it was immensely heartening to be stopped by the Soviet Guards in their gray army coats, to say just "English," and to be waved straight on. It was a Russian pilot who flew me out, a Russian pilot, an English traveler, an American plane. I could say, as the Yugoslavs regularly do, "Long live the alliance of the freedom-loving nations.'"[16]

An American *faux pas* might have caused a serious rift between the Russians and the West. "I remember in 1944," Lord Beaverbrook declared years later, "when Kesselring was willing to surrender the German Army in Italy, negotiations with the Americans took place in Switzerland. General Schmidt was the negotiating medium. The first condition of the negotiations was, 'Don't tell the Russians!' The condition was accepted by the Americans. Somebody did tell the Russians. Who was it? And Russia had once feared a separate peace, and Russia was greatly disturbed." [17]

Roosevelt was well aware that the alliance had to be laid on an institutional basis in order to last, to be done while the common war aim held them together. He took the initiative, "inviting the British, Russian and Chinese allies to consult together on the framework of the future peace organization, the 'new, better League of Nations,' to which President Roosevelt referred this week," an English weekly reported.[18] "Press reports speak of five main points: of a United Nations council of the Big Four with a few small states appointed by election and serving in rotation; a United Nations Assembly later to include all nations; a police power composed chiefly of the forces of the Big Four; a world court; and machinery for mediation. . . . It is an improvement on the League in so far as it lays military responsibility where it alone can lie—with the Great Powers. One of the chief drawbacks of the old League was that the police power was everybody's business and therefore nobody's."

It was through a trusteeship council of the United Nations that Roosevelt intended to provide for ultimate independence of colonies not yet ready for it. He was well aware that he would find himself in opposition to his friend Churchill, but this regrettable fact did not restrain him from meeting the Sultan of Morocco and the ruler of Saudi Arabia, assuring them of the independence of the colonies after the war in the same way America had freed the Philippines—by setting a date for freedom and in the meantime preparing the nation for self-government. Churchill insisted, however, that the Atlantic Charter had no relevance to the British Empire. "It should be recalled that Mr. Churchill, by his reservation with respect to India, has with one stroke destroyed India's faith in it [the Charter]. Of course, other English spokesmen have subsequently attempted to explain away Churchill's reservation, and President Roosevelt was compelled to reaffirm the universal character of the Charter. But Churchill, the co-signator of the Charter, has maintained discreet silence up till now." Lately Henry Wallace, Vice-President, visiting Asia in behalf of the President, stated in Chungking, "In Asia there are other racial political entities now in a state of colonial dependency, whose aspiration to self-government should receive prompt and positive attention after victory." [19]

Wallace's journey was due to the President's concern over China. An on-the-spot survey was to discover the true source of China's present troubles and ways to keep her in the fight until the American army was able to move over to the Pacific area. "Mr. Wallace goes to China at one of the most critical moments in the history of Asia," an Indian daily commented and advised.[20] "The problem of China must not be approached in a spirit of carping criticism, but with a determination to understand the causes that have led to her present weakness. It is the result of blockade and of seven years of memorable resistance. If China is to be saved, she must be helped—not only because she deserves it for her own sake but also because she is a valuable springboard for attack against Japan. Her national fabric has been corroded, but is not beyond repairs."

"Past centuries put the Caucasian race in the position of avant-guard of civilization but this period has been short, representing no more in the life of the world than a drop of water in the ocean. The years to come may again restore Asia's superiority that will overshadow Europe," a pro-Nazi magazine warned.[21]

Japan's attempt to assume leadership over awakening Asia was proving preposterous. She provoked America to clear the way for a spontaneous upsurge of movements for national independence and self-government. The European war was as yet unfinished but America's power was already unfolding in the Pacific. The Japanese "know to what prodigious strength the American Navy has grown," an English weekly recorded.[22] "They know with what . . . rapidity the shipyards of San Francisco, the aeroplane plants of Seattle and Los Angeles, have grown. They feel the reflection of the confidence that a series of unbroken, desperately fought for, and more and more fruitful victories has bred in the American armed forces, especially in the Navy. It is no longer a case of desperate holding actions like the Coral Sea or the almost Pyrrhic victories like Guadalcanal or Tarawa. Now the Americans move with the confidence of predestined victors, bringing their forces to bear with an almost impudent indifference to the counter-measures of the Japanese."

Meanwhile, the Nazi leaders were expecting the great Allied assault on the Continent, becoming less arrogant as the initiative slipped from their hands on both fronts. "We have to take things as they come," Goebbels wrote in his diary. "It surely grates on one's nerves, particularly when he realizes that we are perhaps not equipped to face them." [23]

Hitler prepared his people for coming setbacks, but he exhorted them, "It is the last battle that will be decisive, and the German people will win it. . . . What I demand from the German soldier to-day is something enormous. It is the duty of the front to make the impossible possible, and it is the duty of the people at home to enable the front to achieve the impossible."

An almost unbearable tension strained the nerves not only of the belligerents but also of the neutrals following the Teheran conference which heralded the imminence of the Allied invasion. "The enemy's intention is to make the conference the starting-point for a general offensive against the morale of the German people and the German forces," said General Dittmar, spokesman of the German High Command. "To that end," an English magazine insisted,[24] "it was essential that the Allied triumvirate should again emphasize the imminent upshot of an invasion of the Continent from all sides and should make that prospect as formidable as words and stage could make it. . . . In the now prevailing disposition of every single people in the world, undermined as they are by the strain, any definite crack anywhere is bound to have an incalculable repercussion."

However, Roosevelt finally decided against an invasion of the Balkans, a plan to which Churchill stuck to the end. Roosevelt, "by the end of the Teheran Conference, had long-term reasons for wishing to keep out of South Eastern Europe," an Australian historian of the war noted.[25] "He wanted to make certain of Russia's promised participation in the establishment of the

United Nations. Accordingly, he was determined to avoid any action which might make Stalin suspicious of Anglo-American intentions."

In June the day of the invasion for which the Allied armies had been preparing in Britain for a year arrived. How President Roosevelt heard the news that the invasion had started was told in an Indian daily on the basis of an American report: [26] "After broadcasting to the nation at 8:30 P.M. he retired to his bedroom. He waited for the first news of the landing to come. Mr. Roosevelt began to write and the words he wrote came slowly, for the President was composing a prayer. Occasionally the silence in the President's bedroom was broken by the ring of the telephone. It was a telephone connected directly to the place where the first word of the landing would be flashed from England. At 11:20 P.M. the ring of the phone broke upon the President's writing and meditation and across the line came the long-awaited word. A voice told the President that the first boatload of American troops had pushed off from Britain's shores to France. Throughout the period during which the first boatload of Americans forged its way through the choppy waters of the English Channel, the voice from England talked to Washington. Through moments of terrible strain the President followed the historic progress. At last the ordeal ended as the words came: 'Mr. President, the first boat has landed!' "

While the battles raged in Normandy, the Nazis behind the frontlines carried on "their annihilation campaign against the 'world-enemy, the Jew' to the end. It was senseless to the extent that brains conditioned to any Machiavelism were incapable of understanding it. . . . But," a Swiss author noted in bitter contempt,[27] "even this orgy of hatred was corrupted. From the annihilation camps established for the Biblical scapegoat, the foremost financiers of Hungary with their relatives, altogether 32 persons, were allowed to escape to Lisbon in German-chartered planes. They had bought their lives for a few millions, as Baron Rothschild had in Vienna. The heads of the Chorin and Weiss families yesterday owned huge mining and metal industry plants which since last year have produced full steam for the armament of the Third

Reich. . . . This makes the picture of our time perfect: that the Nazis are not honest even in their dreadfulness, not respectable even in their horrible madness. Their 'total brutality' is but a front of a total rottenness."

While the invasion was gaining momentum, the Nazis perfected their much advertised secret weapon with which their people expected to win the war, despite their retreat on all fronts. They began to shoot flying bombs on London and South England at the rate of one in every forty minutes, causing great damage to life and property. The rockets compelled the cities to evacuate children and to return to the shelters deserted after the Battle of Britain. Again the British could take it, but perhaps chiefly because wherever they looked, the Allies were advancing toward the nerve center of the enemy. Victory could not be far away.

However, in America waves of strikes broke the steady rhythm of war production. "After coal and steel, the railways are passing through their crisis with more than a million men involved," an English weekly commented.[28] "The President then intervenes by taking over the plant of the industry, runs it with the aid of the army under military discipline and then imposes a solution which is always found to be favorable to the men. This procedure deeply offends American traditions. . . . But it does serve two ends. It recognizes, however spasmodically and illogically, that these industries, dominated though they are by the profit motive, are in the last resort public services, over which the community has sovereignty. Secondly it allows every one concerned to yield without loss of prestige. . . . It is probable that wages, limping after the cost of living, will now tend to rise all around, and the spiral of inflation will twist inexorably upwards. Mr. Roosevelt may still do something to check it by the bold use of his executive powers. But in the long run an Administration which cannot carry its taxes against a hostile Congress can hardly hope to stop inflation. Can the President, by the use of his personal ascendancy and his prestige as Commander-in-Chief, recover anything of his authority? He might for the moment achieve something by a broadcast or a powerful message to Congress. But for the next months his authority is likely to touch even lower levels, while the whole political world is absorbed in preparing for the election November next."

The President made spectacular moves to demonstrate that everything was to be subordinated to the aim of carrying the war to the soonest possible victorious end. He appointed men of big industry, known as Republicans but at the same time internationalists, to important positions in the departments of State and War. An English paper explained these appointments, which had caused no little disappointment among American liberals, by this comment: [29] "Mr. Roosevelt never forgets that Woodrow Wilson's tactless handling of the opposition leaders gave the isolationists their chance. Therefore he surrounds himself with Republican colleagues and makes a statesmanlike effort to carry Congress with him in international policy so that who ever is President the attitude of the United States will be the same. . . . It is within this context of procuring all-party responsibility for . . . international cooperation after the war that Mr. Roosevelt's first definitive announcement about post-war organization must be understood."

Strictly speaking there were no isolationists any more, since they turned into violent imperialists. "Some recognize the implication of the Pacific scene," an English paper reported,[30] "but refuse to admit the inevitability of the United States' participation in the European theatre. They believe that their country has been manoeuvred into fighting for Europe and for Britain by the satanic Roosevelt. . . . Their argument is that since they have been dragged for the second time in twenty-five years into a war that is not their own, the only way to avoid a third conflagration is to let America run the show after the war is over. . . . Just as in France, where there were many fanatics who said 'Rather Hitler than Blum,' so in America the professional Roosevelt-haters know no limits in their abuse of the President. It is odd to see how these ostensibly patriotic and conservative people seem to be wholly devoid of any respect for the great office of President, quite apart from the question of Mr. Roosevelt's personality."

The President made a great concession to appease these people in the interest of unity for winning the war and the peace. At a press conference he suddenly stated, to the dismay of the liberals, that the New Deal was out. He said, "Dr. New Deal put the patient on his feet again in 1933, but in December 1941 the same patient ran into a different trouble; he had a bad smash up. Dr. New Deal knew nothing of surgery, so Dr. Win the War was called."[31]

This afforded opportunity for Nazi rejoicing. "The President has acknowledged today the fiasco of his New Deal policy and in view of the coming elections gave the order that the words 'New Deal' should henceforth be forgotten. However, in vain will the words disappear if the evil they meant remains. A simple order cannot obliterate this nor can it wipe out the enormous debt burden that had accrued to the people as a consequence of Roosevelt's criminal experiments."[32]

Goebbels had an explanation of his own for Roosevelt's farewell to the New Deal. He twisted a statement by Harry Hopkins who pointed to the probability that America alone of the great powers would emerge from the war intact and with an unprecedented production capacity. But according to Goebbels, Hopkins and his boss Roosevelt did not worry about unemployment, because they expected all other countries to become America's customers. "The in some respects sensible New Deal," Goebbels wrote, "foundered on the resistance of the businessman and on Roosevelt's conversion from a social idealist to idolizing his own power position."[33] Goebbels chided the Roosevelt crowd for taking overproduction as a kind of natural law and for not considering a switch from the eight-hour day to six hours without damage to the economy, although they could set an example to the less developed countries. "But," Goebbels concluded, "the present regime will have no opportunity of doing it, for it clearly lacks of the wherewithal: the superiority of the power of the State over the power of money."

In the center of the political wrangling whirled the question whether Roosevelt was going to run for the fourth time and if so would he be re-elected?

The fact that the election would take place while the country was engaged in a world war made a great impression on the world, although many wondered whether bowing to the democratic process was not damaging the country's vital interests. It certainly proved that Roosevelt's detractors, who kept maintaining that Roosevelt needed the war as a pretext for perpetuating his Presidency without elections, were wrong.

According to a French paper, a Republican suggested extending the Presidential term by one year provided Roosevelt would renounce his candidacy when the additional year expired.[34]

Most people believed that it would depend on the war situation whether or not Roosevelt would run. "If by midsummer and early autumn things are going rather slowly in the war against Germany," an English quarterly thought,[35] "and if, as would be certain, the restrictions and dislocations of the United States home front are bearing heavily on people, their dissatisfaction with President Roosevelt would certainly be reflected at the polls. On the other hand if the war were in a genuinely grave state by autumn, the voters might think a change too risky. And alternatively, if Germany is on the verge of defeat or actually collapsed, the country might either feel grateful and satisfied toward President Roosevelt or relieved enough to risk a change. . . . But the best guess in early January was that President Roosevelt would be re-elected. . . . There is a steady boom for General McArthur, also in the isolationist and conservative circles. . . . It is known that General MacArthur resents the decisions which have limited the support his command has received, and some of his communiqués and statements made by his own staff pointedly resemble a build-up. Yet, even so, his candidature would be a surprise."

Half a year later, the same magazine reported on the outlook on the election in its June issue, "It was felt [Roosevelt] would certainly wish to see the war through, and have a large hand in the immediate planning of the peace. And, in practical politics, it was realized that if he did not run the Democrats could not hope to elect any other candidate. But in recent days more and more doubts have obscured the President's plans. His health has been increasingly troubled. Nothing serious, as far as the public knows, but an increasing susceptibility to minor ailments and growing signs of strain. When old friends come to see the President, who have not observed him for months or years, they nearly always say afterwards that they have been shocked by the marks of strain that have been left on him. There is reason to believe that members of his family would prefer to see him retire.

"Mr. Roosevelt has not only served years longer than any other American President, but he has done so in years of greatest stress. To look ahead to 16 years in the White House is truly Herculean. Of course, Mr. Roosevelt's temperament and character happily enable him to bear responsibility without being crushed beneath it, as several Presidents have been in four years or less. . . . His sense of duty and responsibility is extremely high, and personal considerations will scarcely be considered in the same breath with national and world imperatives; but when the whole situation is analysed there may indeed be reasons for thinking the President might step aside."

The President had contracted influenza in the winter of 1943, after his return from Teheran, and had not completely recovered even in the spring. In April 1944, he accepted Bernard Baruch's invitation to his farm in the South, and spent there a month. During the time of his absence from the capital, a whispering campaign about his health made its rounds, suggesting a much graver illness to influence the voters against his re-election.

Analyzing the chances of Mr. Roosevelt's candidacy, *The Economist* wrote, "One of the main obstacles of Mr. Roosevelt's Fourth Term—his ill health—appeared to have melted away in the Carolina sunshine. Nevertheless the Republicans will hammer away at their candidate's indictment of 'tired war leaders.' In fact the . . . phrase is rather like the visible part of an iceberg; the largest and most dangerous position—in this case the inevitable whispering campaign—is out of sight" [36]

Meantime two important public figures were discarded from the pre-election scene. The formidable Republican candidate of 1940, Wendell Willkie, started to force his candidacy on the Convention through mobilizing the voters against the party old guard, but was rebuffed at the Wisconsin primary. He withdrew after this defeat and died not long after. The Republican party nominated Thomas Dewey, Governor of New York. The other statesman left out was Vice-President Henry Wallace whom Roosevelt dropped, bowing to the hostility of the conservatives in the party, recommending Senator Harry S. Truman instead, a Missourian who had shown remarkable energy and independence at the revision of war contracts.

"Nobody votes for the Vice President, the Republican delegates were saying," an English monthly commented,[37] "but the Democrats had reason to think otherwise. For them the question was highly contentious because important for a specific reason which has never before been brought out. If Mr. Roosevelt should be re-elected, his term would last until 1949—that is for 16 years from his first inauguration. So long a reign has not hitherto found a place in American political consciousness. The Vice-President succeeds if his chief dies in office. The Democrats and their opponents, therefore, gave thought openly to the chances of succession. . . . Mr. Wallace has given a new prominence to the Vice-Presidency, but his remarkable record as a crusader made his nomination impracticable. The convention agreed to the compromise choice of Senator Truman from Missouri. He is a safe Democrat who has supported the New Deal."

"America often wastes her leaders," an English weekly was deploring the exit of both Willkie and Wallace.[38] "The big event of the Republican mobilization for the coming contest happened before the Convention met: Mr. Wendell Willkie eliminated himself. The Democrats conducted their affairs with a livelier sense for drama: Mr. Wallace fought hard and came near to winning the Convention by sheer sincerity and courage. We should like to think that Wallace's influence will survive his defeat. . . . But he is not a Senator, and will have no recognized place in the life of the Republic when he steps down from the high office he now holds. The same thing is true of Mr. Wendell Willkie. . . . Neither the President's speech nor the Platform held out any hope that if the Democrats win again they will enlarge the scope of the New Deal. . . . The creative phase in the life of the

Democratic Party may be over, but it will not destroy its own work."

The same magazine, in a later issue, asserted [39] that Roosevelt's "sacrifice of Vice-President Wallace on the altar of the city bosses and their machines makes it clear that he has a hard fight to retain the mastery of his party," and it added, "It is true that [Roosevelt] has many great measures to his credit; it is also true that he will be, like Woodrow Wilson, a President who can offer a great victory to his people. But it must not be forgotten that his very virtues have made him perhaps the most hated President since Abraham Lincoln. . . . But, when all is said, Mr. Roosevelt emerges as a really great man, capable of large visions and able, even when temporarily defeated, to keep firm hold of the big end he has in view. Mr. Dewey is as far below the class to which the President belongs as a student who knows mathematics up to matriculation standard is below a Cambridge wrangler. I think this is realized by the mass of the American people, and I think it points to a Roosevelt victory."

"If he does not run a fourth time, as an American statesman, as a citizen of the world, and as one of the most powerful and influential rulers of the period, the President has a moral and historical duty to run," an English magazine insisted.[40] "His twelve years of international and national policy will be at stake. If his health does not prevent him, he will presumably take the risk. He is said to have confessed privately that he is a poor administrator. He does not want to pretend what is not in the line of his nature. He is a genius of intuition and improvisation; he does not like to be bored. . . . Mr. Roosevelt, like all great statesmen, loves high gambling. He has often changed his mind in technical questions, since he needed a practical solution as the moment asked it. But there is a power in him which cannot be compared to anxious reform suggestions in the Hoover style or the One-World wisdom quickly accumulated by Wendell Willkie. He possesses the unique gift of military, political and diplomatic strategy with which world history endows very few of her special favorites. Therefore, we guess, he will fight for his work, which means to him and to many contemporaries the future of America and the world."

If the English magazine believed that it was Roosevelt's moral duty to run again, many Republicans "genuinely felt as a high patriotic duty defeating the Fourth Term," as a noted author viewed it.[41] Further elaborating on the description of Republican minds he asserted, "There is something healthy in the refusal of many Republicans to admit that there can be an indispensable man. It is a natural and healthy reaction in a Republican or a Democrat. If, to Europe and Asia, Mr. Roosevelt bestrides the narrow world of American politics like a colossus, to the Brutuses and Cassiuses who will be gathering in Chicago . . . he is simply one of themselves, inordinately lucky and ambitious. . . . If the outside world does not understand it, so much the worse for the outside world!"

Once he decided to run, Mr. Roosevelt was bound to be nominated by the Democratic party and to win the election, an English weekly held: [42] "In 1942 a great hue-and-cry went up around the nation about the sanctity of American traditions, and especially about the unwritten tradition set by Jefferson of 'no third term.' Lawyers and bar associations distributed literature and got out posters warning that there would be an end of American constitutional government if Mr. Roosevelt broke with the holiest of American traditions. Well, as you know, he did, and somehow the Republic seems to be getting along, though Governor Bricker made the gloomy promise yesterday that it could not be expected to last much later than November 8 if Mr. Roosevelt were re-elected, because he would then be serving as President longer than one-half of Britain's kings and queens, which, according to Mr. Bricker, would constitute not a presidency but a reign. . . . The Americans feel in their bones that the war, and the stalking shadows of the peace and its problems, are the issues of today and tomorrow, and of November 7; and it looks now as if that man will win who on that day seems to the voters to be best able to face those issues; not election issues as such, nor domestic issues as such, but the universal issue of understanding the sowing of the peace."

It would be easier for Roosevelt to win this time than it was in 1940, when, in the words of a magazine,[43] "the opposition put up an attractive candidate and organized a model campaign to bring out every anti-Roosevelt vote that the country could produce. Mr. Roosevelt emerged from the balloting with a popular majority of 5 millions. In 1944 the opposition has put up a candidate who from across the Atlantic seems certainly no more attractive than Mr. Willkie. The problem posed seems, then, to turn on a single question: Are there more anti-Roosevelt voters now than then? It would seem unlikely."

"His best election propaganda is the victories of the American armies, especially the recent important victories in the Pacific," a Swiss newspaper assumed.[44] "It speaks for Roosevelt furthermore that he has collected experience in his twelve years in the Presidency and established an international prestige that a new President would not command. . . . The peace will set hardly less claims than the task had been that Roosevelt faced in the beginning of his third term when the powerful industrial capacity of the country had to be mobilized, the production network with its millions of workers, in one word the whole highly developed economy of the United States had to be converted into the service of the war. Roosevelt filled that task undoubtedly in a sovereign way. This important achievement may suggest to the masses of the voters the hope that he may also succeed in mastering the economic and social problems of the post-war era."

A French newspaper expounded the reasons why it was important that Roosevelt direct foreign policies after the war was over. "The war aims of Mr. Roosevelt and Mr. Dewey are, in essence, the same (healthy countries have no two sets of foreign policy), but it appears, it is even probable, that the old isolationist currents are, whether or not he wanted it, behind Mr. Dewey. When the war is over and the task is to pull the world from the chaos into which the war plunged it, it would be extremely regrettable if the policy of the United States would be subjected to the influence of those who are responsible for the political withdrawal that followed the previous war; a withdrawal that unluckily distorted the reasonable evolution of the peace. . . . The

American people have faced magnificently for the last three years the great responsibilities thrust on them, a fact that demands that a continuity of view, a firm consistency, without which Europe and the world would not be able to recover, should characterize American policy also after hostilities have ceased. This is why it appears indispensable that President Roosevelt continue to exert his guidance during the decisive years to come."[45]

An American columnist summed up European expectations in connection with the election. "With more unanimity than they manifest in their politics they are voting for Roosevelt," she asserted.[46] "This is partly because the French who follow international events are fearful of a return to isolationism in the United States, but it is largely because of confidence in the President as a world leader. Despite criticism directed against him by the Gaullists resentful of delay in recognition of the Provisional Government, the people as a whole are convinced he is a consistent friend of France and a powerful factor in support of a truly international organization of peace. The same feeling prevails in Italy, Belgium and Greece. Liberated Europe is self-centered to the last degree. Its interest in the continuity in the policy which the Roosevelt Administration represents rises primarily from the selfish desire that the power of the United States, so decisive in war, shall not diminish in the councils of peace. They don't know Dewey, so to them Roosevelt is the figure of Uncle Sam. The interesting point is that in European eyes he is not so much an idealist in the Wilson tradition as an expert politician, a shrewd negotiator able to hold the balance between Britain and Russia in the Big Three control of the post-war world which most people over here accept as inevitable."

Analyzing the potential voters for Roosevelt, an English magazine concluded,[47] "By and large, the average American industrial worker is a political supporter of Mr. Roosevelt, *in an apathetic sort of way*. For eleven years he has been hearing his own union leaders praising the social and economic programme of the Roosevelt administration. Despite . . . the relatively minor irritations of the war, the war worker's economic position is better than it has been within living memory. It is doubtful that many workers would vote against Roosevelt. In the Congressional elections of 1942 they stayed away from the polls in large numbers, strengthening by default the anti-Administration forces in Congress. In November, however, assuming, as everyone does, that President Roosevelt will be a candidate for re-election, there may possibly be a return of a little of the political verve of the industrial cities." As to the South, "it has special reasons, among which habit is not the least, for remaining regular. One is the popularity of the President's foreign policy; another the race question. Despite the Presidential commission to ensure equal treatment for Negroes in industry, and even despite the poisonous rumors concerning Mrs. Roosevelt and her interest in Negro advancement, the Republicans remain the party of Negro emancipation."

The President visited Hawaii to meet the American commanders of the Pacific war in August. Upon his return, a magazine compared the two war leaders who both liked journeys. "The two leaders of the English-speaking peoples," the paper stated,[48] "have the rare capacity of apprehending the war in its global character, with the imagination no less than intellectually, and each endeavors to make the picture complete in his own mind by seeing with his own eyes samples of the fighting areas and knowing what men are doing in the far extremities of the combat zone. . . . It is symptomatic of the direction of the war at the highest level that it should be conceived imaginatively and realistically, by President Roosevelt and Mr. Churchill, as a whole, in terms of Europe and Asia and Australia, the Atlantic, the Mediterranean and the Pacific, a global war, determining the fate of all mankind."

Among the former isolationists, many had often expressed their doubts that Britain, after the war in Europe was over, would massively participate in the Pacific war. As far as Russia was concerned, the press related how scrupulous the Russians were not to take part in any conference in which hostilities against the Japanese were on the agenda or in which China was a partner. Stalin kept an army in Siberia near the Manchurian border, but he was no more anxious than the Japanese to have the fight on two fronts and jealously guarded his neutrality. Stalin made vague promises in Teheran, however, that he would join the war on the Japanese after the defeat of Nazi Germany, but so far he had publicly given no sign of hostile intentions toward Japan.

The day before the American election, Stalin made a speech in which he did give such sign. The Soviet leader surveyed the general situation and said among other things, "The decision of the Teheran conference for joint action against Germany and the brilliant putting into practice of those decisions constitute one of the clear indications of the stabilization of the front against the Hitlerite coalition. . . . The decision of the conference at Dumbarton Oaks in the question of the organization of post-war security should be regarded as an equally clear indication of the stability of the front of the United Nations." Stalin then went on to explain the initial successes of the Nazis, and it was at this point that he treated Nazi Germany and Japan in the same breath. He said: "It would be naïve to explain the facts by the personal qualities of the Japanese and the Germans, their superiority over the British, Americans and Russians. . . . It is not a question of their personal qualities but of the fact that the agressive nations, interested in a new war, as nations preparing for war over a long period and accumulating forces for this purpose usually are—and must be—more prepared for war than peace-loving nations." [49]

This speech thus vouchsafed Russia's participation in the new international organization for the preservation of peace, so dear to Roosevelt, and hinted at her taking a fresh look at the Japanese war.

The official German news agency hastened to brand Stalin's speech as a campaign effort for Roosevelt. Experience had taught that events close to election day do not always influence the voters. Lest this opinion prove wrong, the organ of the Soviet government ran an editorial on the election the day before it took place, which in its clumsiness might well have so angered independent voters who resented foreign interference with their most jealously guarded national election, that they could have changed their minds and voted for the Republican candidate.

The Economist, recalling what sharp attacks had appeared in the American press when an unimportant church magazine took a stand for Roosevelt, rather amused, acquainted its readers with the joining of the Russian government paper in campaign oratory at its worst.

"*Izvestia* chose the closing week of the election campaign," the magazine wrote,[50] "to announce joyfully that Mr. Roosevelt's return was secure and that Mr. Dewey's chances were negligible. Displaying an enviable freedom, not only of opinion, but with the facts, it included the *Herald Tribune* as one of Mr. Roosevelt's supporters; denounced elements in the Republican party as not only Fascists, but pro-German; and concluded by the sensational suggestion that to retrieve their waning fortunes the Republicans would stage a fake attempt upon the life of their own candidate, which was to be ascribed to the Communists and submerge President Roosevelt at the polls. . . . The *Izvestia* writer, who predicted another Zinoviev letter, or Reichstag fire, seems not to have realized that, had the article appeared sooner, it might have been used against the President with fatal effect; or that had Governor Dewey been elected, Russian-American relations might have been strained by the suspicion that Moscow had less than perfect confidence in the new administration."

Roosevelt carried the election by 3,600,000 votes. It was a few weeks after the Americans landed in the Philippines, and when the European war appeared to be nearing final victory for the Allies.

"He will see from now on that the American people have again legalized his power position even more, endeavor to satisfy the wishes of Moscow as an acknowledgement of the help Stalin had tendered him by the speech the Soviet chief had made on the eve of the election," the spokesman of the German government stated.[51]

The Latin American press indulged in such enthusiastic slogans as "President Roosevelt's victory is our victory!" or "He is the hope of the Continent," except the Argentine press which called the election a farce and was particularly sarcastic about the soldiers' vote, "so secret that not even they themselves will know whom they voted for." De Valera's mouthpiece, *Irish Press,* dwelt on Roosevelt's merits: "In twelve years," the paper stated, "he has brought a nation through the worst financial crisis in its history. He has given a new philosophy to worker and employer . . . he organized American economy in the certainty that war would engulf the nation and when it came the nation was all but prepared."

The Communist press registered the victory with satisfaction. "The election of Mr. Roosevelt is the guarantee of the enduring union of the allied nations which has been indispensable in the crushing of Hitlerism and no less indispensable for establishing a just and durable peace." [53]

"There can be no dispute about the political mastery which has welded together the conservative South, the city machines, the labor vote, many nominal Republicans, and still more independents into a triumphant, if not always easy, alliance. . . ." *The Economist* commented.[54] "The President's great strength . . . was his record in the management of the war and in fostering international cooperation. It was the main virtue of the campaign which in some respects was as unscrupulous as any that have gone before, that, although foreign policy was the great issue, there was no partisan division on the question of American participation. . . . On the evidence of the campaign, there was little to choose between them. But it is plain that to many Mr. Roosevelt still stands for the crusading liberation which marked his early terms; and that his faith has not been alienated by his failure to insist on the need of preserving some of the war controls. There is a belief that once the election has been won, Mr. Roosevelt will retrace his steps, that he will be both more daring, more imaginative and more constructive than his opponent. . . . Mr. Roosevelt has become a great symbol not only of American willingness to share in international responsibilities, but of progressive politics at home. His re-election contradicts the cynics who predicted that all the American people wanted was a return to the 'normalcy' of Harding."

This election again disclosed the gulf between the press and popular opinion. "It is said," the same magazine reported,[55] "that only about 15 per cent of the newspapers actively supported Mr. Roosevelt with about 60 per cent in the Republican camp and the remainder on the fence. . . . In part the decline of the influence of the press is the measure of radio's gain. Mr. Roosevelt's mastery of the microphone more than outweighed his unpopularity at the editorial desk. It is worth remembering that the lower the income group, the greater the tendency to look to the radio, rather than to the newspaper, for news and comment."

A Swiss newspaper reviewed Mr. Roosevelt's years in the Presidency. "Soon it will be twelve years," the article ran,[56] "that Mr. Roosevelt ascended his first term, a few weeks after Hitler came to power by having been appointed *Reichskanzler*, a position that he built up to an unlimited dictatorship. In the scene of world politics, Roosevelt has become the decisive opponent of Hitler. This was not immediately obvious. The beginnings of Roosevelt's administration took place in similar conditions as that of Hitler's rule. . . . For a time one nurtured the hope in Berlin that the parallel of the by-play on the two political scenes would foster National Socialism and win Roosevelt for the spirit of the Third Reich. . . . But with the 'unparalleled armament' that Hitler introduced, the road of Germany and the United States parted. Roosevelt was one of the first statesmen who recognized the political consequences of the German armament for the world. . . . Anyway, when Roosevelt was first re-elected in 1936, Berlin knew well that the event indicated a negative factor in the evolution of German policy and that its effects might one day cross the plans of National Socialist imperialism. . . . Although American support for England in her worst plight was very limited, yet it was of incalculable moral import. First of all, this Roosevelt policy started the mobilization of the potentiality of the American armament industry, a fact that developed to full effect only after the Japanese attack. Within a year after this event, America together with England assumed the initiative in both the Atlantic and the Pacific Oceans."

The British Broadcasting Company summed up the importance of Roosevelt's re-election for the world,[57] "In the past week or two, the momentous fact that fifty million Americans were going to decide by free ballot where they meant their country to stand in the new world of the peace—this noisy and tremendous fact, like the cry of a new-born baby, seemed to burst in on the world, and the returns were chalked up in France and heard over loudspeakers through the main cities of Russia and in the streets of Chunking. Berlin broadcast them ceaselessly, and decided on Wednesday that America was a victim of a disease it seems unable to shake. The Nazi name for the twelve-year old infection was Franklin Roosevelt.

". . . We can lean back and begin to see what Americans have committed themselves to, and some of the reasons why. First, of course, they have paid a unique tribute to the personality of Mr. Roosevelt. . . . There are Americans who were toddlers of four years of age when he first took office, who will be twenty when he finally retires to his home on the Hudson. Even a famous news magazine that had done its best to bring magnetism to the name of Dewey, grudgingly allowed yesterday that Franklin Roosevelt is the most popular American political figure in history. . . . It is easy to be tempted into thinking that Roosevelt's election was an inevitable thing—a pledge from the American people that they are ashamed of their old ways and will live henceforth only by unselfishness and high principles. Elections are not won on principle. There is a technique of winning friends and influencing voters, and if anybody misunderstands this warning as cynicism, let me say that nobody alive respects the truth of it quite so much as Franklin Roosevelt.

"Mr. Roosevelt never directly answered the really dangerous rumor about the state of his health. He merely undertook to drive in an open motor-car through New York and some of the industrial towns of Pennsylvania, and to speak at night in the open air in Philadelphia. By the grace of God the heavens opened and drenched him pitilessly each time on the only rainy days of the autumn. And he appeared, all the more, a man of laughing courage and defiance. . . . It was assumed by all the experts that Mr. Roosevelt would go back to a mainly Republican House of Representatives. But the big surprise of the election is that by present count the Democrats will have a majority there. . . .

The American people have without doubt endorsed the working strategical partnership of Roosevelt, Churchill, Stalin and Chiang Kai-shek. They have backed up the men in Congress who committed them to the next try for a really workable League of Nations. They have committed themselves. . . .

"In authority to commit the United States to a new responsibility for the state of the world, [Roosevelt] has a new power vastly greater than any he previously had. In this sense he has gone to the people as Wilson did and the people have said 'Yes,' where they broke Wilson's heart by saying 'No.' That, I hope, is rousing news enough for one week from America."

14

THE LAST TERM

The inauguration in January, 1945, as unceremonious as a fourth wedding, finally freed President Roosevelt to undertake the long trip to the Crimea for a most important conference of the Big Three.

In the West, the public was recovering from the scare roused by the initial successes of a violent German counterattack in the Ardennes and in Hungary that had threatened to delay final victory in Europe indefinitely.

The first weeks of disconcerting confusion past, the German offensive proved to have been a desperate last attempt to reverse or at least hold up defeat.

"We know the aims of our enemies of the past and present," Hitler's New Year's message read. "We know what the Anglo-Americans intend to do with the German Reich, subject as they are to the Bolshevik master and to international Jewry behind them. Should their aim be realized it would mean not only the dismemberment of the German Reich, the deportation of 15 to 20 million Germans to foreign lands, the enslavement of the rest of our people, but also the mass starvation of further millions of Germans. Apart from that, however, we are left with the choice of living in freedom or dying in slavery."

After the conspiracy against Hitler was crushed, the Germans had no alternative to Nazi leadership and the Nazis had none to fighting until anyone of authority ordered unconditional surrender, or to the complete disintegration of army and population.

This last furious assault compelled a revision of time-tables, plans, and prospects. "There was a moment last December and early January," an English magazine commented,[1] "when the faint-hearted thought they detected the flavor of dead sea fruit in such measure of fulfilment of Allied hopes as had then been achieved. Disappointment at the failure of the Allied armies in the West to continue far into Germany their sweeping advance from the Normandy beaches through France and Belgium, had been turned into vocal discontent by the initial success of Rundstedt's massive thrust through American lines into the Ardennes. Though it was not fully realized that this thrust was nothing more than a forlorn German hope of breaking through to Antwerp, and of cutting off the large group of Allied Armies in Southern Holland, so as to give Germany a chance of peace by negotiation, the position was widely held to be so disconcerting that audible murmurs could be heard on both sides of the Atlantic. The dour, uncalculating bravery of American troops, and very skillful cooperation between Field Marshal Montgomery and General Omar Bradley, thwarted the desperate German venture and transformed it into a considerable disaster for German arms. Still, Rundstedt did succeed in dislocating the Allied plans and in delaying the resumption of a strong Allied offensive against the Siegfried Line in the direction of Cologne and the Ruhr. Directly and indirectly this enemy success prompted ill-considered and acrimonious outbursts of feeling in the United States and in this country, outbursts which gave German propaganda an opening it was careful not to miss. In all this there was a savor of dead sea fruit. . . . 'The people of the United States were at the lowest spiritual level of the war' (an American correspondent in Britain said). 'This,' he believed, 'was partly an effect of disappointed reaction from anticipations of speedy victory' with which his fellow-countrymen were vibrating last August. . . . Other causes were the conflict in Greece, dislike of British behavior in Italy, and the suddenly discovered weakness and basic disunity in China.' "

"The year 1945 is opening gloomily for the Allies," an English weekly said in introduction to a survey.[2] "Fighting still goes on in Athens. The Lublin Committee (a Soviet picked outfit) has added another twist to the tangled knot of Polish politics by declaring itself the provisional government of Poland. Across the Atlantic, American criticism of Britain and distrust of Russia show but little sign of abating. Militarily, too, the outlook is disappointing. The Rundstedt offensive has been checked, but that it should have succeeded at all grievously contradicts the high hopes of last summer. The Russians' encirclement of Budapest and advance in Austria are bright lights in an otherwise sombre picture, but they are at a standstill in Poland and East Prussia.

"The two chief factors in the Allied crisis—military deadlock and political disunity—naturally interact on each other. Now, as always, political differences are accentuated by military frustration. In turn, the political differences have helped to create the military situation by giving the Nazis hope to fight for—the hope that the coalition against them will, after all, collapse.

". . . The most obvious reason for insufficient reserves in the Western front can be found in the two conferences at Quebec. In 1943, President Roosevelt and Mr. Churchill decided to put increased emphasis on the war with Japan, and in 1944 the decision appears to have been taken to wage the two wars simultaneously with equal energy. . . . The Allies' responsibility for the restoration of German morale is even more direct. . . . It has arisen as a by-product of the Russian-Polish dispute. If the Russians had displayed less intransigence in their claims on Poland, the folly of 'compensation' for Poland in the West up to the line of the Oder would not have been even considered. Yet once dismemberment was put forward in the East, it was inevitable that France should return to the Rhineland project, rejected in 1919. Thus haphazardly, almost by default, terms have been laid down for Germany which will probably leave the Germans fighting to the bloody and bitter end."

The President's State of the Union Message "gave the balance, and the perspective which have been so hard to find in recent weeks," the same weekly asserted.[3] "Mr. Roosevelt's insistence on the need for unity among the Allies was accompanied by a frank recognition of the differences which are bound to emerge as the problems of peace supplant the simpler demands of the war. . . . Of the Atlantic Charter, which internationalists and isolationists alike have chosen to regard as an inflexible yardstick, the President sanely observed that although it is essential to have guiding principles, they do not provide rules of easy application to each and every one of 'this war-torn world's tangled situations."

In Britain there was some uneasiness about reports, or as *The Economist* [4] called them, "inspired reports, appearing in the American press, that the United States Government intends to make some proposal at the San Francisco conference on the general subject of colonies. Just what the proposal is has not emerged, but it is apparent that the general idea behind the American proposals is that of 'collective trusteeship' which is opposed to 'exclusive imperialism.' Clearly this might mean anything from affirmation of the mandate system and its extension to all colonial territories to the complete disappearance of colonial empires and their replacement by a system of international administration."

A left-wing English magazine sharply pointed out the danger inherent in the situation. "Americans who nearly ruined our relations with France," it argued,[5] "may not be entitled to censure our even more deplorable performances in Greece. . . . In a grave passage the President himself faced the danger that American perfectionism may again destroy the world's hopes of an effective, international organization, as it did after the last war. The retreat to isolationism a quarter of a century ago was started not by a direct attack against international cooperation, but against the alleged imperfections of the peace."

An English magazine wondered whether a common Anglo-American policy could develop with respect to Poland.[6] "Both governments, probably both peoples, certainly want the question of Poland's eastern frontier, and for that matter her western frontier, settled after reasonable discussion. . . . But Russia is taking a different line, which is frankly regretted here as it is regretted in the United States. She has imposed a unilateral decision, without the concurrence either of Britain and America or of the Polish government which Britain and America and every other Allied State except Russia herself has so far continued to recognise. What is to be said or done in fact of this situation? What does America want said and done? Without Russia, Germany is not likely to be defeated. Without Russia, Poland will quite certainly not be liberated. Unless therefore the United States is prepared for an open break with Russia—of which disastrous development there is fortunately no sign—to attack this country for accepting a Russian decision which it cannot alter, and speak of Anglo-Russian policy of reaction in Europe, is unfair, censorious and destructive of that good understanding between the two Atlantic nations without which no stable peace can be imagined.

"Take again Greece, about which American conscience seemed troubled too. That British troops should be fighting Greeks in Greece is more repugnant to every Englishman than it can be to any American. But what does America want? . . . How do our aims differ from America's? Mr. Churchill has asserted again and again for weeks past that we care not whether the Greeks are under a republic or monarchy, whether they choose a government of the Right or the Left, provided they choose it freely by a peaceful electoral process in the absence of all armed intimidation. . . . The Prime Minister prevailed over the Greek king to meet the wishes of almost all Greeks by appointing a Regent. Does America not concur in that? It is true that British troops have been involved in a most distasteful warfare in an endeavor to fustrate an armed coup in Athens. . . . Soon, though not soon enough, the three heads of State will meet, and it may be hoped that Britain and America, surveying the present relationship between them, may well decide that, in a simple and classic phrase, this will never do."

On the Western front, the Allies resumed their march, more cautious than before in their estimates of final victory. The question remained whether the Nazi chieftains would succeed in leading the unredeemable troops underground to wage a long drawn-out guerilla war, or would one of them muster enough resolution and power to offer a general surrender?

The decision might be long in coming, but on the other hand it might be taken all of a sudden, finding the Allies without an agreed plan of handling the surrender, the armistice, the administration of the defeated countries, and the broad lines of peace.

Moreover, the end of the war in Europe was to be the opening of the great offensive against Japan. This fanatical enemy was not expected by the military to be subdued and forced to surrender his freshly conquered, giant empire except by the invasion of his home islands, an operation that must be preceded by inexorable bombing and would take the lives of hundreds of thousands, mainly American. Such an offensive required the wresting from the Japanese of bases on the mainland facing Japan, and according to unanimous intelligence reports, Japan kept a huge, well equipped and intact army in Manchuria. All military leaders were in agreement that the Russian land armies ought to engage the Japanese on the mainland, in place of a costly invasion from the sea by the Anglo-American forces.

A conference of the Big Three offered the President opportunity to elicit from Stalin a definite obligation, complete with date, to take part in the war on Japan. Roosevelt had no doubt but that Stalin would set a price, but he hoped to convince Stalin that co-leadership in organizing the future world order, a position of supreme power in the United Nations equal to that of America, a cooperation with America even against Britain in orderly de-colonizing of territories inhabited by a billion people, would confer a higher benefit on him and his country than the gaining of new territories.

Immediate subjects for the conference, like Poland and Greece, were thorny, but they served eventually to show that any breach in the alliance could be cemented by a compromise solution. Churchill had made a hasty agreement with Stalin in October, 1944 concerning the liberated countries in Eastern Europe and the Balkans, that worked remarkably well except that it aroused public opinion in America as well as in Britain when the existence of an agreemen on spheres of influence became known. Stalin had made no protest when Churchill ordered British troops to prevent the left-wing majority of resistance groups in Greece from assuming power, since he thought that natural sympathies would draw such government toward the Soviet Union even without his encouragement. Stalin expected Churchill also to comply with and support his moves in forming governments in

Poland and other countries which, on the strength of the agreement, belonged to the Soviet sphere. Churchill might have assented, but America was not bound by the agreement and Roosevelt believed that the United Nations organization would make spheres of influence obsolete and unnecessary. Public opinion charged the Allied leaders with breach of the Atlantic Charter, and it did not by any means appease people when Roosevelt remarked that nobody had, in fact, ever signed the Charter. Public discontentment was too extensive and noisy to be calmed down with face-saving measures. Moreover, German propaganda harped on the split in the Allied ranks, this time a true one, to revive the German people's fading hopes.

Roosevelt hastened, after the inauguration, to embark on the 14,000 mile voyage on the sea and in the air to Yalta to meet Stalin and Churchill.

Many friends found him intermittently frail and worn, cheerful and energetic, but the sea usually restored his health and vigor. ". . . in Yalta I noticed," Churchill said later, "that the President was ailing. His captivating smile, his gay and charming manner, had not deserted him, but his face had a transparency, an air of purification, and often there was a far-away look in his eyes. When I took my leave of him in Alexandria Harbor I must confess that I had an indefinable sense of fear that his health and his strength were on the ebb." [7]

Yet the President endured the exacting conferences and negotiations in full command of his charm and authority. His sincerity and broad view made a great impression on Stalin, although his obvious conspiratorial siding with Stalin against the British Prime Minister at times disgruntled the latter. The Big Three now had time and opportunity to take full measure of each other's strength and weaknesses; none could deny the other's superb qualities. Stalin appeared to have been captivated by the sincerity of friendliness that the President professed toward Russia when he stressed the primacy of postwar cooperation in peace between her and America.

At long last Roosevelt received what, at that time, was the most urgent wish of the military, of the Congress, and of the public:

Stalin's promise to turn against Japan three months after the end of hostilities on the European front. As compensation, Roosevelt made territorial concessions to Russia, to the detriment of China and Japan, but Stalin's argument was that he had to justify to his people going to war against a nation that had maintained scrupulous neutrality toward them, even when she would have run little risk in attacking the beaten Russians in the back.

The President also gained Stalin's assent to the United Nations organization, with the right of veto in the Security Council for its permanent members.

On the tough Polish question, a test case for the other small countries overrun by the Soviet army, a compromise solution was reached; its text dealt with salient points in terms that were ambiguous enough to make a compromise possible. It was acknowledged that the Russians had the right to ensure that the governments of their neighbors would be friendly to the Soviet Union. On the other hand, the West insisted that free and unfettered elections ought ultimately to determine the set-up of such governments. In such elections only democratic parties would be allowed to take part, but the terms "democratic" or "non-Nazi" remained undefined. The Soviet Union had entered the class of democratic nations, adhering to the Atlantic Charter without meeting objection or reservation although she had not changed her form of government. A similar government in Poland may have passed the scrutiny as well. It was left to the foreign ministers to cope with the problem.

One of the most important results of the Yalta conference was, as *The Economist* stressed, that it put "an end once and for all to the 'spheres' established in Teheran. . . . Thus the Great Power responsibility," the magazine commented further, "covers all phases of liberation and . . . the emphasis is laid on the *joint* nature of their responsibilities. This decision will, no doubt, be hailed in the American Press as a victory won by the President over British and Russian policies, with their desire of exclusive spheres. If to regard it in this way will make the policy of American intervention in Europe more popular and more enduring, it would be foolish to cavil." As to Poland, the magazine remarked that everything turned on the interpretation of the terms left undefined. "If they mean what they say and what British and Americans understand them to mean, then a great advance has been made."

However, after Churchill's report to the House of Commons, *The Economist* became disquieted. "As it is, his speech gave the unhappy impression," the paper stated,[9] "that all initiative in Polish problems has now been handed over to Moscow and that the British Government would be prepared to back any Russian decision provided a certain amount of face-saving appearances were preserved."

In America, the "first impressions of the Yalta meeting were good," an English quarterly reported,[10] "although a sharp attack began on the Polish settlement by Polish-Americans and their friends, notably in Roman Catholic circles, and among old isolationists. But nobody suggested what the United States could do to obtain a more favorable settlement from the Soviet Union. Opposition, as so often before, was taken out largely in political and editorial oratory. Unfortunately this sort of attack did nothing to render more confident and cooperative our relations with Russia. . . . On the voting agreement (in the United Nations) . . . there was considerable reassurance for American isolationists, if they would only be logical. For the absolute veto given the Great Powers meant that none of them would be obligated to sanctions contrary to its own positive decision at the time."

The Japanese guessed right about the most substantial agreement at the conference. The newspaper *Asaki Shimbun* in Tokyo reported on February 14: "The main problem in the manifold background of the conference was to make the warfare against Japan a common cause of the Allies. At present the United States alone wages that war. The political manoeuvres by the means of which the United States reached her aim characterized the conference. The planned conference in San Francisco is nothing else than an attempt by America to make the war against Japan a war of all the United Nations."

Government circles in Berlin expected the conference to issue an appeal to the German people for surrender, sugar-coated in some vague promises. Correspondingly, the German press cautioned the public not to believe the promises. When the conference ended without such an appeal, this was the official reaction: [11] "Blind hatred and the will of annihilation permeated the politicians who took part in the decisions. What they intend to do with the German people can be called a Morgenthau-plan with certain specifications that originated in hatred but will never be realized. The enemy failed to count on the will of the German people to resist. . . . As to the rest, it results in the unlimited triumph of Stalin in all areas, as he was assured decisive influence in Europe. He has become in some respects the High Commissioner of the three Great Powers on the Continent."

A Swiss newspaper saw the result of the Yalta conference in a different light: [12] "The Yalta agreements show that, although the Soviet regime follows stubbornly and ruthlessly the line of the traditional Russian imperialism, in the long run it accommodates itself to a cooperation with the western powers. . . . There is no controversy between the two Anglo-Saxon countries in respect to such questions of principle as the democratic methods, even though there might be political and economic rivalry between them on the old Continent. It was the Soviet regime that had to make concessions in the principles, although their exploitation by America would, of course, depend on a steadfast and clever pol.-icy. Stalin took that step in assuming that Russia, as one of the world powers, would be able to protect her universal interests in lasting agreement with her equals in power in this enormous war and against the acknowledgment of the same right for America on the European continent. But for the price of acknowledging this right Moscow could hardly receive the economic and financial aid from America needed for the rebuilding of the Soviet Union at favorable conditions."

Yet it was difficult "to establish and maintain a trustful partnership with the Russia of Stalin and Molotov," in the judgment of an English monthly.[13] ". . . We fought on the same side because Hitler left us no choice, and neither of us could have won or perhaps even survived without the other. Yet, this valiant and loyal cooperation when our backs were to the wall was preceded by twenty years of open or scarcely veiled antagonism which left deep furrows of mistrust. We must never forget that the rulers of Russia regard the capitalist system of their Western partners with the same unfriendly gaze as the governing classes in the democracies survey the totalitarian experiment. . . . We are all children of our own past and we cannot toss it away like an old garment. Inexhaustible patience, infinite tact, unfailing goodwill are needed if the alliance concluded in 1941 . . . is to be more than a scrap of paper." The article emphasized how effective in this field "the wisdom and courage, the buoyancy and broad humanity" of the President had been.

Roosevelt has been attacked for the Yalta agreements by Europeans with hindsight wisdom, who make him responsible for the presence of the Russians in the middle of the Continent. They lose sight of the fact that Roosevelt's first responsibility was to safekeep what he thought to be of vital interest to the United States, since he was President of this and not of East-European countries. If he misjudged this country's vital interest, he did so in reliance on the unanimous advice of the American military chiefs, as he had always done, according to the quoted testimony of the British Chief of Staff, in matters military. However, another hindsight viewed the Yalta agreements differently. ". . . unless one argues that the Western Powers should have prepared to fight Russia as soon as Germany collapsed, or to break off their battles against the Nazis and the Japanese short of victory—both of which would have been inconceivable at the time—it seems only fair to say that the concessions made at Yalta to Stalin were no more than their recognition (and in the case of Poland, only partial recognition) of the existing military balance of power."

Yet, as the article continued it left the firm plane of the factual situation that determined the attitudes and actions of the President, venturing instead into the morass of psychology, even extending the President's alleged psychological inadequacy to that of the West in general. It seemed to have overlooked that Winston Churchill at least had given tangible proofs, in October 1944 if not also at other times, that he enjoyed the game of sheer power politics. It went on to say: "Practical compromise between principle and expediency . . . had been the keynote of Roosevelt's whole career in domestic American politics and, with the combination, he had worked wonders. When he attempted to apply similar methods to international relations . . . his wonder-working power abruptly vanished. . . . Roosevelt failed to take adequately into account the enormous intellectual and moral gulf which divided him and the West generally from Stalin and Russia. Without a more extensive adherence to similar moral principles, without . . . a more genuine community of mind, workable compromise was impossible. . . . Only by . . . unreservedly espousing the amorality of power could more durable agreements have been reached. But that would have seemed to Roosevelt a cynical betrayal of the best hope of humanity." Yet, perhaps, America's improved situation, as a consequence of the atomic bomb and Japan's immediate surrender, as well as the discovery that the Japanese forces in Manchuria were much weaker than intelligence had reported, had more to do with the attitudes toward the Yalta agreements than the President's psychological make-up.

In the end of March the President left for Warm Springs, Georgia, his usual place of rest, where he enjoyed the carefree relaxation approximating the vacation of a very busy private person. "He also took there the cure he always felt would restore him to health and vigor," a French author wrote.[15] "On April 11 he finished writing a speech to be made two days later over the radio, on the occasion of the yearly Jefferson dinner." The end of this speech would have sounded as a distanct echo of his profession of faith at his first inauguration, when he said: "So, first of all, let me assert my firm belief that the only thing we have to fear is fear itself." "Now, on the last day of his life he stated, with the same force: 'The only limit to our realization of tomorrow will be our doubts of today. Let us move forward with strong and active faith.' "

"On the twelfth," the author continued, "the program of the day included a picnic near Warm Springs in the company of a few persons of his staff, at which a snack with local specialties, chosen by the President, was to be consumed. At four o'clock the guests began to wonder why the usual commotion preceding the President's coming was absent. As each minute passed, the disquiet mounted. Some went to the telephone, calling the information service at the Presidential cottage. The answer sounded confused and evasive. A party descended the hill toward the settlement and heard there that the President had died at 3:25 P.M.

"Some of the guests reminisced about three images of the President's last year, in their sliding scale of change, as the man was dying amidst full activity. Manifestly, his life had been fading away even as his strength betrayed him. Had those next to him realized it? Probably they had yielded to the known inclination of human nature not to see what they were afraid to see."

On his last day, the President drafted two cables with significant messages. "The first was to Churchill, who had consulted the President about what he should say to the House of Commons about Poland," an Australian correspondent noted.[16] "In this cable Roosevelt said: 'I would minimize the general Soviet problem as much as possible because these problems, in one form or another, seem to arise every day and most of them straighten out. . . . We must be firm, however, and our course thus far is correct.' The second cable was to Harriman in Moscow. In this Roosevelt revealed once again his tolerance and his faith that he would carry into the peace the 'Great Power unity' which, under his leadership, had brought them to the point of victory.

"This was the last message that came from Franklin Roosevelt's hand. An hour later, as he was sitting for an artist who was painting his portrait, he fainted in his chair. That afternoon he died."

"The annals of the modern age may be searched without our coming upon a personal event to compare with the death of President Roosevelt," an English magazine registered.[17] "The passing at a critical moment of a great man of action, especially one who has manifestly changed the course of history, is a most rare occurrence, and the death which makes memorable the 12th of April has no parallel. It bears the marks of a unique ironic tragedy. . . . The absolute victory for which he wore out his life was within the grasp of the Allies when his hour arrived. That was not many days before the first great German surrender and almost on the eve of the international assembly in San Francisco which was to have had the benefit of his directing mind. . . . Every great man is irreplaceable. Between any power and original leader and the man appointed to succeed him there is always a sharp contrast, which gives rise to a fear lest the unfinished work may not be carried to fulfillment."

"Franklin Roosevelt is the greatest casualty of the war," another English magazine asserted.[18] ". . . But what here makes the bitterness of death, not for him but for mankind, is the tragedy of uncompleted service. . . . The man who had led his country to the eve of a victory built largely on his wisdom and inspiration might well have asked release when that goal was reached. But he never would have. . . . Roosevelt was far more than Chief Magistrate of his country. He was a leader as no American President since Lincoln could claim to be. The war has demonstrated that beyond all misunderstanding, that while the war no doubt developed Roosevelt's character, as it must have developed any President's with a character worth developing, the qualities it illuminated were latent in his personality from the first. . . . If this country had enjoyed political leadership comparable to Roosevelt's from the time when he became leader in America the whole of history might have been different. . . . Nobly and discerningly as Franklin Roosevelt has served his own generation, generations yet to come may have even greater reason to pay tribute to him than we have today."

The British made no secret of it that they had particular reasons to cherish Roosevelt's memory.

"No Englishman who lived through those dreadful twelve months from June 1940 to June 1941," a magazine asserted,[19] "is ever likely to forget how completely the nation's hope for ultimate victory rested on that buoyant figure in the White House, and how, stage by stage, the hopes found response in action. . . . We have learnt, in Mr. Roosevelt's years in office, to appreciate how much of our own safety and welfare depend upon the American colossus. To the average Englishman, it is a friendly monster, but an erratic and unpredictable one. Mr. Roosevelt had mastered the art of managing the unmanageable. Through all the shoals of

American politics, with constant tacking in the varying winds, blown sometimes a long way off course, nevertheless this master pilot had demonstrated his ability to bring the vessel into port, sometimes only just in time, it is true, often with much argument among the crew, but never failing. With him at the head of affairs, it was possible to feel sure that, in the end, sound policy would prevail."

"He was beyond all question the truest and mightiest external friend the British Commonwealth of Nations has ever known," a quarterly dedicated to Commonwealth affairs asserted,[20] even though it knew how firmly Roosevelt had stood for the liquidation of colonialism. He "was mourned as sincerely from London to Wellington as in Washington and New York."

The magazine questioned the idea that Roosevelt had probably been more revered abroad than in his own country, by stating: "To claim more, to suggest that because for us, who were not concerned with the acute controversies in which so much of the President's public life was passed, his transcendent greatness stood out in clearer relief than for his own nation, would be unjust to the political discernment of Americans, who have shown as much reverence by their actions under his leadership as by their tributes to his memory. . . . In the last years Americans, including those who continued to oppose him stoutly in domestic issues, were proud to recognize as true the image of Roosevelt that had been conceived in the minds of millions in the suffering nations of Europe, as the incarnation of the hope of liberty that had sunk so low in the years of defeat that without his championship it might have seemed to be extinguished forever."

Prime Minister Churchill received the cable reporting the death of the President next morning, which was, as he stressed in his Memoirs, Friday the 13. He eulogized his friend also in behalf of Parliament on April 17, which adjourned immediately after. "I felt as if I had been struck a physical blow," he wrote.[21] "His love of his own country, his respect for its constitution, his power of gauging the tides and currents of its mobile public opinion, were always evident, but added to these were the beating of that generous heart which was always stirred to anger and to action by spectacles of aggression and oppression by the strong against the weak. It is indeed a loss, a bitter loss to humanity, that those heartbeats are stilled forever."

It must be that in mysterious ways an earlier message had reached the four corners of the globe, announcing that the most powerful nation had elected a chief who extended his sympathy and protection to the weak, the opressed and persecuted everywhere, since it has never before happened that upon the death of a chief of state a huge number of people spontaneously registered their grief by writing to the American legations, or directly to Washington or addressing their messages to the widow of the President. All these foreigners, and their fraternal organizations, appeared to feel the President's demise as a personal loss. This personal attachment to Roosevelt of common people abroad had astounded Joseph C. Grew, American Ambassador to Japan until Pearl Harbor, who wrote [22] of "the regard, verging on reverence, that was felt for Franklin D. Roosevelt by millions of humble people in every part of the world. Those people looked upon our late President as their friend. They saw him as the champion of all humanity in a hard and ruthless world. And, in the eyes of these foreigners, all other Americans somehow shared in the reflected glory of the great man whom they had chosen as their President."

Indeed, the *New York Times* reported on April 14: "Everybody felt personal about Roosevelt. It is true abroad as well as at home. There is a great loneliness in many parts of the world because he is gone."

University students from Yunan, China, wrote: [23] "For years past we have been travelers in endless darkness, and Mr. Roosevelt was the bright lantern to guide us on the way."

Love rose to adoration in many a man and woman in the liberated countries. "You were for us, Mr. President," a Belgian wrote,[24] "a sort of God, less distant, less inaccessible than the other. A God who held our liberty in his providential hands."

The same personal grief was expressed in Paris, as reported in an article describing the mood in that city upon the sad news.

"A brave man . . . a friend. . . . The people of Paris murmured these words so heavy with affection. . . . Our little people hide their grief bashfully. But yesterday they let it be seen that they were beset with sorrow—all. I heard an old woman in the subway saying: 'When one was in trouble one turned to him as to a God. Yes, as if he were a God.' We should remember the anxieties in 1937 and 1938 when Europe was prostrated before the blows of the Germanic force. In the hours of despair a question always came from trembling lips: 'What is Roosevelt going to do?' Later, when we passed as defeated soldiers through villages, deserted by the panic, there was always one who, before he fell asleep on some pallet in a barn, murmured: 'Patience! Roosevelt has not said his word yet.' And the thought alone of that man with his large hat, clear regard behind his glasses, held the promise for us that one day the great trial would come up for appeal." [25]

Each national group, no matter how it hated the others, mourned the President's death as the loss of its particular protector. A truly classic example of this was presented by the condolences of five national groups in Tunisia.[26] The Muslim intellectuals sent this message: "The high, very high idea which we Tunisians have today of the American democracy—it is mainly to Roosevelt that we owe it. Hearing him speak, seeing him fight, this generous Giant, we have, indeed, learned to know and admire the great American nation."

The Zionists wrote: "The Jewish people will never forget President Roosevelt, the great statesman who understood the importance of the Jewish tragedy and worked earnestly to bring about the necessary solution."

The National Union of Spanish people in Tunisia asked: "Please consider us among those who are today beside the great American people in their national sorrow."

The Italian anti-Fascists in Tunisia assured that "They do not forget the friendly declarations of the President regarding the Italian people and the aid given by the United States to the liberated Italian population."

Finally, the Fighting French in Tunisia sent their condolences, stating: "The President's death has deeply affected the French and Tunisian patriots and democrats."

"Not one person raised his voice loudly," the *New York Times* reported from London. "It was as if they were talking of a very dear relative who had died suddenly. And not a word was spoken to the President's detriment."

"The Russian people has experienced sorrow to an unprecedented degree," the paper's reporter in Russia related, "upon the late President Roosevelt's death, which they feel both in political and in a personal sense all the way from the top of officialdom to the man in the street." [27]

"The Russian people will forever revere the memory of the great statesman Roosevelt, who did so much to strengthen the friendship between the Soviet Union and America. All freedom-loving peoples will remember him as the outstanding fighter for the cause of democracy and progress and the great organizer of the fight of the free peoples against the common enemy," [28] *Izvestia* commented. ". . . The cornerstone of Roosevelt's political activities," *The War and the Working Class* wrote in a lengthy review of the President's foreign policies, "was the development and strengthening of cooperation between the great Trans-Atlantic Republic, Great Britain and the Soviet Union. In broad perspective, the President regarded this friendly cooperation, based not on temporary and transient factors but on the fundamental and lasting interests of the great trinity of powers and of all the democratic countries, as the only conceivable way not only of routing the fascist aggressors but also of building a durable peace on the foundation of durable security. . . . The finest monument that can be erected to this splendid man would be the realization of the main idea which inspired his political activities, viz., to ensure mankind peace and security. This is the noble legacy Frankin Delano Roosevelt left to the American people and to all fighters for freedom and democracy."

The Tokyo radio interrupted its program on April 13, announcing the death of President Roosevelt with these further words: "For some minutes we are going to emit music suitable to the circumstance in honor of the death of that great man." Prime Minister Suzuki the next day expressed his deepest sympathy to the American people on the passing of their President.

The news of the death of Roosevelt was hailed by the top Nazi leaders as the long overdue miracle turning defeat into victory.

"I will remember," Frau Inge Haberzettel, Goebbels' secretary related, "Friday, April 13th. . . . While Goebbels was on his way back to Berlin by motor-car, we received the news of the death of President Roosevelt. Goebbels, as usual, returned very late at night (from visits to the Eastern Front). A very heavy bombardment was going on and the Chancellery and the Adlon Hotel were burning. We met Goebbels on the steps of the Propaganda Ministry. A reporter said to him, 'Herr Reich Minister, Roosevelt is dead!' Goebbels jumped up out of his car and stood for a moment as if transfixed. 'Now,' he said, 'bring out your best champagne and let us have a telephone talk with the Fuehrer.' We went into his study, and champagne was served. Goebbels spoke to Hitler on his private line, and said, 'My Fuehrer, I congratulate you! Roosevelt is dead! It is written in the stars that the second half of April will be the turning point for us. This is Friday, April the thirteenth. It is the turning point.' Hitler said something to him, and then Goebbels put down the receiver. He was in ecstasy." [30]

"Death wanted him to disappear from the world scene," the German official news agency commented on April 13. Had the attempt on the life of the Fuehrer succeeded on July 21, he would have greeted the news with a burst of pleasure. Now, he was the one to go while that same destiny allows his enemy to live and finish the fight for the existence and freedom of Germany." The comments of the remaining neo-Fascists in the north of Italy ran in the same vein, but in unprintable words.

The *Times* of India interpreted the worries of many people in many parts of the world, when it wrote: [31] "To think of the coming weeks and months without the guiding wisdom of Mr. Roosevelt is to look to a bleak, sad future."

A groundswell of eulogies in Latin America praised the President for having instituted the Good Neighbor Policy. Soil from twenty Latin American Republics was flown to America to be shaken over the President's grave.

"About half a million people waited in silence for hours for the funeral train, and many cried when the hearse drawn by six horses passed by. All Washington, from the highest officials to the smallest children, wished to say a last goodbye to their dead leader. The deep, genuine grief of the people is a unique testimony to the humanistic virtues of the departed President. A particular trait of his character was his love of the people with whom he had been in close touch till his last breath," a Swiss paper reported.[32]

"Some personalities make their effect by masterfulness," Arnold J. Toynbee wrote.[33] ". . . Others get their way by persuasion. Roosevelt played both roles. It was by masterfulness that he rallied the American people from the economic depression; it was by persuasiveness that he afterwards led them, step by step, to oppose the aggressor powers in World War II. In this, however, Roosevelt was aided by an impersonal force: the ending of America's isolation through the 'annihilation of distance' by technology. Roosevelt's art lay in inducing America to face the political and military implications of this technological revolution."

"One had to see him to be able to talk about him truly. His speeches were not basically different from those made by other statesmen; his photo gave some indication, since his figure was beautiful, but his smile appeared to be completely under control; his voice, over the radio, was captivating, a golden voice, and it sufficed that he begin 'My Friends,' to conquer his hearer even though he did not see him in flesh and blood," André Siegfried reminisced.[34]

"Yet, knowing all this I felt that I did not understand his astonishing popularity, his extraordinary ascent, as long as I had not entered into direct contact with him. Then I understood that his effect on people was due to the single fact that he spoke as a human to other humans. This attitude is so rare that it is irresistible. . . . At times the truth is improbable. Well, when one approached the President, when he offered you his hand to shake, with his famous smile, one really had the feeling that he was glad to meet you. The genuine human likes other human beings, is glad to know them, he is sorry for their troubles and would like to help them. One read these feelings on this engaging figure, on that large smile so little affected, so natural that one had the impression that he smiled for you, exclusively for your sake, and for the first time. When Roosevelt told me: 'I am glad to see you,' I dare say I believed him. The radio allowed him to penetrate in the reach of everybody. . . . Every American was able to say to himself that the President counted on him, trusted him, knew him. Should he have thought that the President loved him, he would not have been mistaken."

"The corpse rests lifeless today, but his fervent love of suffering humanity and his invincible courage will survive forever," Mme. Chiang Kai-shek's message said.[35]

"We Jews and immigrants are particularly attached and obligated to the dear departed," Albert Einstein wrote.[36] "Rarely has he whose heart is in the right place also the political genius and will power through which gifts alone can a man influence, decisively and lastingly, historic developments. . . . He successfully intervened within the frames of the politically possible in behalf of the security of the weak and for the improvement of economic relations. Although he had to carry an immense burden, a healthy humor allowed him to remain inwardly free—which is rare among those who have to make decisions of fateful consequences. He was consistent to the extreme with respect to his ultimate aims, and yet admirably elastic in overcoming the grave obstacles that are set against a far-seeing statesman, especially in democratic countries, in which an office—even the highest one, gives slight authority. . . . It is tragic that he is not able to take part, with his unique abilities, in the solution of the problem of internatonal security. It is tragic, especially for us Jews, that he has not lived to carry on, with his alert feeling of justice, the decisive negotiations, upon which might depend whether our gravely tested people will find a refuge, whether the doors of Palestine will be open to the refugees and persecuted among us."

Another great exile, Thomas Mann, paid this tribute to the President: [37] "He had the amiableness and captivating charm of Julius Caesar, indeed his greatness was of similar quality to that of the Roman.

"Like him," continued Mann, "Roosevelt was an aristocrat,

child of wealth and friend of the people, protector of the little man. . . . Clever as a snake and bare of malice like pigeons, tender and strong, refined and simple like a genius, enlightened with intuitive knowledge of the needs of the time and the spirit —including the wisdom that he who serves well with the most courageous obedience, with the most flexible toughness, is lucky like the man of 'faith' of whom Goethe says that he rises steadfastly, at times dashing boldly forward, other times plying patiently so that Good will be carried into effect, to thrive, to avail. Thus I see him, have I known and admired and loved him, and I was proud of having, under his aegis, become *Civis Romanus*."

"Nature endowed him with a heart and spirit commensurate to the immense country that Providence gave him for a time to administer," Paul Claudel wrote.[38] ". . . The adroitness and experience of a fighter lived in him side by side with the calculating patience of a sick man whom circumstances permitted to meditate. . . ."

A strangely pessimistic message stood out in the avalanche of condolences. "My humble condolence and congratulations; latter because your illustrious husband died in harness and after war had reached a point where Allied victory was certain; he was spared humiliating spectacle of being party to peace which threatens to be prelude to war bloodier still if possible," the cable from Mahatma Gandhi read.

A thoughtful broadcast from London summed up the President's career upon the anniversary of his death. Isaiah Berlin related his thoughts, memories and appreciation of President Roosevelt.

Speaking of the time of the New Deal, he said: [39] "Over this vast, seething chaos presided a handsome, charming, gay, intelligent, delightful, very audacious man, Mr. Franklin Delano Roosevelt. He was accused of many weaknesses. He had betrayed his class, he was ignorant, unscrupulous, irresponsible. He was ruthless in playing with lives and careers of individuals. He was surrounded by adventurers, slick opportunists, intriguers. He made conflicting promises, cynically and brazenly, to individuals and groups and representatives of foreign nations. He made up, with his vast and irresistible public charm and his astonishing high spirits, for a lack of virtues considered more important in the leader of the most powerful democracy in the world: the virtues of application, industry, responsibility.

". . . He believed in his own strength and ability to manage and to succeed, whatever happened. . . . It was this, perhaps, more than any other quality, which drew men of very different outlooks to him. In a despondent world which appeared divided between wicked and fatally efficient fanatics marching to destroy, and bewildered populations on the run, unenthusiastic martyrs in a cause they could not define, he believed in his own ability, so long as he was in control, to stem the terrible tide.

"He had all the character and energy and skill of the dictators, and he was on our side. He was, in his opinion and public actions, every inch a democrat. All the political and personal and public criticism of him might be true; all the personal defects which his enemies and some of his friends attributed to him might be real; yet as a public figure he was unique.

"As the skies of Europe grew darker, in particular after war broke out, he seemed to the poor and unhappy in Europe a kind of benevolent demigod who alone could and would save them in the end.

"His moral authority, the degree of confidence which he inspired outside his own country—far more beyond America's frontiers than within them at all times—has no parallel. Perhaps President Wilson in the early days after the end of the First World War, when he drove in triumph through the streets of London and Paris, may have inspired some such feeling; but it disappeared quickly and left behind it a terrible feeling of disenchantment. It was plain even to his enemies that President Roosevelt would not be broken as President Wilson had been. For to his prestige and to his personality he added a degree of political skill —indeed virtuosity—which no American before him had ever possessed. . . . Roosevelt was a magnificent virtuoso of this type, and he was the most benevolent as well as the greatest master of his craft in modern times. He really did desire a better life for mankind.

". . . The great majorities which he obtained in the elections . . . during his four terms in office . . . were ultimately due to an obscure feeling on the part of the majority of the citizens of the United States that he was on their side, that he wished them well, and that he would do something for them. And this feeling gradually spread over the entire civilized world.

"He became a legendary hero—they themselves did not know quite why—to the indigent and the oppressed far beyond the confines of the English-speaking world.

". . . His illness and the support and encouragement and political qualities of his wife—whose greatness of character and goodness of heart history will duly record—seemed to transfigure his public personality into the strong and beneficent champion who became the father of his people, in an altogether unique fashion.

". . . Mr. Roosevelt's example strengthened democracy everywhere—that is to say, the view that the promotion of social justice, and individual liberty does not necessarily mean the end of all efficient government; that power and order are not identical with a straitjacket of doctrine, whether economic or political; that it is possible to reconcile individual liberty and a loose texture of society with the indispensable minimum of organization and authority. And in this belief lies what Mr. Roosevelt's greatest predecessor once described as the last best hope on earth."

On the first anniversary of his death, this message flashed across the Atlantic:

"We do well to honor his name and be proud that we have lived in his time." [40] Signed: "Winston Churchill."

NOTES

Chapter One

1. Dixon Wecter, *The Age of the Great Depression* (New York: Macmillan, 1948).
2. François de Tessan, *Le President Hoover et la Politique Américaine* (Paris: Baudinière, 1935).
3. Stanley H. Bailey, *Mr. Roosevelt's Experiment* (London: Hogarth, 1935).
4. Richard Lewinsohn, *Die Welt aus den Fugen* (Dresden: Reissner, 1933).
5. François de Tessan, *op. cit.*
6. Bertrand de Jouvenel: *La Crise du Capitalisme Americaine* (Paris: Gallimard, 1933).
7. André Maurois, *L'Amerique Inattendue* (Paris: Mornay, 1931).
8. François de Tessan, *op. cit.*
9. Helmut Magers, *Roosevelt* (Leipzig: Kittler, 1934).
10. Paul Einzig, *The World Economic Crisis* (London: Macmillan, 1932).
11. Raymond Las Vergnas, *Franklin D. Roosevelt* (Paris: Ed. Universitaires, 1944).
12. *Economist* (London), November 8, 1930.
13. Raymond Las Vergnas, *op. cit.*
14. *New Statesman and Nation,* (London), May 10, 1930.
15. Jean Lescure, "Les Podromes de l'expérience Roosevelt," *Revue Economique Internationale* (Bruxelles), December, 1938.
16. Otto Bauer, *Zwischen Zwei Weltkriegen* (Bratislava: Prager, 1926).
17. Karl Polanyi, *The Great Transformation* (New York: Rinehart and Co., 1944).

18. Paul Alpert, *L'Amérique de Roosevelt* (Paris: Nouv. Éd. Latines, 1936).
19. Bertrand de Jouvenel, *op. cit.*
20. Richard Lewinsohn, *op. cit.*
21. Helmut Magers, *op. cit.*
22. Bertrand de Jouvenel, *op. cit.*
23. Jaime Gurza, *Logic, Roosevelt and the American People* (Mexico City, 1935).
24. Bertrand de Jouvenel, *op. cit.*
25. Paul Alpert, *op. cit.*
26. R. Recouly, *L'Amérique Pauvre* (Paris: Ed. de France, 1933).
27. *Economist* (London), June 21, 1930.
28. Dixon Wecter, *op. cit.*
29. Richard Lewinsohn, *op. cit.*
30. Richard Lewinsohn, *op. cit.*
31. N. J. Bonn: *The Crisis of Capitalism in America* (New York: John Day, 1932).
32. *New Statesman and Nation* (London), May 10, 1930.
33. Stanley H. Bailey, *op. cit.*
34. *Revue de France* (Paris), November 1, 1932.
35. André Maurois, *op. cit.*
36. *Neue Zurcher Zeitung* (Zurich), November 1, 1932.
37. Jaime Gurza, *op. cit.*
38. *Neue Zurcher Zeitung* (Zurich), November 13, 1932.
39. Sir Frederick Whyte, *President Roosevelt and the New Deal,* London: Nineteenth Century, May, 1933.
40. Arnold J. Toynbee and V. M. Boulter (eds.), *Survey of International Affairs* (London: Royal Institute of International Affairs, 1932).
41. Mary Agnes Hamilton, *In America To-day* (London: Hamish-Hamilton, 1932).
42. T. E. Gregory, *The Spectator* (London), October 15, 1932.
43. *The Spectator* (London), October 15, 1932.
44. *New York Times,* May 5, 1933.
45. *The Round Table* (London), March, 1933.
46. *L'Europe Nouvelle* (Paris), October, 1932.
47. Dixon Wecter, *op. cit.*
48. *L'Europe Nouvelle* (Paris), November, 1931.
49. *Neue Zurcher Zeitung* (Zurich), November 1, 1932.

50. *Contemporary Review* (London), November, 1930.
51. *Ibid.*, June, 1930.
52. Quoted in Edgar Eugene Robinson, *American Democracy in Time of Crisis* (Stamford, Calif., Stamford Univ. Press, 1934).
53. *Times* (London), October 6, 1930.
54. *Contemporary Review* (London), June, 1930.
55. *New Statesman and Nation* (London), October 11, 1930.
56. *Contemporary Review* (London), June, 1930.
57. Richard Lewinsohn, *op. cit.*
58. *Ibid.*
59. Speech at Buffalo, October 20, 1930.

Chapter Two

1. Paul Hazard, *Revue des Deux Mondes* (Paris), December 1, 1932.
2. *Spectator* (London), November 11, 1932.
3. Georges Lechartier, *Revue des Deux Mondes* (Paris), December 1, 1932.
4. *Ibid.*
5. François Herbette, "*F. D. Roosevelt,*" *Revue de France* (Paris), November 1, 1932.
6. *Neue Freie Presse* (Vienna), November 8, 1932.
7. *Round Table* (London), December, 1932.
8. *Revue des Vivants* (Paris), March, 1933.
9. Helmut Magers, *Roosevelt* (Leipzig: Kittler, 1934).
10. Johannes Stoye, *U.S.A.* (Leipzig: Lernt Um, 1933).
11. Helmut Magers, *op. cit.*
12. Richard Law, *Time and Tide* (London), January 14, 1939.
13. Stanley H. Bailey, *Mr. Roosevelt's Experiment* (London: Hogarth, 1935).
14. *Neue Freie Presse* (Vienna), November 1, 1932.
15. Bertrand de Jouvenel, *La Crise du Capitalisme Américain* (Paris: Gallimard, 1933).
16. *Neue Zurcher Zeitung* (Zurich), November 6, 1932.
17. Raymond Recouly, *L'Amérique Pauvre* (Paris: Ed. de France, 1933).
18. F. W. von Pittwitz, *Preussische Jahrbuecher,* Heft 1, (Berlin: July 1, 1934).
19. *Neue Zurcher Zeitung* (Zurich), November 6, 1932.

20. Bertrand Fay: Roosevelt et son Amérique, quoted by L. Bonnichon: *Des Aspects Sociaux de la Réforme Roosevelt* (Paris, 1934).
21. A. S. J. Baster, *The Twilight of American Capitalism* (London, King & Son, 1937).
22. *Ibid.*
23. Dixon Wecter, *The Age of the Great Depression* (New York: Macmillan, 1948).
24. Georges Boris, *La Révolution Roosevelt* (Paris: Gallimard, 1934).
25. *Neue Zurcher Zeitung* (Zurich), November 28, 1932.
26. Georges Boris, *op. cit.*
27. *New York Times* (from London), June 11, 1933.
28. *Revue de France* (Paris), July 1, 1933.
29. Helmut Magers, *op. cit.*
30. *Yale Review,* June 18, 1933.
31. *The Roosevelt I Knew* (New York: Viking Press, 1946).
32. *London Week End Review,* quoted in *New York Times,* October 28, 1933.
33. *Revue de France* (Paris), September, 1933.
34. *Ibid.*
35. Frédéric de Jantze, *La Revue des Vivants* (Paris), March, 1933.
36. George Boris, *op. cit.*

Chapter Three

1. *Economist* (London), November 18, 1932.
2. *Neue Zurcher Zeitung* (Zurich), November 11, 1934.
3. The Public Papers, Vol. 3. Introduction.
4. Basil Rauch, *History of the New Deal* (New York: Creative Age Press, 1950).
5. Basil Woon, *Roosevelt, World Statesman* (London: Peter Davies, 1942).
6. Rexford Tugwell, *The Democratic Roosevelt* (Garden City: Doubleday, 1957).
7. Raymond Recouly, *Revue de France* (Paris), August 5, 1933.
8. *Looking Forward, The Re-appraisal of Values,*
9. Carlos Davila in B. P. Adams: *You, Americans* (New York: Funk and Wagnalls Co., 1939).
10. Jaime Gurza, *Logic, Roosevelt and the American People* (Mexico City, 1935).

11. Louis Bonnichon, *Des Aspects Sociaux de la Réforme Roosevelt* (Paris, 1934).
12. *China Press* (Shanghai), May 5, 1935.
13. Otto Hoetzsch, "Die Vereinigten Staaten von Amerika im ersten Halbjahr 1933," *Zeitschrift fuer Politik,* Berlin, 1934.
14. August 15, 1934.
15. *Sunday Dispatch* (London), July 29, 1934.
16. Albert Caprile in B. P. Adams *You, Americans* (New York: Funk and Wagnalls, 1932).
17. *New York Times,* June 5, 1933.
18. *New York Times,* July 23, 1933.
19. *New York Times,* July 25, 1933.
20. *New York Times,* December 22, 1933.
21. O. Kuusinen, *La Position de la Communiste Internationale* (Paris: Bureau d'Edition, 1934).
22. Paul Alpert, *L'Amérique de Roosevelt* (Paris: Nouv Ed Latines, 1934).
23. Bertrand de Jouvenel, *La Crise du Capitalisme Américaine* (Paris: Gallimard, 1933).
24. Kushat, Talaksi Shah, *World Depression* (Madras, 1933).
25. *New York Times,* May 17, 1933.
26. *Journal des Débats* (Paris), July 22, 1933.
27. *Revue des Vivants* (Paris), March, 1933.
28. Helmut Magers, *Roosevelt* (Leipzig: Kittler, 1934).
29. "The New Deal Swindle," *The Labour Monthly* (London), July, 1934.
30. Georges Boris, *La Révolution Roosevelt* (Paris: Gallimard, 1934).
31. *New York Times,* November 6, 1933.
32. *American Magazine,* July, 1934.
33. *New York Times,* December 22, 1933.
34. *New York Times,* January 21, 1934.
35. *New York Times,* March 4, 1934.
36. *New York Times,* August 14, 1934.
37. *New York Times,* August 14, 1934.
38. Georges Boris, *op. cit.*
39. Robert de St. Jean, *La Vraie Révolution de Roosevelt* (Paris: Grasset, 1934).
40. "While the World Watches," *Collier's,* December 29, 1934.
41. *New York Times,* October 13, 1934.
42. *New York Times,* September 3, 1934.

43. *New York Times,* November 4, 1934.
44. March 5, 1934.
45. August 13, 1934.
46. *New York Times,* April 3, 1934.
47. *New York Times,* April 25, 1934.
48. *New York Times,* June 27, 1934.
49. *New York Times,* June 6, 1934.
50. *New York Times,* November 26, 1933.
51. *New York Times,* October 14, 1933.
52. Georges Boris, *op. cit.*
53. *Survey of International Affairs* (London: Royal Institute of International Affairs, 1936).
54. Roland Leslie Warren, Comparison between the economic opinions of Roosevelt and Hitler, University Heidelberg, 1937.
55. Jaime Gurza, *op. cit.*

Chapter Four

1. *Neue Zurcher Zeitung* (Zurich), February 8, 1935.
2. Bernard Fay, "Impressions from America," *Neue Zurcher Zeitung* (Zurich), February 3, 1935.
3. Stephen Kemp Bailey, *Roosevelt and His New Deal.* (London: Fact, 1938).
4. A. Fenner Brockway, *Will Roosevelt Succeed?* (London: Routledge and Sons, 1934).
5. Juan Guixé, *L'Expérience Roosevelt* (Paris: Édit., Contemporaines, 1938).
6. Wilhelm F. Walter, *Das Experiment Roosevelts* (Essen: Glueckauf, 1936).
7. Seymour Houghton, *Carrefours Américains* (Paris: Jean Flory, 1938).
8. Stolberg and Vinton, *Economic Consequences of the New Deal* (New York: Harcourt, Brace and Co., 1935).
9. S. K. Bailey, *op. cit.*
10. Carlos Davila in B. P. Adams, *You, Americans* (New York: Funk & Wagnalls, 1939).
11. Quoted by Gerald White Johnson, *Roosevelt, Dictator or Democrat?* (New York: Harpers, 1941).

12. Taraknath Das, *Foreign Policies of President F. D. Roosevelt* (Calcutta, 1934).
13. Ibid.
14. S. K. Bailey, *op. cit.*
15. David Marshal Mason, August 24, 1935.
16. *Journal Des Débats* (Paris), January 4, 1936.
17. *Le Temps* (Paris), January 4, 1936.
18. *Corriere della Sera* (Milan), January 7, 1936.
19-26. *New York Times,* January 5, January 6, and February 5, 1936.
27. Jay Pierrepont Moffat, *The Moffat Papers* (Cambridge, Mass.: Harvard Univ. Press, 1956).
28. Fritz-Konrad Krueger, *Wandlungen in der Politik der Vereinigten Staaten, Zeitschrift fuer Politik,* Berlin, 1937.
29. *Oesterreischische Zeitung* (Vienna), January 4, 1936.
30. Quoted by Paul Alpert, *L'Amérique de Roosevelt* (Paris: Nouv. Éd. Latines, 1936).
31. Le Petit Havre (Le Havre), December 18, 1937.
32. *The New Deal* by the Editors of *The Economist* (New York: Alfred A. Knopf, 1937).
33. *New Statesman and Nation* (London), October 10, 1936.
34. Quoted by James MacGregor Burns: *Roosevelt, The Lion and the Fox* (New York: Harcourt, Brace and Co., 1956).
35. *New Statesman and Nation* (London), March 6, 1936.
36. *Ibid,* April 18, 1936.
37. *The New Deal* by the Editors of *The Economist* (New York: Alfred A. Knopf, 1937).
38. Carlos Davila, *op. cit.*
39. *New Statesman and Nation* (London), January 11, 1936.
40. *Revue de Paris* (Paris), December, 1936.
41. *Ibid.*
42. *The Economist* (London), November 21, 1936.
43. *Revue de Paris,* December, 1936.
44. *Observer* (London), November 8, 1936.
45. *Zeitschrift fuer Politik* (Berlin), December, 1936.
46. *Voelkischer Beobachter* (Munich), November 5, 1936.
47. *Revue de Paris,* December, 1936.
48. *The Economist* (London), November 21, 1936.
49. November 6, 1936.
50. *New York Times,* November 7, 1936.

Chapter Five

1. *Hochschule fuer Politik*, Berlin; Jahrbuch, 1939.
2. Max Lambert, *Les États-Unis* (Paris: Blond and Gay, 1944).
3. *New York Times,* February 2, 1937.
4. *New York Times,* September 26, 1937.
5. Basil Maine, *Franklin Roosevelt* (London: Nicholson and Watson, 1942).
6. R. Baumal, *La Démocratie Americaine* (Bruxelles: Heraly, 1946).
7. Louis R. Franck: *Démocraties en Crise* (Paris: Rieder, 1937).
8. Basil Maine, *op. cit.*
9. *The Twentieth Century* (Allahabad, India), November, 1939.
10. R. H. Kiernan: *President Roosevelt* (London: Harrap and Co., 1948).
11. Firmin Roz, *Roosevelt* (Paris: Dunod, 1948).
12. *New Statesman and Nation,* (London, April 3, 1937).
13. *Ibid.* September 11, 1937.
14. *Economist,* (London: June, 1937).
15. *Weltwoche* (Zurich), December 3, 1937.
16. *L'Europe Nouvelle* (Paris: May 7, 1938.)
17. *Ibid.*
18. Max Lambert, *op. cit.*
19. *Hochschule fuer Politik*, Berlin, Jahrbuch, 1939.
20. *Weltwoche* (Zurich), June, 1937.
21. Aymé Guerrin, *Trois Expériences* (Paris: Denoel, 1938).
22. *New Statesman and Nation* (London), November 20, 1937.
23. Stephen Kemp Bailey, *Roosevelt and his New Deal* (London: Fact, 1939).
24. *New York Times*, November 21, 1936.
25. *The Round Table* (London), December, 1938.
26. *Ibid.*
27. R. De Roussy de Sales in *Revue de Paris,* May, 1937.

Chapter Six

1. *Survey of International Affairs* (London), 1938.
2. *Esprit* (Paris), October, 1938.

3. André Maurois, *États-Unis* (Paris: Ed. de France, 1939).
4. *New Statesman and Nation* (London), April 3, 1937.
5. *Survey of International Affairs* (London), 1938.
6. Alfred Max, *Politique Extérieure des États-Unis* (Paris: Hartmann, 1939).
7. *Welwoche* (Zurich), January 1, 1937.
8. April 20, 1938.
9. Alfred Max, *op. cit.*
10. *L'Europe Nouvelle* (Paris), March 5, 1938.
11. Alfred Max, *op. cit.*
12. *Japan Times Weekly,* September 15, 1938.
13. Alfred Max, *op. cit.*
14. *New York Times,* January 4, 1938.
15. Wickham Steed in *Contemporary Review* (London), April, 1938.
16. Wilfred Roberts in *Contemporary Review* (London), June, 1938.
17. *Survey of International Affairs* (London), 1938.
18. *L'Europe Nouvelle* (Paris), June 4, 1938.
19. *Survey of International Affairs* (London), 1938.
20. R. Roussy de Sales in *L'Europe Nouvelle* (Paris), June 4, 1938.
21. *Survey of International Affairs* (London), 1938.
22. Raoul Crabbé in the *Revue Belge* (Brussels), June 15, 1938.
23. André Siegfried Preface to Alfred Max, *op. cit.*
24. Firmin Roz, *Tableau des États-Unis* (Paris: Spid, 1946).
25. Alfred Max, *op. cit.*
26. Norman A. Ingrey in *Contemporary Review* (London), August 19, 1938.
27. *France-Amérique* (Paris), April, 1939.
28. *Weltwoche* (Zurich), January 1, 1937.

Chapter Seven

1. S. K. Ratcliff in *Contemporary Review* (London), August, 1938.
2. Rexford G. Tugwell, *The Democratic Roosevelt* (Garden City: Doubleday, 1957).
3. Paul Hazard in *France-Amérique* (Paris), April, 1939.
4. Leo F. Hausleiter, *Hanseatische Verlagsanstalt* (Hamburg, 1941).
5. *News Chronicle* (London), January 3, 1938.
6. Hans Schadewaldt, *Was will Roosevelt?* (Duesseldorf: Voelkischer Verlag, 1941).

7. *Time and Tide* (London), January 14, 1939.
8. Jay Pierrepont Moffat, *The Moffat Papers* (Cambridge, Mass.: Harvard University Press, 1956).
9. Paul Hazard, op. cit.
10. Robert Waithman, *Report on America* (London: Frederick Muller, 1940).
11. *Zeitschrift fuer Politik* (Berlin), January-February, 1937.
12. Raymond Las Vergnas, *Franklin D. Roosevelt* (Paris: Ed. Universelles, 1944).
13. Max Lambert, *Les États-Unis* (Paris: Blond and Gay, 1940).
14. Odette Keun, *I Think Alone in America* (London: Longmans Green and Co., 1939).
15. Basil Maine, *Franklin Roosevelt* (London: Nicholson and Watson, 1942).
16. *Survey of International Affairs* (London), 1938.
17. *Le Populaire* (Paris), September 24, 1938.
18. *The Japan Chronicle* (Tokyo), July 28, 1938.
19. *Nineteenth Century* (London), October, 1938.
20. (Paris), September 27, 1938.
21. *France-Amérique,* April, 1938.
22. R. H. Kiernan, *President Roosevelt* (London: George G. Harrap, 1948).
23. Ibid.
24. *France-Amérique* (Paris), April, 1939.
25. Max Lambert, *op. cit.*
26. *Japan Times* (Tokyo), November 17, 1938.
27. James MacGregor Burns. *Roosevelt The Lion and the Fox* (New York: Harcourt, Brace & Co., 1956).
28. Raymond Las Vergnas, *op. cit.*
29. Adolf Halfeld, *U.S.A. Greift in die Welt* (Hamburg: Broschek & Co., 1941).
30. The *Nineteenth Century* (London), October, 1938.
31. *Survey of International Affairs* (London), 1938.
32. *Ibid.*

Chapter Eight

1. *Contemporary Review* (London), June, 1939.
2. Quoted by *Manchester Guardian Weekly,* March 17, 1939.

3. *Manchester Guardian,* January 6, 1939.
4. March 8, 1939.
5. *L'Europe Nouvelle* (Paris), February 4, 1939.
6. *Ibid.,* May 6, 1939.
7. Adolf Halfeld, *U.S.A. Greift in die Welt* (Hamburg: Broschek & Co., 1941).
8. *Contemporary Review* (London), April, 1939.
9. *Ibid.,* June, 1939.
10. February 18, 1939.
11. *Contemporary Review* (London), April, 1939.
12. *L'Europe Nouvelle* (Paris), January 7, 1939.
13. *Ibid,* April, 1939.
14. *Economist,* (London), April 22, 1939.
15. *Hamburger Fremdenblatt* quoted by *Manchester Guardian Weekly,* February 3, 1939.
16. *Contemporary Review* (London), June, 1939.
17. *Survey of International Affairs* (London), 1939.
18. *Spectator* (London), April 7 and May 5, 1939.
19. July 8, 1939.
20. *Round Table* (London), September, 1939.
21. R. H. Kiernan, *President Roosevelt* (London: Harrap and Co. Ltd., 1948).
22. *Voelkischer Beobachter* (Berlin), April 16, 1939.
23. *Homme Libre* (Paris), April 16, 1939.
24. *Weltwoche* (Munich), June 2, 1939.
25. R. H. Kiernan, *op. cit.*
26. June 17, 1939.
27. *Neue Zurcher Zeitung* (Zurich), April 3, 1939.
28. April 5, 1939.
29. *Neue Zurcher Zeitung,* June 14, 1939.
30. June 17, 1939.
31. *Japan Times* (Tokyo), May 18, 1939.
32. June 29, 1939.
33. Asahi Tokyo, June 6, Nichi Nichi, (Tokyo), August, 1939.
34. *Round Table* (London), December, 1939.
35. Firmin Roz, *Roosevelt* (Paris: Dunod, 1948).
36. *Survey of International Affairs* (London), 1939.
37. *Contemporary Review* (London), December, 1939.
38. Raymond Las Vergnas, *F. D. Roosevelt* (Paris: Ed. Universelles, 1944).

39. December 30, 1939.
40. *Spectator* (London), May 5, 1939.
41. *Round Table* (London), June, 1939.
42. Dr. Frank Darval in *Contemporary Review* (London), April, 1939.
43. Raoul Roussy de Sales in *L'Europe Nouvelle* (Paris), January 6, 1940.

Chapter Nine

1. Quoted by *France-Amérique* (Paris), February, 1940.
2. *Spectator* (London), December 29, 1939.
3. *L'Europe Nouvelle* (Paris), January 13, 1940.
4. *New Statesman and Nation* (London), January 20, 1940.
5. *Round Table* (London), March, 1940.
6. *Contemporary Review* (London), April, 1940.
7. *Revue des Deux Mondes* (Paris), March, 1940.
8. *Ciano's Diplomatic Papers* (London: Odhams Press Ltd., 1943).
9. *Round Table* (London), December, 1939.
10. *Ibid.*, June, 1940.
11. *Arbeiderbladet* (Stockholm), December 4, 1939.
12. *Revue des Deux Mondes* (Paris), May, 1940.
13. *Revue de Paris*, March 15, 1940.
14. Frank William Ikle, *German-Japanese Relations, 1936-1940* (New York: Bookman Associates, 1956).
15. *Round Table* (London), March, 1940.
16. *Contemporary Review* (London), January, 1940.
17. *The Nineteenth Century* (London), July, 1940.
18. *L'Europe Nouvelle* (Paris), June 8, 1940.
19. Firmin Roz, *Roosevelt*, (Paris: Dunod, 1948).
20. *Ibid.*
21. *The Nineteenth Century* (London), June, 1940.
22. *Japan Chronicle* (Tokyo), June 12, 1940.
23. General Okamato, quoted by Firmin Roz, *op. cit.*
24. R. H. M. Worsley, *Europe versus America* (London: Jonathan Cape, 1942).
25. *Ibid.*
26. *Round Table* (London), September, 1940.
27. *Ibid.*

28. *Contemporary Review* (London), July, 1940.
29. Raymond Las Vergnas, *Franklin D. Roosevelt* (Paris: Ed. Universelles, 1944).
30. *New Statesman and Nation* (London), April, 1940.
31. *Australian Quarterly* (Sydney), June, 1940.
32. *L'Europe Nouvelle* (Paris), February 17, 1940.
33. *New Statesman and Nation* (London), July 27, 1940.
34. November 2, 1940.
35. August 10, 1940.
36. September 28, 1940.
37. November 2, 1940.
38. *New Statesman and Nation* (London), November 9, 1940.
39. *Economist* (London), November 9, 1940.
40. *Dagens Nyheter* (Stockholm), November 7, 1940.
41. *New York Times*, November 7, 1940.
42. Quoted by Lewis Broad: *Winston Churchill* (London: Hutchinson and Co., 1945).
43. *Nineteenth Century* (London), October, 1940.
44. Mainichi, quoted by *Japanese Chronicle* (Tokyo), November 8, 1940.
45. Asahi, *ibid.*
46. Adolf Halfeld: *U.S.A. Greift in die Welt* (Hamburg: Broschek & Co., 1941).
47. *La Sociologie Haitienne* (Port-au-Prince), November-December, 1939.
48. Raymond Las Vergnas, *op. cit.*

Chapter Ten

1. *Contemporary Review* (London), February, 1941.
2. *Listener* (London), March 13, 1941.
3. *Spectator* (London), January 10, 1941.
4. Basil Woon, *Roosevelt, World Statesman* (London: Peter Davies, 1942).
5. *Deutsche Allgemeine Zeitung* (Berlin), January 8, 1941.
6. *Neue Zurcher Zeitung* (Zurich), February 20, 1941.
7. *Giornale d'Italia* (Rome), February 24, 1941.
8. *Neue Zurcher Zeitung* (Zurich), February 24, 1941.

9. Alfred Fabre-Luce, *Journal de la France* (Brussels): Éditions de la Toison d'or, 1942.
10. *Le Mois Suisse Montreux,* June, 1941.
11. *New York Times,* January 9, 1941.
12. Theodor Seibert, *Das Amerikanische Rätsel* (Berlin: Franz Eher Verl, 1941).
13. *Contemporary Review* (London), July, 1941.
14. *Round Table* (London), December, 1941.
15. *Contemporary Review* (London), June, 1941.
16. September 30, 1940.
17. *New Statesman and Nation* (London), July 12, 1941.
18. *Round Table* (London), March and June, 1941.
19. *Zeitschrift fuer Politik* (Berlin), December, 1941.
20. Pierre Monniot, *Les États-Unis et la Neutralité* (Paris: A. Pédone, 1946).
21. *Neue Zurcher Zeitung* (Zurich), February 23, 1941.
22. Firmin Roz, *Roosevelt* (Paris: Dunod, 1948).
23. *Le Mois Suisse Montreux,* June, 1941.
24. *Neue Zurcher Zeitung* (Zurich), June 23, 1941.
25. *Round Table* (London), September, 1941.
26. *Nineteenth Century* (London), July, 1941.
27. *New Statesman and Nation* (London), September 6, 1941.
28. *The Observer* (London), September 14, 1941.
29. *Hochi,* quoted by *Japanese Chronicle,* Tokyo, July 10, 1941.
30. *Neue Zurcher Zeitung* (Zurich), August 14, 1941.
31. *Ibid,* June 22, 1941.
32. Rexford G. Tugwell, *The Democratic Roosevelt* (Garden City, New York: Doubleday & Co., 1957).
33. *New Statesman and Nation* (London), September 13, 1941.
34. *Round Table* (London), September, 1941.
35. August 15, 1941.
36. *Deutsche Allgemeine Zeitung* (Berlin), August 15, 1941.
37. Raoul de Roussy de Sales, *The Making of Tomorrow* (Reynal & Hitchcock, New York, 1942).
38. J. C. Wedgwood in *Contemporary Review* (London), February, 1941.
39. *Observer* (London), March 16, 1941.
40. *Round Table* (London), September, 1941.
41. *New Statesman and Nation* (London), May 17, 1941.

42. *Ibid.*, March 1, 1941.
43. *Ibid.*, June 14, 1941.
44. *Ibid.*, March 1, 1941.
45. *Round Table* (London), September, 1941.
46. *Australian Quarterly* (Sydney), September, 1941.
47. Quoted by Basil Woon, *op. cit.*
48. January 7, 1941.
49. *Listener* (London), January 9, 1941.
50. Adolf Halfeld, *USA Greift in die Welt* (Hamburg: Broschek & Co., 1942).
51. *Neue Zurcher Zeitung* (Zurich), August 12, 1941.
52. *Ibid.*, August 5, 1941.
53. Quoted by *Japanese Chronicle* (Tokyo), May 22, 1941.
54. Alistair Cooke in *Listener* (London), January 2, 1941.
55. Isaiah Berlin in *Listener* (London), April 17, 1957.

Chapter Eleven

1. *Round Table* (London), June, 1942.
2. *Neue Zurcher Zeitung* (Zurich), December 10, 1941.
3. *Spectator* (London), December 12, 1941.
4. *Round Table* (London), March, 1942.
5. Kurt von Tippelskirch, *Geschichte des zweiten Weltkrieges* (Athenäum, Bonn 1951).
6. Firmin Ros, *Roosevelt* (Paris: Dunod, 1948).
7. *Manchester Guardian*, December 9, 1941.
8. *Listener* (London), December 18, 1941.
9. *New Statesman and Nation* (London), December 20, 1941.
10. *Spectator*, January 30, 1942.
11. *Neue Zurcher Zeitung*, December 10, 1941.
12. *Ibid.* from Tokyo, December 5, 1941.
13. N. G. Jog, *Will War Come to India* (Bombay: New Book Co., 1941).
14. *Spectator*, December 11, 1942.
15. *Contemporary Review* (London), December, 1942.
16. *Round Table* (London), December, 1941.
17. *Neue Zurcher Zeitung* (Zurich), December 9, 1941.

18. *Zeitschrift fuer Politik* (Berlin), March, 1942.
19. *Ibid.*
20. *Ibid.*, December, 1941.
21. *Neue Zurcher Zeitung*, January 2, 1942.
22. *Times* (London), December 12, 1941.
23. *Spectator* (London), January 9 and February 27, 1942.
24. J. Goebbels in *Das Reich*, September 2, 1942.
25. *Neue Zuricher Zeitung* (Zurich), January 3, 1942.
26. *Ibid.*, January 8, 1942.
27. *Ibid.*, March 26, 1942.
28. *Economist* (London), March 14, 1942.
29. *Spectator* (London), September 11, 1942.
30. *Ibid.*, October 2, 1942.
31. *Neue Zurcher Zeitung*, September 16, 1942.
32. *Ibid.*, September 9, 1942.
33. *Round Table* (London), March, 1942.
34. *Spectator* (London), July 31, 1942.
35. *Neue Zurcher Zeitung*, September 28, 1942.
36. *Ibid.*, October 14, 1942.
37. *Ibid.*, November 8, 1942.
38. *Contemporary Review*, December, 1942.
39. *Neue Zurcher Zeitung*, November 9, 1942.
40. *Ibid.*, December 12, 1941.
41. *The Ciano Diaries*, May 28, 1941 (Garden City Publ., New York, 1945).
42. *Round Table* (London), March, 1942.
43. Basil Woon, *Roosevelt, World Statesman* (London: P. Davies, 1942).
44. *Times* (New York), June 18, 1942, from Stockholm.
45. *New Statesman and Nation* (London), December 5, 1942.
46. Basil Woon, *op. cit.*
47. D. W. Brogan in *Spectator* (London), October 30, 1942.
48. *New Statesman and Nation*, May 16, 1942.
49. *Ibid.*, October 3, 1942.
50. *Neue Zurcher Zeitung*, October 9, 1942.
51. R. G. Menzies, *The Forgotten People* (Sydney, Australia: Angus and Roberts, Ltd., 1943).
52. J. A. R. Marriot in *Nineteenth Century* (London), May, 1942.
53. *New Statesman and Nation* (London), March 14, 1942.

Chapter Twelve

1. Sir John Pratt, *War and Politics* (London: Jonathan Cape, 1943).
2. Joseph W. Stilwell, *The Stilwell Papers* (New York: W. Sloane Assoc., 1948).
3. *Contemporary Review* (London), August, 1943.
4. Firmin Roz, *Roosevelt* (Paris: Dunod, 1948).
5. *La Marseillaise* (London), May, 1943.
6. *La Revue du Caire,* September, 1943.
7. *Neue Zurcher Zeitung,* February 6, 1943.
8. Alexander Werth, *France 1940-1955* (New York: Henry Holt & Co., 1956).
9. *Round Table* (London), September, 1943.
10. *Economist* (London), January 16, 1943.
11. *Zeitschrift fuer Politik* (Berlin), January, 1943.
12. *Observer* (London), May 16, 1943.
13. *Listener* (London), October 23, 1943.
14. *Round Table* (London), September, 1943.
15. *New Statesman and Nation* (London), January 29 and February 5, 1943.
16. *Spectator* (London), February 5, 1943.
17. *Contemporary Review* (London), March, 1943.
18. *Svenska Dagbladed* (Stockholm), September 21, 1943.
19. *Spectator* (London), January 29, 1943.
20. *Le Mois Suisse* (Montreux), October, 1943.
21. The *Observer* (London), January 24, 1943.
22. *Weltwoche* (Zurich), April 16, 1943.
23. February 13, 1943.
24. *Australian Quarterly* (Sydney), March, 1943.
25. Firmin Roz, *Tableau des États-Unis* (Paris: Spid, 1946).
26. *Ibid.*
27. *Spectator* (London), February 5, 1943.
28. *New Statesman and Nation* (London), July 24, 1943.
29. Firmin Roz, *op. cit.*
30. *Spectator,* January 29, 1943.
31. *Neue Zurcher Zeitung* (Zurich), August 16, 1943.
32. *Economist* (London), November 13, 1943.
33. *Listener* (London), December 16, 1943.

34. *Contemporary Review* (London), October, 1943.
35. *Weltwoche* (Zurich), May 7, 1943.
36. Arthur Bryant, *The Turn of the Tide* (London: Collins, 1957).
37. *Dialogues of A. N. Whitehead* (Boston: Little Brown & Co., 1954).
38. *New York Times,* April 14, 1943.
39. *Contemporary Review* (London), October, 1943.
40. *Economist* (London), June 5, 1943.
41. *Round Table* (London), September, 1943.
42. D. W. Brogan in *Nineteenth Century* (London), January, 1943.
43. *New Statesman and Nation* (London), January 9, 1943.
44. *Spectator,* February 5, 1943.
45. *Observer,* November 7, 1943.

Chapter Thirteen

1. *New York Times,* December 19, 1943.
2. *Contemporary Review* (London), April, 1944.
3. Firmin Roz, *Roosevelt* (Paris: Dunod, 1948).
4. *Contemporary Review* (London), June, 1944.
5. *Neue Zurcher Zeitung* (Zurich), July 1, 1944.
6. *Contemporary Review,* February, 1944.
7. *Basler Nachrichten* (Basle), Nos. 339, 343; 1943.
8. *Spectator* (London), September 29, 1944.
9. *Listener* (London), September 21, 1944.
10. Firmin Roz: *op. cit.*
11. November 2, 1943.
12. *Listener* (London), December 28, 1944.
13. *New Statesman and Nation* (London), July 29, 1944.
14. *Round Table* (London), September, 1944.
15. March, 1944.
16. *Listener* (London), December 7, 1941).
17. *Listener,* November 12, 1959.
18. *Economist* (London), June 3, 1944.
19. *Times of India* (Bombay), June 23, 1944.
20. *Times of India* (Bombay), June 8, 1944.
21. *Le Mois Suisse* (Montreux), August, 1944, quoting K. K. Kawakani: *Asia at the Door.*
22. *Spectator* (London), October 6, 1944.

23. October 9, 1943, quoted by Herbert A. Quint *Die Wendepunkte des Krieges* (Steingruben Verlag Stuttgart, 1950).
24. *Contemporary Review,* January, 1944.
25. Chester Wilmot, *The Struggle for Europe* (London: Collins, 1952).
26. *Times of India* (Bombay), June 10, 1944.
27. Herbert Luethy: *St. Gallener Tagblatt,* July 8, 1944.
28. *New Statesman and Nation* (London), January 1, 1944.
29. *Ibid.,* June 24, 1944.
30. *Contemporary Review,* November, 1944.
31. *Times* (London), December 28, 1943.
32. *Voelkischer Beobachter* (Munich), January 15, 1944.
33. *Das Reich* (Berlin), April 2, 1944.
34. *La Marseillaise* (London), February 19, 1944.
35. *Round Table* (London), March, 1944.
36. *Economist* (London), May 31, 1944.
37. *Contemporary Review,* November, 1944.
38. *New Statesman and Nation* (London), July 29, 1944.
39. *Ibid,* October 21, 1944.
40. *Contemporary Review* (London), February, 1944.
41. D. W. Brogan in *The Spectator,* June 30, 1944.
42. *Listener,* October 12, 1944.
43. *Spectator* (London), November 3, 1944.
44. *Neue Zurcher Zeitung* (Zurich), November 4, 1944.
45. *Le Figaro* (Paris), November 5, 1944.
46. Ann O'Hare McCormick in *New York Times,* November 6, 1944.
47. *Economist* (London), May 13, 1944.
48. *Spectator* (London), August 18, 1944.
49. *New York Times,* November 7, 1944.
50. November 11, 1944.
51. *Neue Zurcher Zeitung* (Zurich), November 9, 1944.
52. *New York Times,* November 10, 1944.
53. *L'Humanité* (Paris), November 9, 1944.
54. November 11, 1944.
55. November 25, 1944.
56. *Neue Zurcher Zeitung* (Zurich), November 9, 1944.
57. *Listener* (London), November 16, 1944.

Chapter Fourteen

1. *Contemporary Review* (London), March, 1945.
2. *Economist* (London), January 6, 1945.
3. *Ibid.*, January 13, 1945.
4. Ibid., March 31, 1945.
5. *New Statesman and Nation* (London), January 13, 1945.
6. *Spectator* (London), January 5, 1945.
7. House of Commons, April 17, 1945.
8. *Economist* (London), February 17, 1945.
9. *Ibid.*, March 3, 1945.
10. *Round Table* (London), June, 1945.
11. *Diplomatische Information* (Berlin), February 13, 1945.
12. *Neue Zurcher Zeitung* (Zurich), February 15, 1945.
13. *Contemporary Review* (London), May, 1945.
14. *Survey of International Affairs* (London), 1945.
15. Firmin Roz, *Roosevelt* (Paris: Dunod, 1948).
16. Chester Wilmot, *The Struggle for Europe* (London: Collins, 1952).
17. *Contemporary Review* (London), May, 1945.
18. *Spectator* (London), April 20, 1945.
19. *Economist* (London), April 21, 1945.
20. *Round Table* (London), June, 1945.
21. *Triumph and Tragedy* (Boston: Houghon, Mifflin Co., 1953).
22. Joseph C. Crow, *Turbulent Era* (Vol. II. Boston: Houghton, Mifflin Co., 1952).
23. From the Archives, Roosevelt Memorial Library, Hyde Park, N.Y.
24. *La Dernière Heure*, Bruxelles, April 15, 1945.
25. *Le Figaro* (Paris), April 14, 1945.
26. From the Archives, Roosevelt Memorial Library, Hyde Park, N.Y.
27. April 13, 1945.
28. April 14, 1945.
29. April 15, 1945.
30. H. R. Trevor-Roper, *The Last Days of Hitler* (New York: Macmillan, 1947).
31. April 14, 1945.
32. *Neue Zurcher Zeitung* (Zurich), April 16, 1945.

33. *New York Times Magazine*, November 8, 1959.
34. *Le Figaro* (Paris), April 14, 1945.
35. *Combat* (Paris), April 14, 1945.
36. *Aufbau* (New York), April 27, 1945.
37. *Ibid.*, April 20, 1945.
38. *Le Figaro* (Paris), April 17, 1945.
39. *Listener*, April 17, 1957.
40. *New Republic* (New York), April 15, 1946.